Mysteries of Celtic Britain

Mysteries of
Celtic Britain

by
Lewis Spence

SIENA

This edition published and distributed by Parragon, 1998

Parragon
13 Whiteladies Road
Clifton
Bristol
BS8 1PB

ISBN 0 75252 682 0

A copy of the British Library Cataloguing-in-Publication Data
is available from the British Library.

Printed and bound in the EC

PREFACE

THAT the island of Britain was the seat of the development of a *cultus* and secret tradition of extraordinary vitality and individuality is no new thesis, but, so far, it is one which has not been dealt with in any tolerable or scientific manner, nor has the evidence concerning it been examined in the light of modern research, especially as regards recent valuable conclusions in Folklore and Archæology. All I can claim to have done in the present volume is to have collected the data concerning it and to have made an effort to systematize the same, with the dual intention of proving its authentic character and value to British mystics as providing them with a horizon of native and, therefore, sympathetic lore and practice ; and its long survival in these islands—a survival which, in certain districts, appears to have lasted until a time which we are now accustomed to regard as comparatively recent.

That the cult we call " Druidism " possessed a much higher mystical tendency than the generality of British people are aware has, of course, been frequently advanced as a serious contention. But, because of the bizarre method by which this view has formerly been advanced, a perfectly sound hypothesis has not only been seriously damaged, but has been greeted with unmerited contempt. I have striven, in setting it forth in a more catholic manner, to employ only such sources as appeared to me absolutely worthy of credence and to eschew anything in the nature of the extreme or the empirical—in short, to let the evidence plead for the theory by virtue of its copiousness, its obviousness, and its generally overwhelming character. At the same time, I have made every endeavour to arrange and select this in such a manner that the orderly presentation of facts would not in any way derogate from their weight or possible acceptance, and to digest them into the beginnings of a system which will at least give pause to those who altogether deny the former presence of a highly intellectualized *cultus* and mystery in our islands, or its survival in a more or less official form until recent times.

The nucleus of proof is, naturally, to be sought in Wales, the last stronghold of official Druidism, where a quite extraordinary treasure of manuscript material relating to it still exists. It has been far too much the fashion to assume a problematical or comparatively recent origin for ancient Cambrian literary sources. But I believe I have brought sufficient evidence to bear to show conclusively that this great *corpus* of venerable material is not only authentic in essence, but of such preponderating value as it is scarcely possible to overestimate. Especially do I believe the writings preserved by Iolo Morganwg in *Barddas* to have been handed down from an immemorial antiquity, as his editors maintained, and to enshrine the beliefs, ideas, and practices of the Secret Tradition of Britain, and I feel that the unbiassed reader will, after having perused the evidence relative to this, find himself in general agreement with this view.

The evidence concerning the rites and ceremonies of initiation is, I think, clear and conclusive, and should once for all lay at rest any dubiety on this particular head. It should also be of peculiar value to British mystics, as providing them with a general view of a system or code of conduct by which their ancestors sought to gain a knowledge of that higher existence which they personally seek to attain, and I am not without hope that it may induce them to consider the propriety of examining further, and perhaps embracing a soul-philosophy more in natural conformity with our native psychology than any exotic system can possibly be.

We Britons are, alas, too prone to find in alien systems, æsthetic and philosophic, that which is seemingly more desirable than anything of native origin. So far as mystical philosophy is concerned, we have not until the present, perhaps, had any real opportunity of gauging the values of a tradition developed in accordance with Western, and more exclusively Britannic, mentality. But I feel that with the mass of fact I have been enabled to place before him, the British mystic may no longer believe himself compelled to seek guidance from Oriental cults and philosophies of arcane origin, but may turn for the purposes of psychical instruction and enlightenment to the noble and venerable tradition of his fathers, in which he cannot but discover ideals and beliefs which strike a familiar and hereditary chord, to his refreshment, encouragement, and final illumination. I have also carefully indicated the sources from which he may gain a more comprehensive knowledge of the system in its entirety.

I cannot close without expressing my sincere thanks to Miss Wendy Wood for the eight excellent drawings which she has made for this book. Deeply imbued with the Keltic spirit and versed in the details of Keltic antiquity, she has also infused them with the richness of Keltic imagination and

mysticism.   I have also to thank my daughter Rhoda
for tireless assistance in gathering and arranging the
materials which are the foundations of this attempt
to rebuild the house of our decaying British tradition
—an edifice which, I am convinced, the patriotic
mystic will lend every aid in gloriously rebuilding !

L. S.

66 Arden Street,
    Edinburgh.

CONTENTS

—

CHAPTER I
INTRODUCTORY

CHAPTER II
THE CULT OF THE DEAD

CHAPTER III
THE MYSTERY OF KELTIC PHILOSOPHY

CHAPTER IV
"BARDDAS"

Contents 11

CHAPTER V
THE ARCANE TRADITION IN BRITISH MEDIÆVAL LITERATURE

CHAPTER VI
THE MYSTERY OF THE GRAIL

CHAPTER VII
THE SECRET TRADITION IN RITE AND LEGEND

12 Contents

CHAPTER VIII
THE HIGHER PHILOSOPHY OF BRITISH MYSTICISM

CHAPTER IX
THE WAY OF INITIATION

Contents

Mysteries of Celtic Britain

The Mysteries of Britain

CHAPTER I

INTRODUCTORY

To the peoples of antiquity the isle of Britain was the very home and environment of mystery, a sacred territory, to enter which was to encroach upon a region of enchantment, the dwelling of gods, the shrine and habitation of a cult of peculiar sanctity and mystical power. Britain was, indeed, the *insula sacra* of the West, an island veiled and esoteric, the Egypt of the Occident. Legends of its strange and perilous marvels were current among the semi-civilized races who dwelt over against its ghostly white cliffs ; it was regarded as the haunt and refuge of giants, demons, and spirits ; by not a few, even as the paradise and resort of the dead. The early accounts of its terrors show how varied were the wonders ascribed to it. Perhaps that instinct or policy of secrecy which inspired early traders to surround an area of mercantile monopoly with tales of dread was responsible for much of this supernatural reputation. But the fame of Britain as a territory withdrawn and occult cannot altogether be explained by such a theory.

The intention of this book is to explain the ancient status of Britain as a country of almost unique sanctity in the ancient world, and to demonstrate the survival of the mysticism and occult tradition which were certainly developed among our British ancestors to an extent unrivalled on the continent of Europe. I shall also endeavour to make it plain, by arguments founded upon authority, that the tradition of mysticism which flourished in our island was of equal antiquity and sanction with that developed in Egypt and the East, and in no sense derivative from it so far as its origins were concerned.

The romance of distance has, indeed, played havoc with our native occult philosophy. Either because the East appears to us more glamorous than our own environment, or because we have become conventionally used to the notion, we assume that she is the mother of all mystery, that her ancient civilizations—Egypt, Babylonia, and India—were the sole and world-originators of secret lore. Yet it is demonstrable that on our insular and isolated soil there arose an arcane tradition as potent and as majestic as any similar system fostered by the Orient, and better accommodated to our racial psychology.

Although it is impossible to dogmatize concerning the origins and earlier affinities of this separate British tradition, we can affirm with confidence that through long and insular segregation it developed a system entirely its own, which was handed down through the ages and is still capable of extensive recovery. Just as in the early centuries of our era, and before them, Britain was regarded as specifically sacred, an enclosure of the gods, so throughout the Age of Romance was she thought of as peculiarly the island of faerie glamour and enchanted adventure. This secondary phase was merely a survival of the much more venerable belief in her religious sanctity. But if she is no longer the haunted and magical island of Spanish and French romancers, the elder conception of her as the birthplace of a distinct occult tradition should hold a vivid and abiding interest for those of her sons and daughters who still feel inspired by her mystical significance. The attempt will be made in these pages to reconstruct the fragments of the ancient British esoteric philosophy in such a manner that the salient outlines at least of its edifice may be apparent and distinct, and that its system may be at the disposal of British mystics for their use and comprehension as more suited by its genius to the native mentality and disposition than the exotic *cultus* so long in vogue.

Evidences regarding the belief in the sacred and mystical character of the British Isles in early times are readily forthcoming. Julius Cæsar, who almost certainly received his information from the Æduan Druid Diviciacus, the friend of Cicero, says of the Druid cult : " It is believed that this discipline was first instituted in Britain, and from thence transferred to Gaul, for even at this day those who desire to be perfect adepts of their art make a voyage thither to learn it." [1] It is thus clear from Cæsar's testimony that the Gaulish Druids regarded Britain not only as the birthplace of their cult, but in some respects as its official headquarters, its Tibet. Every religion looks with veneration toward the place of its origin, and the mere fact that the Gaulish Druids not only believed the British Isles to be the first home of their faith, but that they actually sent their neophytes for instruction to its seminaries is perhaps the best testimony the experienced student of religious science could desire in arriving at a conclusion favourable to the inception of Druidism in our island.

Procopius, the Byzantine historian, who flourished in the sixth century (A.D. 500-565) unquestionably

[1] *De Bello Gallico*, Bk. VI, 13.

refers to a late form of the belief in the mysterious reputation of Britain in his *De Bello Gothico*.[1] Speaking of the Isle of Brittia, by which he means Britain, he states that it is divided by a wall. Thither fishermen from the Breton coast are compelled to ferry over at darkest night the shades of the dead, unseen by them, but marshalled by a mysterious leader. The fishermen who are to row the dead across to the British coast must go to bed early, for at midnight they are aroused by a tapping at the door, and someone calls them in a low voice. They rise and go down to the shore, attracted by some force which they cannot explain. Here they find their boats apparently empty, yet the water rises to the bulwarks, as if they were crowded. Once they commence the voyage, their vessels cleave the waves speedily, making the passage, usually a day and a half's sailing, in an hour. When the British shore is reached, the souls of the dead leave the craft, which at once rise in the sea as if unloaded. Then a loud voice on shore is heard calling the name and style of those who have disembarked. How hard Keltic lore dies is illustrated by the fact that it is still usual at Treguier in Brittany to convey the dead to the churchyard in a boat over a part of the river called the " Passage de l'Enfer," instead of taking the shorter way by land.[2]

As has already been said, the argument to be upheld in these pages is that European civilization, both Eastern and Western, arose from a common centre. It follows from this that the religious and mystical ideas which flowed from that common fount had also a single and primitive origin. Just as the

[1] Dindorff's edition, Vol. II, p. 559.
[2] See my *Legends and Romances of Brittany*, p. 383.

Cult of the Dead, which appears to have been the native and pristine religious impulse of this early culture, developed certain special tendencies and characteristics in Egypt and the East, there is reliable evidence that it similarly developed in Britain, taking on the colour of its insular environment and evolving an occult tradition of equal potency and authority capable of revealing to us a mystery as majestic and more in consonance with our peculiar psychology.

With this theory are indissolubly associated those problems of the origin of our race which for so long have aroused the fiercest controversy, but which modern archæology has to a great extent succeeded in resolving. It has been the bane of that species of mysticism which drew authority from alien sources that many of its most powerful apologists were unconversant with the sciences of archæology and anthropology, and that they have recognized sources of dubious character and alleged inspiration whilst neglecting the proven conclusions of science. These notions have, however, been utterly wrecked by recent archæological demonstration and need not detain us here.

The race now generally called "Iberian" or "Mediterranean" by the majority of ethnologists, was probably the last wave of a well-marked stock having its origin in North-Western Africa, and which during thousands of years sent out impulses to both East and West. Its precise place of origin we do not know, but Sergi, perhaps the most competent and experienced of its historians, believed this to be situated in the region of the Sahara, which was not always prone to desert conditions. That it gave Egyptian civilization its first impetus I hope to show, and if it flourished more exceedingly in the

Nile-land than elsewhere, that was almost wholly on account of the propitious environment it encountered there.   Similarly it took on special attributes in Britain, the Cult of the Dead which it carried with it to our island, as it did to Egypt, culminating in the sublime and intellectual system of Druidism, which found here its natural home and environment, which survived in Britain long after it had perished elsewhere, and lingered on, affecting the entire process and history of British mystical thought even to the present time.

In order to justify the above statements a digression into the sphere of archæology and ethnology is essential.   This will draw its facts and sustain its arguments from the writings of authorities who have given the most recent attention to the problems of European archæology and those of the Near East.   In Europe, the history of civilization may be said to begin with the Aurignacian or Crô-Magnon race, who appear to have entered our continent about 23000 B.C.   Certain authorities believe them to have had an African origin.   The Capsians, who followed them, roughly about 10000 B.C., were admittedly of African origin, and their culture was superior to that of their predecessors, in the domestication of the dog and the use of the bow. Like the Aurignacians, the Capsians were artists who left their paintings on the walls of their rock-shelters in the central parts of Spain, only these display a much more marked conventional treatment of the subject and were nearly all of a religious or magical character.

Bosch Gimpera, a Spanish archæologist of experience,[1] has given it as his opinion that the

[1] See his *Ensayo de una reconstruction de la etnologie prehistoria de la Peninsula Iberia* (Barcelona, 1923).

Capsians were a mixed race, comprising "Mediterranean" or "Iberian" elements, negroid and "Armenoid" strains. Their culture, characterized by small finely-worked flakes, has been allied by some authorities with that of Tardenoisian (about 6000 B.C.) which shows certain superficial resemblances to it. But the affinity is now regarded as questionable. The Azilian culture, a degeneration of that of the Aurignacian, is discovered in Britain, at the Victoria Cave near Settle, and in the island of Oronsay and at the MacArthur Cave near Oban. Further, a culture having widespread centres in France, Belgium, Germany, and parts of Italy, and known as the Campignian (about 4000 B.C.) and characterized by unpolished flint implements, is also encountered in Britain. All these cultures are associated with the period of low development occurring between the Old and New Stone Ages.

Coming to Neolithic or New Stone Age times, the stream of culture seems to have arrived by sea from the south.

Since the close of the War, British archæology has experienced a process of reconstruction more fundamental than that applied to many departments of our national life equally in need of reorganization. More, indeed, has been achieved during this decade in the solution of vexed questions than during the preceding century, and the enthusiastic revival of antiquarian effort in France, Spain, and Scandinavia has placed an extraordinary stream of new and convincing data at the disposal of British students. Obscurities in British prehistory were due chiefly to a poverty of Continental analogies, but comparison of the results of recent excavations abroad has made it possible not only to point with precision to the Continental areas of origin of the several primitive cultures whose remains are found on British soil, but even in some cases to the actual localities and identical sites in Spain, in Gaul, and elsewhere whence they must have been carried to our shores some twenty to forty centuries ago.   At first, conservative antiquaries were chary of giving assent to conclusions so novel and far-reaching in their consequences to British prehistory.   But the evidence has been so overwhelming in its character and so universal in its acceptance as to justify complete agreement with its deductions.

These most surprising results have been arrived at chiefly through painstaking comparison between British and Continental megalithic or rough stone forms of architecture, pottery, and artifacts in stone and bronze, and by the rise of a wonderful European journalism of antiquity hitherto unapproached in accuracy, perception, and distinction.   The remarkable conclusions alluded to are to a great extent due to the excellent pioneer work accomplished in Spain by Señors Obermeier and Bosch Gimpera, and in Great Britain by Messrs O. G. S. Crawford, E. H. Stone, and Professor V. Gordon Childe.

Concentration on the question of the trade-routes blazed by the ancient peoples of the Mediterranean and Atlantic areas during the New Stone and Bronze Ages has, indeed, revolutionized our comprehension of the Western World four thousand years ago, and has made it clear that the traders of Spain and Brittany even at that dim era regularly engaged in a continuous and well-organized commerce with our islands.   Not only did they carry with them such articles of merchandise as they could barter for gold, amber, and jet, but they instructed our rude forefathers in their own system of rough stone building to such purpose that in many cases the result was an almost exact model of structures to be found on Continental sites to-day.

From Los Millares in Almeria in the South of Spain is a far cry to lone Rhinaire, in Caithness. Yet, as has been definitely proved, the horned cairn at the Scottish site reproduces exactly the plan of some ancient tombs at the Almerian station, and exhibits the selfsame system of corbelling. Four thousand years ago men from Southern Spain in large dug-out boats plugged with Spanish cork were coasting the Iberian sea-line, rounding the horns of Brittany, and making slow passage by the aid of leathern sails up the West Coast of Scotland and through the Pentland Firth to Denmark in search of gold and amber. Some of these vessels have actually been found in the raised beaches of Scotland, still containing the green-stone adzes they brought with them. The rectangular chambers with lateral niches in the Orkneys repeat above ground the subterranean chambers of Anghelu Ruju in Sardinia, the brochs or dry-stone towers which stud the coasts of Scotland are practically identical with the nuraghi of Sardinia, even if somewhat later in period than the latter, and the remarkable series of tombs scattered along the western and northern coasts of Scotland serve to indicate the line of the trade-route from Southern Spain to Denmark. On the other hand, Danish amber and English jet are found in the graves at Los Millares, and help to indicate the precise kind of treasure which the early traders were anxious to secure.

These early traders to Britain seem to have introduced first the "dolmen" type of grave, a large stone raised on three or four monoliths. A later form is the chambered long barrow and the cairn, which penetrated inland in Britain as elsewhere.

The long barrows were used as collective sepulchres in which the dead were usually buried, although in Yorkshire and some parts of Scotland undoubted evidences of cremation are forthcoming.

The men who constructed these long barrows were long-skulled and short in stature. That they came by sea and from the South-West is certain, as the distribution of their burial-places reveals, and the barrows they built can be referred only to similar structures in Spain and the Western Mediterranean, especially in Almeria.

These long barrow men were traders, voyaging from Spain to Denmark by way of the northern coasts of Scotland, as the series of these tombs shows, and the Danish amber and British jet found in their Spanish burial-places are eloquent of the far-flung traffic in which they engaged. But few signs are evident of any colonization on a large scale by this enterprising race of maritime merchants, which may be dated at about 2000 B.C., and is contemporary with the Middle Minoan civilization in Crete. But the long barrow culture did not impinge on our eastern coasts, or, indeed, press far inland, although it seems improbable that it may have been "taken over by the natives from traders touching on the shore," as Professor Childe suggests. Surely had such been the case such precise similarity to Iberian models as he alludes to could scarcely have resulted.

The lives of the builders of the long barrows were evidently almost entirely conditioned by the Cult of the Dead. That these New Stone Age people were originally of African origin is now clear.[1] In Spain, extraordinary numbers of religious objects associated with this cult have been found, made chiefly from bone, idols of a flat or "plaque" shape, and

[1] See Childe, *Dawn of European Civilization*, p. 136.

"croziers" of schist. These objects, taken from tombs, show how elaborate the Cult of the Dead had become in the Iberian peninsula at that early period.

Regarding the race and culture of the folk who followed the men of the long barrows in Britain there is now no dispute. In the Rhineland, a fusion between the "bell-beaker" people and the "battle-axe" folk of Thuringia had taken place. The former were probably of Italic origin, and had opened up the Brenner route from Italy for the amber trade, linking up the Elbe Valley with the Adriatic about 2000 B.C. They were a race of prospectors and traders. The battle-axe folk were users and makers of bronze implements, coming from Hungary and Transylvania. These, mingled with a small proportion of "Alpines," or short-skulled people, invaded Britain. This mixed race was short-skulled, although certain structural peculiarities seem to show that they were not without "Nordic" or Northern racial affinities. They spread rapidly in Britain, introducing a metal culture into the island for the first time, manufacturing gold objects on a fairly large scale, and a peculiar shape of food-vessel with a bell-shaped mouth. Their contribution to British culture was certainly greater than that of their Atlantic predecessors. But the cultures overlapped and mixed. And there is sufficient evidence that the religious and mystical ideas of the earlier Iberian peoples triumphed, completely dominating in the end those of the Central European new-comers, and giving for all time a peculiarly "Iberian" aspect to British religious and mystical thought. Britain was, indeed, destined to remain Iberian in a religious sense long after the Iberian Cult of the Dead had vanished in its own original milieu. Once introduced, this Iberian form appears to have taken a powerful hold on the imagination of the native stock and its successors, and even the later Celtic invaders seem to have adapted its basic principles and to have grafted their mythology upon it. This then it was which rendered British mystical thought unique in Europe, and which caused it to be looked upon by the peoples of the Continent at the beginning of the Christian era as the exemplar and prototype of the ancient faith of the West.

Controversy rages on the question of the priority of civilization in East and West. Those who maintain the more venerable character of Eastern civilization regard the Iberian culture of Spain as a reflection of that of the Eastern Mediterranean, or, at least, a carrier of its benefits to more northern lands. But the bare fact that the megalithic or rough stone monuments of Spain exhibit exactly similar, if more conventionalized, paintings to those of the more ancient Capsian culture which came from North-West Africa, should give the protagonists of Eastern civilization considerable pause. It is precisely the great centres of megalithic architecture in Europe which have obviously the closest affiliation with survivals from the Old Stone Age of the West, an age pre-dating anything that the Nile and Mesopotamia have to show.

Even the Old Stone Age in Spain and France was not only demonstrably native to the West and more ancient than the cultures of the East, but it assuredly exhibits the earliest known germs of the great Cult of the Dead. Late Aurignacian burials display the first steps in the development of mummification at a period at least 14000 years B.C. The flesh was removed from the bones and these were painted red, the colour of life. "The dead man was to live again in his own body, of which the bones were the framework," says Professor Macalister. "To paint it with the colour of life was the nearest thing to mummification that the Palæolithic people knew; it was an attempt to make the body again serviceable for its owner's use." Microscopic examination has proved that the bones so painted were in several cases wrapped around by skins, the first rude prototype of mummy-swathing. The simple fact is that Egypt has nothing so ancient to show in the way of early efforts at embalming.

Several gifted writers among the "Orientalists" have attempted to prove Eastern influence in the megalithic culture of the West by showing that the structure known as the "dolmen" was modelled on the Egyptian mastaba. Among these Elliot Smith[1] and Perry are the most outstanding British defenders of this theory. But the Egyptian mastaba differs radically from the dolmen in that it was a funerary chapel built over the actual tomb cut in the rock, whereas the dolmen was the substructure of a grave-mound. Elliot Smith, Perry, and Professor Peake, observing the association between European megalithic structures and gold, have inferred therefrom that Eastern prospectors for the precious metal built these monuments, Peake believing them to have been Sumerians, while Elliot Smith and his school lean to an Egyptian origin. The religious urge in Egypt, the latter think, the need for life-giving substances employed in the Cult of the Dead, aroused a spirit of exploration in Egypt and stimulated distant voyages. But no metal in a worked state is to be found in the megalithic monuments, and the explanation that the Eastern voyagers refused to initiate the

[1] See his "Evolution of the Rock-cut Tomb and Dolmen", in *Essays Presented to Sir William Ridgeway.*

natives into the art of metal-working, while instructing them in the art of dolmen-building (that is, according to Smith and Perry, mastaba-building) will scarcely recommend itself as being well founded or reasonable.   Why the "prospectors" should have taught the rude populations of Spain and Brittany the rudiments of their religion and the art of imitating the mastaba and yet have refused them the boon of instruction in ore-working, is not sufficiently made plain.   There is no real reason to believe that the dolmen was not the invention of the late survivors of the Old Stone Age civilization of the Atlantic or Western region.   "The great centres of megalithic architecture in Europe are precisely those regions where the Old Stone Age survivals are most numerous," remarks Professor Childe.   He goes on to remark that this thesis, too, has its difficulties. "How did megalithic architecture spread from the Atlantic Coast to the Caucasus, to say nothing of India or the Pacific Islands?   If the comparison drawn (in a preceding chapter) between the early civilizations of the Near East and the West has any weight, it would be absurd to argue that the Western barbarians taught the Egyptians and Cretans the Cult of the Dead."

So it would certainly appear to one who was not armed with a third and alternative theory—the thesis that both West and East drew the idea of the Cult of the Dead from a common source, a North African source.   My own belief is that this great and ancient cult, dating from the late Palæolithic times, spread from some centre in North-West Africa to Egypt on the one hand, and to Spain, Gaul, and eventually to Britain on the other.   That it had already begun to develop in Spain in late Aurignacian times we have seen, and that it invaded Britain through "Spanish"

influence about 2000 B.C., and Egypt about the
First Dynasty, is also clear. My contention is that
it was this very ancient cult which brought to Britain
the elements of that faith which later took shape as
Druidism, a religion which came to have an especial
hold and sanction in our island, and which was,
indeed, the root and beginning of British mysticism.
Britain, we know from Cæsar, was regarded as the
official home of Druidism. Let us see precisely what
evidence we possess of the North-West African
origin of the Cult of the Dead.

Mummification, the preservation of the human
body after death in order that it might once more be
revivified by the return of the spirit, seems to have
arisen in Egypt out of the Cult of Osiris, god of the
dead and the Underworld. Osiris does not make his
appearance in Egypt before the period of the First
Dynasty, or about 3400 B.C., when a centre of his
worship is found at Abydos. The so-called Book
of the Dead, or early fragments of it, are known to
have been in use in Egypt early in the Osirian era.

Now the Book of the Dead is obviously, in its
earlier fragments, the written expression of a much
older ritual dating from prehistoric times, and
digested into writing in early Dynastic or late pre-
Dynastic times. It is also the book of Osiris and
the Osirian cult. Dr. Budge says of Osiris "his
home and origin were possibly Libyan," that is, he
came from the West.

Sanconiathon, the Carthaginian writer, tells us
that the cult of the Cabiri, a mysterious religion,
originated in North-West Africa, and was delivered
among others "to the Egyptian Osiris." The
Cabiri are said by Sanconiathon to have been the
inventors of boats, of the arts of fishing, building and
agriculture, writing and medicine. There is little

doubt, indeed, that they were the old civilized race of the West, whom we have seen penetrating to British shores in their dug-out canoes. If Osiris was one of its apostles, then the religion of the Cabiri was merely the Cult of the Dead, as Sanconiathon asserts. Cicero calls the Cabiri the "Sons of Proserpine," goddess of the Underworld, which is to say as much. Dionysus of Halicarnassus, Macrobius, Varro, and others, regarded the Cabiri as the Penates of the Romans, that is the dead presiding as household familiars, and Vossius thought them the ministers of the gods who were deified after their death. Strabo regarded them as the ministers of Hecate, and Bochart recognized them as "infernal deities."[1]

This Cabirian cult, then, hailing from North-West Africa, is evidently nothing but a dim survival or memorial of the ancient civilized race of that region, which made its way into Spain, and after undergoing many phases there from Palæolithic to Neolithic times, gradually found its way, or sent its doctrine of the Cult of the Dead, to Egypt on the one hand and to Britain on the other. This theory explains in a word all the notions of Egyptian influence in Britain, and the many apparent resemblances between Egyptian and British mysticism and folk-belief.

But it may be said, and with some justice, that all this is scarcely of the nature of evidence. Who, after all, was Sanconiathon, someone may ask, the problematical Carthaginian model of a late Roman writer? It has, however, been proved long ago that Sanconiathon's account was in all probability genuine enough. Still, let us get on to firmer footing. We have it on the soundest authority that more than one race of African origin invaded or crossed over to

[1] See Rich, *Occult Sciences,* p. 160 ff.

Europe in Palæolithic and Neolithic times. Great theories, indeed, stand or fall by this assertion, and they are backed by sturdy proofs enow. The Capsian Culture, which came to Europe as we have seen, emanated from North-West Africa; it is, indeed, named after Capsa or Gafsa in Tunis. The Azilian culture is also indisputably African. "With the Capsian culture," says Professor Macalister, "must undoubtedly be associated the Spanish wall-paintings at Alpera, Cozul, and elsewhere . . . the Capsian flint industry is the parent of the Azilian-Tardenoisian." The Azilian culture in its earliest phase is to be found in North-West Africa.

Now my point is that these ancient cultures were flourishing in North-West Africa and Spain at a period about 10,000 years ago and more, when Egypt had no definite culture of any kind whatsoever, save the Badarian (ca. 9000 B.C.) in itself an echo of the Solutrean or late Aurignacian. The North African *cultus* had, indeed, been preceded by that of a much older race, the Crô-Magnon, which seems to have arrived in Spain about 20,000 years ago, and which certainly laid the foundations of the art of mummification. Yet in face of these facts the "Orientalists" insist that "civilization" is of older origin in Egypt and the East! Is it contended that the early culture of the Aurignacians, Capsians, and Azilians, primitive though it was, did not precede anything Egypt had to show, that they perished utterly and transmitted no traditions either to the peoples who succeeded them or to the East? Is it quite improbable that their cultural and religious ideas, however elementary, did not gradually and in the course of ages find their way to Egypt (where they developed under more favourable conditions) as

c

they certainly did to Britain at a later time by a much more difficult and dangerous route? Or is it contended that the similarity between their beginnings and that of Egypt is merely fortuitous?

Professor Macalister, in a memorable passage in his *Handbook of European Archæology*, gives it as his opinion that the Aurignacian race originated in Central Africa. All authorities agree that the Capsian and Azilian cultures developed in North-West Africa. That this culture reached the East and may have sent back cultural gifts in a superior form to Western Europe at a later period, I do not for a moment deny. But that is altogether another matter, and in any case the " Orientalists" have grossly exaggerated the importance of the "come-back". The point is that the earliest signs of civilization appear in North-Western Africa and Western Europe, and that nothing analogous appears in Egypt until about 9000 B.C., and even that date is dubious.

Now it cannot be questioned that the earliest civilized inhabitants of Egypt were of Iberian stock. Mr. H. R. Hall, an excellent authority, speaking of the earliest inhabitants of Egypt, says : " We see Egypt originally inhabited by a stone-using Hamitic race (the Iberians) related to the surrounding Semites, Libyans, and Mediterraneans." Again, he says : " In the Delta, they (the invading Armenoids) probably found a civilization of a primitive Mediterranean type much more advanced than in the Upper country. . . . The hiero-glyphic system, and all the accompanying culture that it implies, may have been theirs, but was more likely Mediterranean."[1]

No one gave closer or more prolonged study to

[1] *Cambridge Ancient History*, Vol. I, p. 264.

the origins of the Mediterranean or Iberian race than the late Professor Sergi of Rome. He writes : " But that original stock could not have its cradle in the basin of the Mediterranean, a basin more fitted for the confluence of peoples and for their active development ; the cradle whence they dispersed in many directions was more probably in Africa. The study of the fauna and flora of the Mediterranean exhibits the same phenomenon and becomes another argument in favour of the African origin of the Mediterranean peoples."

He proceeds to say that a study of the Hamitic race has assisted him in arriving at a conclusion. In the description "Hamitic" he includes ancient and modern Egyptians, Nubians, Abyssinians, Gallas, Somalis, Berbers, Fulahs, and the Guanches of the Canaries. The physical characteristics of all these peoples he finds to be essentially the same, and he looks for their place of origin in Africa. At first he did so in East Africa, in the region of the great lakes, near the sources of the Nile and in Somaliland, chiefly encouraged to do so by the fact that the race was so frequently and anciently portrayed on the Egyptian monuments, and by the presence of flint implements of the Palæolithic Age in the Nile valley. But extensive finds of worked flints are also found in North Africa and the Sahara. " The idea has thus arisen that Western rather than Eastern Africa was the original home of these peoples." That the Iberians of North-West Africa carried their culture to Egypt seems, therefore, much more than probable. The Western sites pre-date those of Egypt, and that fact alone should weigh with us, for the Iberians were merely the cultural descendants of the Capsians and Azilians. Moreover, as I shall show at a later stage, some of the rites and customs of the early Iberian peoples of Britain are still to be found in their pristine entirety among their Iberian kindred in North-West Africa. That the entire rite of Beltane, a rite adopted from the British Iberians by the Kelts, should survive in Morocco is, perhaps, the best proof not only of the Iberian origin of Druidism, but of the fact that an Iberian people actually brought it to our island.

The earliest notices of religion in Britain allude to a strange cult called Druidism, which, as we have seen, the Gauls believed to have originated in the country. An extraordinary mass of ponderous nonsense has been accumulated through the centuries relative to the nature and beliefs of this cult, and it is only recently that modern methods of study have been applied to the examination of such fragmentary material relative to it as is worthy of examination and has come down to us. In his remarkably interesting book *The Druids, a study in Keltic Prehistory*[1] Mr. T. D. Kendrick, of the British Museum, has succeeded in placing the entire question on a much more tolerable basis than formerly, and has made it possible to draw certain more or less final conclusions regarding the origins and nature of Druidism.

He is of the opinion that the Saxon invasion blotted out all memory of the Druids in Britain, and that this was gradually recovered only by the scholarship of the sixteenth century, a conclusion which is certainly open to challenge, as I hope to show later. But he is abundantly justified in his statement that the romantic revival ridiculously exaggerated the tradition of Druidism, describing it, however alluringly, in an unnatural and theatrical manner, at the same time disseminating the mendacious

[1] 1927.

legend that the Druids were actually the builders of the great stone monuments of a prior age.

Who, then, were the Druids? What were the origins of Druidism, what was its nature and forms of worship? To these questions which have agitated British archæology for nearly four centuries it is still impossible to supply definite and concrete answers, but they are now capable of being replied to in a sufficiently satisfactory general manner.

Although at the dawn of British history we discover Druidism as a cult practised officially by a people of Keltic race, there is every reason to believe that it was not of Keltic origin, but had been adopted by the Keltic invaders of Britain from her older and preceding population. But Mr. Kendrick refuses to discuss Druidic origins in Britain other than in the light of what we know of Druidism in Gaul, on the grounds that in Britain " it is too nebulous a thing to allow a reasonable basis for discussion." Nor can he square Druidic ascendancy in Gaul with Cæsar's statement that it originated in our island, to which the Kelts had penetrated only after their arrival in Gaul. Cæsar, he believes, merely recorded an opinion, not a statement of fact, which, however, was associated with the information that serious devotees of Druidism betook themselves to Britain for its closer study.

Proceeding, Mr. Kendrick reasonably infers that, did Druidism originate in Britain, it must have been established here long before Cæsar wrote. From a passage in Diogenes Lærtius (Vitæ, intro. 1.) we are aware that Sotion of Alexandria had alluded to Druidism as early as about 200 B.C. in the twenty-third book of his *Succession of Philosophers*, now lost. Its origin in Gaul, and, *a fortiori*, in Britain, were this the place of its beginning, must thus be of still greater antiquity, and, accepting the statement in Cæsar's writings as an expression of a general belief, Mr. Kendrick finds it "difficult to resist the conclusion that at the beginning of the La Tène period (the Iron Age) at the time of the first Keltic traffic with England, there existed in our country some novel religious element that after the Keltic invasion was grafted upon Keltic faith and spread throughout Gaul, giving rise to what thenceforward was termed Druidism."

But what was the specifically British element in Druidism? he asks. Was it the priesthood itself, or the Druidic theology or dogma? It does not seem likely to have been the first, in view of the complete subjugation of the conquering Kelts by a defeated caste which it implies. Nor were the Roman invaders particularly impressed by the Druid hegemony in Britain, to which they vouchsafe only passing mention.

But certain of the Keltic tribes and confederates did not have Druids, who seem to have been confined to Gaul and Britain. The original Keltic province lying between Switzerland and Hungary where the La Tène iron culture arose was certainly not peopled by a homogeneous race, if it enjoyed a common culture and language, and when at last it broke up in emigration its different elements were unlikely to retain the self-same religious ideas. For this and other reasons, Mr. Kendrick believes Druidism in Gaul to have been of Keltic origin, and he can find nothing in its beliefs "that was not also known to one or other of the indogermanic peoples." He admits that there is not "much encouragement for inquiry on these lines," however, and "that the time has come to attempt another method of approach."

This, Mr. Kendrick also admits, is "merely a hypothetical reconstruction of events." Summarized, it amounts to this : Gaul and Britain during the Bronze Age had achieved a general cultural unity and enjoyed intimate trade relations. This implies a certain religious unity. Two distinct provinces of culture in this area can be distinguished—one Western Gaul, Ireland, and Western and South-Western England, the other and more important, Northern Gaul and South-Eastern and Eastern England. The common religious bond joining all must have been of high antiquity, as a homogeneous flint culture had prevailed over the entire area for thousands of years.

But at the beginning of the Iron Age Britain became relatively more secluded because of the new Ligurian and East Germanic influences which were changing Continental civilization, and had, therefore, better opportunities for preserving its ancient religion in a pure form. This gave it a "religious distinction" on the Continent, and "native enterprise" may have done the rest. At this juncture the Kelts arrived in Eastern and North-Eastern Gaul, developing their special iron culture of the La Tène type in the Marne area. It has been shown that Stone Age artistic traditions in this very area were preserved until Roman times, and there seems to be "an equal probability of the persistence of native religious tradition." The Keltic invaders adopted the native faith of the land. Then came the Keltic invasion of Britain. But it was an invasion of Kelts whose minds had already been sophisticated by the prehistoric religious ideas of the Marne area. In Britain they encounter the same faith in its pristine purity, and would, therefore, have no difficulty in its adoption.

At the period of the concentration of the Kelts in their ancient home in the Alpine lands and in Central Europe they had not yet organized a priestly class of their own, but when they did so at last, they did so in Gaul, Mr. Kendrick believes, at some time in the fourth or third century B.C.   Thus the origin of Druids and of Druidism are different events due to different causes.   Druidism in Gaul, for Mr. Kendrick, is Keltic religion after amalgamation with the native faith it found in Gaul on its settlement there.   Druidism in Britain is the inclusion in the Kelticized faith of the ancient native British religion, which in itself was a purer form of the Continental native element in Druidism.

But while Druidism in Gaul was governed by a priestly caste, it seems to have been in Britain still under the sway of kings and chiefs rather than a priesthood.   At the time of the Keltic invasion of our island the Continental Kelts of Gaul had not yet developed the system.   Those who called themselves "Druids," when at last the word was introduced, " were only the magicians and soothsayers of a fugitive and desperate people " shattered by the Belgic occupation and the coming of the Romans. In view of evidence to the contrary it is difficult to agree with Mr. Kendrick on this head, and his attitude regarding it appears to me rather deliberately wayward, as I hope to be able to show, although he seems more favourably disposed to the theory of a Druidic official priesthood in Ireland, a " faint reflection " of the Gallic system.

If I have paraphrased Mr. Kendrick's conclusions at some length, I have done so because they agree with my own so completely that on perusing his excellent book I recognized not only the almost entire identity of his views with those held by myself for many years, but a treatment of the subject so convincing, yet so free from dogmatism as to provide a most suitable starting-point for such an inquiry as that on which I have embarked in this volume. Of course, Mr. Kendrick is in no sense responsible for the superstructure which I hope to erect on the bedrock of his conclusions, of which my own, prior to reading his work, were the more nebulous and shadowy duplicates. But a few of his minor findings appear to me rather unjustified, and in this preliminary examination of the Druidic question I feel I should advance my own views before approaching other issues.

In the first place, it is a little surprising to discover that Mr. Kendrick almost entirely ignores the subject of traditional survivals of the Druidic faith. In view of the extraordinary degree of attention which has been paid to this question by writers on Folklore, both accurate and the reverse, this attitude appears to me somewhat unaccountable, but as it is obviously Mr. Kendrick's expressed intention to employ only such materials as might justly be classed as "historical", and as the whole tenor of the present volume is in consonance with tradition, it is unnecessary to stress the point, which we will have abundant opportunity of returning to. But the almost entire neglect of the traditional aspect of his subject takes a more positive form when he gives it as his opinion that the Saxon invasion blotted out all memory of the Druids in Britain, and that the recollection of them was only recovered by later scholarship. The truth is that a hundred customs, chiefly local, scores of little rites and festivals survive in contradiction of this assertion, and these are almost as numerous in allegedly Saxon England as in Keltic Scotland and Ireland. All the same, these may not have been remembered as "Druidic." As in this chapter I am dealing with generalities alone, I refrain from citing instances, and leave for the moment the question of the Druidic nature of these rites, but I hope to adduce testimony that not only did a concrete memory of Druidism survive the Saxon invasion, but that a very powerful traditional recollection of it was handed down, and that the ripest Keltic scholarship is equal to the refutation of the theory that local place-names display only a fragmentary reminiscence of it, as Mr. Kendrick believes.

The argument that no regular and official caste of Druids existed in Britain, and that they were only the magi and sorcerers of "a fugitive and desperate people" at the time of the coming of the Romans seems not only to lack cogency, but to run directly counter to all the evidence. The very circumstance that the Gauls sent their neophytes to our island for instruction, is in itself almost sufficient to refute it. To whom did these apply for instruction in the priestly art and function? To the native kings and chiefs, whom, Mr. Kendrick supposes, took the place in Britain of the official priesthood in Gaul? Not only is this highly unlikely on the face of it, but the existence of a large and powerful caste of Druids in Mona or Anglesea refutes it. Tacitus distinctly alludes to Mona as the last refuge of Druidism in Britain ("insulam incolis validam et perfugarum receptaculum"), and this accounts for the absence of Druids in other parts of what is now England at a certain period. And I shall only remark here that the best possible evidence exists of the presence in Scotland at a much later date of a caste of Pictish Druids who owed nothing to Irish culture, and who were, indeed, hostile to the intervention of Irish Christian missionaries. As is now well known, the Picts were a people of ancient British stock, mingled with aborigines, the very stock, indeed, among which Druidism, or at least its aboriginal phase, was most likely to have flourished most strongly and to have survived longer than elsewhere, on Mr. Kendrick's own showing, and the late existence of Druidism and a Druidic priesthood in Pictavia is beyond dispute.

Not only is this the case, but it must be manifest that if Cæsar does not allude to the existence of Druids in South-Eastern Britain, that he does not do so for political reasons. Students from Gaul were not going all the way to Anglesea for their instruction. One sometimes sighs for a little practical commonsense in modern archæology, and it is badly needed here. It has been made clear by M. Camille Jullian that the Gaulish Druids took a leading part in the rebellion of Vercingetorix, but that Cæsar ignored the circumstance,[1] and Professor Haverfield saw in this studied neglect a desire on the part of the Roman conqueror not to intermeddle with a religious caste.[2] Mr. T. Rice Holmes, dealing very humanly with the question, suggests that " Cæsar may have bought over the Arch-Druid "[3] and thus have considered himself compelled to secrecy.

However this may have been, it seems incredible that no Druid caste officiated between Druidic Northern Gaul and Druidic Anglesea. The historical memory of the Druids was entirely at the mercy of their Roman enemies, and Cæsar, if reasonably just, was certainly not generously disposed to

---

[1] *Vercingetorix,* pp. 107-11, 1902.
[2] *Eng. Hist. Review,* 18, p. 336, 1903.
[3] *Ancient Britain,* p. 298, note.

his foes. I submit that this is a case where the absence of records is more eloquent than their presence. We have also to bear in mind that Cæsar had only a very limited knowledge of Britain, and that he expressly states that only the south-eastern coasts were inhabited by the non-Druidic Belgæ. Mr. T. Rice Holmes reasonably concludes : " It was British Druidism that supported and renovated the Druidism of Gaul, and formed one of the bonds of union between the two Keltic lands."[1] In any case it is sufficient for our purpose that Cæsar distinctly states that Britain was the Mecca of Druid disciples, and that Tacitus makes it clear that Anglesea was an important Druid centre. The two facts combined suffice to demonstrate that Druidism, so far from languishing in Britain, had a powerful hold in the island. It remains to show later that this authority and tradition was not destroyed in Roman times, but was retained as a secondary and secret faith in many parts of the country long subsequent to the introduction of Christianity, and that it contributed largely to the secret arcane tradition of the island of Britain.

The late Sir John Rhŷs was originally of the opinion that Druidism reached Gaul "undoubtedly through the Belgæ, who had settled in Britain". But in a later publication he gave it as his opinion that other people of Brythonic stock preceded the Belgæ in our island. From this he gathered that the date of the first mention of Druidism threw no light on its place of origin. He also believed that no "Belgic or Brythonic people ever had Druids", but received the belief from the older non-Keltic inhabitants.

That the Druids used the stone circles of Britain

for religious purposes is denied almost by the collective opinion of modern archæology. Tradition as unanimously credits them with the erection of most of our rough stone monuments, but tradition, according to the modern archæologist, is "an ass". The writer of the official Government guide to Stonehenge dismisses the theory in a few scathing sentences,[1] as does Mr. T. Rice Holmes, who admits that "in this country also the belief has long been growing that Druidism was of non-Keltic origin".[2] Yet M. Salomon Reinach[3] attributes the megalithic monuments of Gaul to Druidic influence.

The truth is that the stone monuments, or most of them, were constructed at a period so relatively early that it is extremely difficult to posit very much concerning the religion of the people who raised them. Mr. Stevens thinks that "it would not be inconsistent with existing evidence to set the date of Stonehenge roughly at from 1700-1800 years B.C.". Now this is precisely the period at which the men from Spain, whose culture is referable much farther back to North-West African sources, were voyaging to Britain and seemingly settling there. Whether their cult was "Druidism" or not, it certainly had in it the germs of that Iberian faith from which Druidism later resulted, so that if Stonehenge and other circles of the kind were not "built by the Druids", they may at least have been erected by proto-Druids, as I fully believe posterity will discover, by a people who, if they had not yet finally developed the faith of Druidism, which they were found in possession of in Cæsar's time, nearly

---

[1] H. Sumner, *Stonehenge,* pp. 66 ff.
[2] *Ancient Britain,* p. 115.
[3] *Revue Celtique,* XIII, p. 194, 1892.

seventeen hundred years later, were at least developing its tenets.

If the theory I have put forward in this book is worth anything at all, it must stand or fall by proof, to be adduced as we learn more of our megalithic monuments, that the *development* of Druidism was associated with them.   Druidism was a thing "Iberian" in the first instance, and so were they. Stonehenge was built at a period when the bronze culture had begun to overlap that of polished stone. Mr. Kendrick, from technical considerations, believes it to have been erected in the La Tène or Iron Age.   " If," he says, " Stonehenge was not a temple of Druidism, then it must have been a disused ruin in the La Tène period, when Druidism was the religion of the land."   He also points to the fact that a La Tène man was buried within its area, and believes that the "Kelticized population of Wessex took advantage of the ancient *national* sanctity of the old circle-site on Salisbury Plain to construct thereon a temple for their faith that should serve as a rallying-point, and, more than that, a stimulus, for Druidism after the failure of the order in Gaul, that is to say, in the 1st century B.C." He does not, however, class the other British megalithic structures along with Stonehenge, which he regards as relatively "classical" to their type, and sophisticated by Mediterranean architectural models.   But he wisely concludes that the true temples of the Druids in general were natural groves, except when the gradual influence of civilization "prompted them to translate the groves into buildings", such as Stonehenge, thus wiping out the possibility of the megalithic altars and rude stone circles being Druidic.   But, as I have suggested, they *may* have been proto-Druidic.

CHAPTER II

THE CULT OF THE DEAD

In our search for the origins of the ancient mysticism of Britain we are almost immediately arrested by the absorbing question of Druidism, which, like an immense forest, seems to draw all paths to it. As I have shown, efforts have been made to prove that Druidism scarcely flourished with such vigour in our island as in Gaul, and that in any case the Roman occupation speedily stamped it out. But the authorities who have advanced this view have omitted all consideration of the question of its survivals, those festivals and popular rites which can indubitably be proved to have been derived from it, and which not only illustrate its former ascendancy in Britain, but its age-long presence in the by-ways of popular affection for centuries after the Saxon invasion of England.

As I have said tentatively, I believe Druidism to have arisen out of a Cult of the Dead which had gradually been taking form during the long centuries of the Old Stone Age, and which, in the New Stone Age, had in a generalized state been disseminated east and west from some point in North-West Africa to Spain on the one hand and to Egypt on the other. From the former country it gradually found its way, both directly and through Gaul, to Britain. At the commencement of the Iron Age it became more especially segregated in this island, which at that period was more culturally apart from the Continent than during the Bronze Age. That this cult took on the colours of its environment in both Egypt and Britain is scarcely to be wondered at, but that it remained a Cult of the Dead in both countries there is evidence irrefragable.

That evidence, in the case of Egyptian religion, is so generally accepted as to need no demonstration here. But as regards its application to the early British faith, proof is essential, for the reason that so far it has not been tested or even advanced theoretically in any but a rather perfunctory way. Let us see then what evidence exists that Druidism was actually a branch of the great Iberian or Mediterranean Cult of the Dead.

" The Gauls," says Cæsar,[1] " state that they are all descended from a common father, Dis, and say that this is the tradition of the Druids." Now Dis is merely the Latin form of Pluto or Hades, god of the dead, lord of the shadowy region of the departed. To him is ascribed the invention of honouring the dead with funeral obsequies, and he it was who seized upon Proserpine and haled her off to his gloomy dwelling beneath the earth. Black bulls were his victims in sacrifice, the river Styx must be ferried to reach his realm. According to Rhŷs, he is the Keltic god Llyr, or Bran.

" With grand contempt for the mortal lot," says Ammanus Marcellinus,[2] " they professed the immortality of the soul." " One of their dogmas," writes Pomponius Mela,[3] " has come to common knowledge, namely, that souls are eternal, and that there is another life in the infernal regions. . . . And it is for this reason, too, that they burn or bury with their dead things appropriate to them in life, and that in times past they even used to defer the completion

---

[1] VI, 18, 1.   [2] XV, 9, 4.   [3] *De Situ Orbis*, III, 2, 18, 19.

of business and the payment of debts until their
arrival in another world. Indeed, there were some
of them who flung themselves willingly on the funeral
piles of their relatives in order to share the new life
with them."

Valerius Maximus,[1] describing the Druids of
southern France, says : " It is said that they lend to
each other sums that are repayable in the next
world, so firmly are they convinced that the souls
of men are immortal."

That they sacrificed criminals and even the
innocent to the *manes* of the dead or to the gods of
the dead is also clear enough from the statements
of Cæsar, Dion Cassius, Tacitus, Diodorus Siculus,
and other classical writers. This is a practice which
can spring only from one idea, that of placation of
the dead. True, it is occasionally to be observed
as an offering to the powers of growth, a rite of the
resurrection of the "dead", so to speak, but its early
history and origin undoubtedly point in the first
instance to a rite intended for the placation of the
deceased, and its relics are to be found in ancient
Egypt and elsewhere. Cæsar[2] informs us that it was
a custom of the Gauls to immolate the favourite
animals of the dead man on the funeral pile, and he
adds that not long before his time slaves and
retainers had been sacrificed. " Their funerals," he
says, " are very sumptuous and magnificent in
proportion to their quality. Everything that the
deceased person set the greatest value on is cast into
the pile, even animals, and formerly those vassals
and clients whom they held the dearest were obliged
to attend them to the other world." They also
believed " that the gods are never appeased but
by the death of one man for another, wherefore they

[1] II, 6, 10.   [2] VI, 19, 4.

have public offerings of the kind which are committed to the care of the Druids, who have large, hollow images bound about with osiers, into which they put men alive, and, setting fire to the image, suffocate them.   They believe thieves, outlaws, and other offenders to be the most grateful offerings to the gods, but, when honesty has made them scarce, the innocent are forced to supply their places.''

That the Cult of the Dead was well developed among the Kelts there are many other evidences. The bards sang the praises of departed her)es, and the tombs of some of these were regarded as sacred places.   More than one Irish god was believed to have his dwelling in a burial cairn.   In some cases the dead were interred around the family hearth, the spot round which the domestic lares or ghosts were wont to congregate.   On All Souls' Eve the Kelts of Brittany are still accustomed to spread a feast for the hungry dead, as did the Egyptians periodically. The ram and the serpent, Keltic symbols of the Underworld, are discovered as figurines among Gaulish grave-goods.

Canon MacCulloch, writing on the Cult of the Dead in his compendious work *The Religion of the Ancient Celts*, says :

> The dead were also fed at the grave or in the house. Thus cups were placed in the recess of a well in the churchyard of Kilranelagh by those interring a child under five, and the ghost of the child was supposed to supply the other spirits with water from these cups. In Ireland, after a death, food is placed out for the spirits, or, at a burial, nuts are placed in the coffin. In some parts of France milk is poured out on the grave, and both in Brittany and in Scotland the dead are supposed to partake of the funeral feast. These are survivals of pagan times, and correspond to the rites in use among those who still worship ancestors. In Keltic districts a cairn or a cross is placed over the spot where a violent or accidental death has occurred, the purpose being to

appease the ghost, and a stone is often added to the cairn by all passers-by.[1]

The practice of holding funeral games was also a Keltic rite associated with the Cult of the Dead, and recalls the Trojan obsequies. The dead were commemorated at certain of the festivals of fertility, such as Luguasad and Samhain, which symbolized the birth and death of vegetation, and which appear to have arisen out of the notion that certain slain persons represented spirits of fertility. "The time of earth's decay," says Canon MacCulloch, "was the season when the dead, her children, would be commemorated."[2] Sir James Fraser believes that the feast of All Saints (November 1st) was intended to take the place of the pagan Cult of the Dead.[3]

Now this form of the Cult of the Dead, as manifested in Druidism, must not be directly identified with the Pythagorean doctrine of re-birth or metempsychosis, according to which the soul took another bodily shape after death. It is clear that in Druidism we have an ancient and conservative form of the Cult of the Dead preserving a more early phase of it than that which was developed in Egypt. Mr. Kendrick has shown that although Cæsar identified the belief of the Druids in immortality with the Pythagorean doctrine, and was followed in so doing by Hippolytus, Clement, Valerius Maximus, and others, that they probably knew of it only in terms of Cæsar's statement, that it was improbable that any intercourse took place between Pythagoras or his disciples and the Kelts, so brief was the vogue of his doctrine and so circumscribed its scope. Again, "The recorded instances of resemblances between the Druidic and Pythagorean systems are not sufficiently remarkable to justify a claim for their intimate relationship ; and

[1] p. 167.   [2] op. cit. pp. 169-170.   [3] *Adonis*, p. 253 ff.

secondly, in each case the growth of the systems can be explained in local terms without recourse to such distant borrowings''.   He observes, too, that the views of the Gauls on the question of the soul's immortality, quoted above from Mela, show that they did not at all appreciate or profess Pythagoras's teaching, ''according to which such continued enjoyment of one's belongings or the transaction of postponed affairs after death was impossible.   They could not have believed, it is clear, in an instant metempsychosis, perhaps into animal as into other human bodies, but rather in the survival of the identity of the deceased in its recognizable form.''[1]

Mr. Kendrick then proceeds to search Keltic literature for instances of a belief in metempsychosis, and discovers several allegories, which, he demonstrates, although occasionally produced to assist the theory of transmigration, are scarcely illustrative of the belief.

But a far more trustworthy method of arriving at the true significance of the Druidic or ancient British Cult of the Dead, with its belief that souls might return to the body, is to be found in the survival of an idea which can readily enough be linked with ancient Keltic dogma.   The Keltic belief in a race of *sidhe* or fairies, by no means yet abolished, is most definitely a relic of the great Cult of the Dead as it flourished in Druidic times and, indeed, supplies all the evidence required that Druidism was essentially a mystery associated with the Otherworld and the belief in a process of reincarnation—but a reincarnation taking place at a period sufficiently removed from death to permit of a more or less prolonged existence in the Otherworld.

Research has now made it clear that the Keltic *sidhe* or ''fairies'', as the word has rather loosely been translated, are nothing more or less than the spirits of the dead. As the fairies of later folklore they are also, obviously enough, the ghosts of the departed.

That in many countries fairies were regarded as connected with the dead there is proof pressed down and running over. They were thought of as dwelling in a dim, subterranean sphere, in sepulchral barrows, or in a far paradise, like those fays encountered by Ogier the Dane or Thomas the Rymour. The Fairy Queen in the old ballad warns Thomas against eating the apples and pears which hung in her gardens, for to partake of the food of the dead is to know no return. This place of faery seems to be the same as the island of Avallon (the Place of Apples) or the Keltic Tir-nan-Og, the Land of Heart's Desire and renewed youth. A fairy who taught sorcery to the Scottish witches was said to have been killed at the battle of Pinkie some thirty years before. I think, too, that in the wearing of butterflies' wings by the fays of art and folk-tale one can discern a folk-memory of that Keltic belief that butterflies were the souls of the dead. Some races still retain the belief that on the death of a person his soul at once takes up its abode in the body of a new-born child. But the fairies are souls waiting their turn in a dim paradise for an opportunity to recommence the earth-life.

The belief that the fays were a dwarfish race appears to have been a later borrowing from the idea of the small and swarming Teutonic elves. The fays of Keltic folklore are of normal human height. The Irish *sidhe,* Morgan le Fay, the Welsh Y Mamau, or "the Mothers", are all of mortal bulk. So were the Breton fays, and those Scottish fairies who carried off Tamlane and taught witches the lore of the sorcerer. And each and all of them were in some manner associated with the realm of the departed.

The belief in fairy changelings is obviously the survival of an idea that the souls of the dead return to inhabit the bodies of mortal children. Faerie is, indeed, like the Melanesian *mana*, a great reservoir of soul-force, to which the human spirit, its bodily sheath destroyed or outworn, returns, and which is ever ready to pour out its psychic energy into the new-born mortal frame.

The belief in the *sidhe* or fairies, the dead awaiting a return to mortal life, was essentially a feature of Druidic belief, as early Irish and later Welsh literature shows, and this in itself suffices to demonstrate that Druidism was a Cult of the Dead. How far the idea of the *sidhe* was Keltic and how far aboriginal or Iberian is a problem the answer to which is not far to seek, for we find the *sidhe* constantly associated with burial chambers in Ireland and Scotland which were originally of Iberian or "aboriginal" origin. That they were accepted and used as Keltic and Druidic burial-places is certain enough, indeed they were probably employed in many cases as graves by successive generations in Ireland and Britain for centuries, as excavation has abundantly proved.

But if Druidism was, like the religion of Egypt, a Cult of the Dead, it was so with a difference. That cult was of early and rapid development in Egypt owing chiefly to its exceptionally hot and dry climate, which seems to have suggested and even naturally favoured the process of mummification. In Britain the Cult of the Dead passed through the same early phases as in Egypt, that is, coloration of the bones with red pigment, probable wrapping in skins, and cairn-burial accompanied by grave-goods. Here and there, too, large monolithic temples, somewhat resembling the grove-like pillared structures of Egypt, arose in association with it.

But when the Kelts entered Britain, bringing with them the La Tène iron culture, they appear to have introduced a form of thought somewhat opposed to the ancient Iberian or Mediterranean belief in the necessity for preserving the relics of the dead. There seems to have been a clash of ideas between the Keltic conquerors and the Iberian inhabitants which, in the event, resulted in a confusion of ideas, the acceptance on either side of a part of the religious beliefs of the other. The Kelts seem at first to have feared or disliked the Cult of the Dead as they found it in Gaul and Britain. Instead of regarding life as a mere ante-chamber of death, a preparation for the hereafter, as did the Iberians of Egypt and Britain, they rather considered it as one of the main objects of religion to preserve life in the fleshly body, and to keep the world of spirits at bay by placation and other means, as many other primitive people have done and still do. This explains their partiality for the mistletoe, the plant and emblem of life, the divine life-substance or protoplasm, their aversion from thieves, highwaymen, and murderers, whom they burned in the sacred fires along with the beasts of prey which depleted their flocks and herds. In short, any agency destructive of life or sustenance they waged relentless war upon, and this outlook is still, and always has been, typical of British popular philosophy and folk-sentiment. The Kelt was terrified of the *sidhe* or fairies, the spirits of the dead, to whom the Egyptians and Babylonians paid such meticulous reverence. The Oriental has always been comparatively indifferent to or acquiescent in the idea of death ; the Westerner has almost from the first dreaded and disliked it ; and in this difference of attitude we shall probably find grounds for much of the objection to early British survivals in later times.

But the Kelts could not altogether overcome the Iberian predilection for the worship of the departed, and had necessarily to compound with it. This explains, for example, their doctrine that money lent during life might be repaid in the Otherworld. Time and again we find the Cult of the Dead breaking through the structure of Druidism or Iberian-Keltic religion, merging with it at last in a complete pattern to compose a very special type of British Mysticism.

If these conclusions be granted, we are now enabled to take a clearer view of Druidism and to correct, in virtue of the light thus vouchsafed us, older theories concerning its tenets and practice. They may also assist us in allotting to folk-beliefs of later times, traditional festivals and the like, a Druidical significance so far as their manifestations square with the known facts.

All the evidence, classical and otherwise, goes to show that the Druids were a well-defined, priestly class with sub-divisions having different functions, religious, oracular, magical, administrative, and bardic. Diodorus, Strabo, and Timagenes, Cicero and Tacitus, allude to these classes separately or generally. The Irish evidence substantiates their existence. The Gaulish Druids, prophets, and bards are reflected in the Irish Druids, Fathi or Vates, and Filid or poets. In Wales both Druids and bards are found, and long after Druidism had outwardly vanished in the Principality the *derwydd-vard*, or Druid-bard, survived as a repository of Druid philosophy and belief. That both sections of the Keltic race, Goidelic and Brythonic, were under the sway of the Druids is abundantly clear. That Keltic religion and Druidism are interchangeable terms is also indubitable. That is as much as to say that it was not the mere addition of something Iberian and aboriginal as an annexe to Keltic faith, but a long-continued and well-developed fusion of early Keltic belief with Iberian belief, welded as to its parts, as the Kelt-Iberian race had been welded in Spain and Southern Gaul, and thus the psychological concomitant of the physical and racial admixture. The same process took place in Britain as on the Continent, the Iberian and Keltic races fusing in these islands in the same manner, and producing a like religious result. Only, by virtue of segregation from the Continent, Druidism in Britain seems to have taken on a special and insular colouring, and to have survived for a considerably longer period in the more outlying parts of the British archipelago.

Those who exalt the knowledge and philosophy of the Druids to supreme heights of magical and mystical ascendancy are obviously as mistaken as the opposing school who wish to reduce their status to that of mere witch-doctors. The probability is that they were at least the equals in scientific ability and general scholarship with the Egyptian priesthood of the closing centuries of the last pre-Christian millennium. Pomponius Mela refers to them as "teachers of wisdom", and as professing a knowledge of the size and shape of the world, and the movements of the heavens and stars. They were, he says, the instructors of the Gallic nobles.

Cæsar alludes to the Druids as teachers held in great honour, learning a great number of verses by rote as part of their mystery, making use of Greek letters, and versed in astronomical science. Diviciacus, the Æduan Druid, is quoted by Cicero as having "that knowledge of Nature which the Greeks call physiologia". Says Mr. Kendrick:

This, in conjunction with Cæsar's testimony, throws a flood of light on the conditions of service in the priesthood during the first century before Christ, and at once disposes of the quite natural idea that all its members were secluded and mysterious ancients, holding aloof from the common world in a gloomy atmosphere of esoteric ritual and priestly taboos.   For Divitiacus was a man of affairs, acknowledged ruler of the Ædui, and a politician and diplomatist of established reputation throughout the whole of Gaul.[1]

Diodorus Siculus describes the Druids as "philosophers and theologians", and Ammianus Marcellinus tells us that they were "uplifted by searchings into secret and sublime things".   Dion Chrysostom says that "they concern themselves with divination and all branches of wisdom".

Now I submit that all this goes to show that if the Druids were not the possessors of a vast *corpus* of native learning, they were at the least far removed from the status of mere medicine-men, which some obviously rather cynical authorities profess to believe they occupied.   The very fact that they employed written characters disposes of the charge, for it is known that they possessed a system of writing peculiar to themselves.   This is the alphabet known as Ogham, so called after Ogmios, the Keltic god of learning and eloquence, a method of writing which seems to have been confined entirely within the four seas of Britain.   Inscriptions carved in its characters have been discovered on rough stone monuments, cromlechs, and other stones, as well as on fragments of wood, in Cornwall, South Wales, the North and West of Scotland, and in Ireland.   Antiquarians have been familiar with the key to these symbols for upwards of a century (indeed, in some quarters it was never lost), and it was readily found that the language which they embodied was the Old Keltic, the forerunner of the tongue now known as Q-Keltic or Gaelic.

Its characters are of the very simplest and most

[1] op. cit. p. 80.

primitive form. Indeed, it would be extremely difficult to point to a script more artless or more practical in its design and ease of employment. It consists of a series of strokes written or carved on either side, or both, of a dividing line. Thus for the vowels the letter A is merely a single straight stroke meeting the line at right-angles. O consists of two similar strokes, U of three, E of four, and I of five.

H is a straight stroke beneath the line, and D, T, C, and Q or K are represented by from two to five strokes of the same kind. B, L, W, S, and N are indicated by from one to five strokes above the line, whilst M, G, NG, F, and R are slanting strokes crossing the line from right to left. The system can be mastered, so far as its alphabetics are concerned, in less than a quarter of an hour, and bears a close resemblance to the elementary exercises in Pitman's shorthand.

Another variety is known as Virgular Ogham, in which the strokes are indicated by a series of arrow-heads. In this system none of the strokes intersect the medial line. This line frequently consisted merely of the edge or corner of the stone or stick on which the inscription was carved; that is, the letters were carved on two faces of the stone, the edge acting as the dividing line. The majority of inscriptions in Ogham appear to date from the early pre-Christian centuries, and that it was a script in use among the Druids in Ireland, Cornwall, and Scotland there is no reason to doubt.

But, besides the Ogham, the Druids of Britain made use of an even more interesting and certainly more involved system of writing. This, called by a British name, Bobileth, which may be translated "Tree-writing", consisted of thirty-four characters, and in Old Keltic, or Gaelic, was known as

Bethluisnion, from the names of the first three letters, "Beth", the birch tree, "Luis", the quicken, and "Nion", the ash. Of this alphabet each letter was named after a tree. It was written on tree bark, or on smooth tablets of birchwood known in Erse as Taible Fileadh, or "Poets' Tablets", and the characters themselves were described as "twigs" and "branch-letters". It was to this kind of writing that the Welsh bard Taliesin alluded when he sang : " I know every reed or twig in the cavern of the chief diviner." The Bobileth script could be used symbolically by composing a message made up of the leaves of the appropriate trees strung on a cord, a system which recalls the quipus or messages of the ancient Incan Peruvians made of knotted strings. Very probably this was the original—or at least one of the earliest—methods of communication in vogue in Britain before it occurred to the Druidic inventors that to write the hieroglyphs or pictures of the trees themselves was a much more simple and effective process, and we can scarcely doubt that from some such mode of picture-writing the Bobileth alphabet was later developed ; in any case the tree-names of the alphabet are still preserved in the Keltic languages of Britain.

Under Roman persecution the Druids disappeared —or seemed to disappear. Says Strabo : " On account of their evil sacrifices the Romans endeavoured to destroy all the superstition of the Druids, *but in vain*." The Druids were, indeed, the protagonists of their country's liberty, the patriots of an island Keltic in its culture and sentiment, and still preponderatingly so, whatever may be said or written to the contrary. They saw their beloved isle invaded, torn, and despoiled by the crudest of materialists, by men whose whole desire was to loot it of its treasure of gold and pearls, as they themselves declared—first by Julius Cæsar, the decadent of Roman society, "the inevitable co-respondent in every fashionable divorce case", as he has been called, then by Agricola, the sycophantic servant of a wretched tyrant. Did not the Druids appreciate and rightly gauge the character of their enemies? In view of the known culture of Britain, its beautiful craftsmanship and work in enamelling, jewellery, and coinage, the eloquence of its priesthood, the skill of its mariners, whose vessels were of a tonnage and sailing capacity immeasurably superior to the rather primitive galleys of the Romans, the assumption that our ancestors were mere barbarians is indeed one of extraordinary short-sightedness.

The Druids retreated in front of their merciless enemies to the forests and fastnesses of our island.[1] But on the retreat of the Italian conquerors and their rather pitiful native auxiliaries, they returned, as the Irish version of Nennius declares, in the reign of Vortigern.[2] A number of them had revolted against Rome after the death of Nero in the year A.D. 68, which in itself is the best of proof that more than a century after the first Roman invasion of our island the order had not been effaced. In A.D. 70 a diet of them gathered and prophesied the world-empire of the Kelts.[3] Ausonius mentions that even in the fourth century men in Gaul were wont to boast of their Druidic descent.[4] And if the tradition flourished so long in Gaul, how much more must it have done so in the remote and un-Romanized portions of Britain, in Wales, Scotland, and Ireland? In the sixth century the Druids opposed Columba in Scotland as in Ireland they had opposed St. Patrick, pitting their magic against that of the Christian missionaries.

[1] D'Arbois, *Les Druides*, p. 73.   [3] *Tacitus,* IV, 54, 4.
[2] p. 238; and *Hist. Britonum,* p. 40.   [4] V, 12; XI, 17.

I believe that it is not improbable that the Druids flourished for centuries as a *cultus* under the name of Culdees. The Culdees are generally supposed to have been a caste of Christian priests or monks of early British origin, unfriendly to Roman authority and discipline. But there are many circumstances connected with them which seem to show that, if they practised a species of Christianity, their doctrine still retained a large measure of the Druidic philosophy, and that, indeed, they were the direct descendants of the Druidic caste.

We find the Culdees, previously to the arrival of Augustine in 597, in various parts of England, Scotland, and Ireland, and they must have differed in their views very considerably from the Roman priesthood, else they would not have been persecuted by them, as Bede avers. They married, and their abbots held office by hereditary right, so that in Armagh fifteen generations held the episcopate successively. They dwelt in colleges, practising music as well as the mechanical arts. They celebrated Easter at a different period from the Roman hierarchy, holding it a month before the Roman festival. They shaved the head in a tonsure from their foreheads backward, in the form of a crescent, baptized infants by immersion, without the consecrated chrism, were opposed to the doctrine of the real presence, and denied the worship of saints and angels. They condemned the mass, paid no respect to holy relics, and refused to offer up prayers for the dead. In fact, anything less resembling Roman practice than theirs can scarcely be imagined. Many early Christian writers condemn the rudeness of their forms of worship and the unauthorized character of their ecclesiastical government. The second Council of Chalons denounced them as heretics in 813, and the fifth canon of the Council of Ceal-Hythe decreed in 816 that they were not to be permitted to function as priests in England.

At St. Andrew's, in Fife, the Culdees "continued to worship in a certain corner of the church after their own manner", says the registry of the Priory of St. Andrew's, "nor could this evil be removed till the time of Alexander of blessed memory, in 1124", so that Culdees and Roman priests performed their services in the same church for nearly three hundred years !

Now it is only in such districts as Druidism is known to have lingered in for generations that hereditary priestly descent in the Christian Church has been observed. In Brittany it prevailed until it was abolished by Hildebert, Archbishop of Tours, in 1127. At the end of that century Giraldus Cambrensis complains of it as a disgrace to Wales that sons should follow their fathers in the priestly office.

Moreover, it is precisely in these localities where Druidism had been most strongly entrenched that we find the largest Culdee settlements. At Ripon and York they dwelt and flourished in the time of Bede, and they worshipped at the Church of St. Peter in the latter city so late as the year 936. Their chief seat in Scotland was the island of Iona, the ancient name of which was Inis Druineach, or "the island of the Druids".

With the monastery of St. Columba at Iona is associated a weird legend which tells how the saint was unable to found a church there because of the machinations of an evil spirit, who threw down the walls as fast as they were built until a human victim was sacrificed and buried under the foundations.[1] Very probably the story is a survival from the

[1] Jamieson, *Hist. of the Culdees*, p. 21.

Druidic forerunners of Columba. Under each of the twelve pillars of one of the circular temples of Iona, according to Higgins, a human body was found to have been buried.[1] Jamieson remarks that the Culdees succeeded the Druids in Iona at no great length of time. When Columba came to Iona he was opposed by one Broichan, a Druid, and Odonellus relates that on the Saint's landing in the island he was met by Druids, who *disguised themselves in the habits of monks*. They told him that they had come there to preach the Gospel, but he discovered the imposture, and they resigned the field to him.[2]

All this tends to show that the Culdees, who dwelt on Iona and professed the rule of Columba, were merely Christianized Druids, mingling with their faith a large element of the ancient Druidic *cultus*.

The account of the coming of Columba in Adamnan's life of the saint reveals very clearly that he himself was not unacquainted with Druidic lore. Indeed, he opposed the Druids with arts similar to their own. In a striking passage Canon MacCulloch observes :

Since Christian writers firmly believed in the magical powers of the Druids, aided, however, by the devil, they taught that Christian saints had miraculously overcome them with their own weapons. St. Patrick dispelled snowstorms and darkness raised by Druids, or destroyed Druids who had brought down fire from heaven. Similar deeds are attributed to St. Columba and others. The moral victory of the Cross was later regarded also as a magical victory. Hence also lives of Keltic saints are full of miracles which are simply a reproduction of Druidic magic—controlling the elements, healing, carrying live coals without hurt, causing confusion by their curses, producing invisibility or shape-shifting, making the ice-cold waters of a river hot by standing in them

[1] G. Higgins, *The Celtic Druids*, p. 202.
[2] Higgins, p. 204; Smith, *Life of Columba*, p. 92.

at their devotions, or walking unscathed through the fiercest storms. They were soon regarded as more expert magicians than the Druids themselves. They may have laid claim to magical powers, or perhaps they used a natural shrewdness in such a way as to suggest magic. But all their power they ascribed to Christ. "Christ is my Druid"—the true miracle-worker, said St. Columba. Yet they were imbued with the superstitions of their own age. Thus St. Columba sent a white stone to King Brude at Inverness for the cure of his Druid Broichan, who drank the water poured over it and was healed. Soon similar virtues were ascribed to the relics of the saints themselves, and at a later time, when most Scotsmen ceased to believe in the saints, they thought that the ministers of the kirk had powers like those of pagan Druid and Catholic saint. Ministers were levitated, or shone with a celestial light, or had clairvoyant gifts, or, with dire results, cursed the ungodly or the benighted prelatist. They prophesied, used trance-utterance, and exercised gifts of healing. Angels ministered to them, as when Samuel Rutherford, having fallen into a well when a child, was pulled out by an angel. The substratum of primitive belief survives all changes of creed, and the folk impartially attributed magical powers to pagan Druid, Celtic saints, old crones and witches, and Presbyterian ministers.[1]

Still, the people would not have believed these things possible had not a large leaven of the old belief survived. Indeed, its last echoes have not yet died away, even in the great cities of Scotland, much less in the Highlands and islands.

I think I have said enough to prove that Druidism had not died out in Scotland at least in the sixth century, and that is all I wish to do at the moment. I might speak of Columba's magical war with the Druids of Inverness, or of the proof that Druids survived in other districts of the North, but the above evidence surely suffices.

The evidence of the survival of a Druid priesthood in Ireland until comparatively late times is sufficiently plentiful. In Erin they were not only the companions

[1] op. cit. pp. 331-2.

but the tutors of the native kings and princes, and they sat in judgement in criminal cases, as did the *filid*, their descendants and successors. That they had written records we know, for King Loegaire requested that the books of Saint Patrick and those of the Druids should both be subjected to the ordeal by water to prove which were the more efficacious. They were in the habit of baptizing children, and of one hero it is told that they chanted the baptismal rite over him as an infant. They also took part in burial rites, and presided over the sacrifices which were made at the entombment. They practised the healing art, and of Cuchullin it was said that had Fergus been ill "he would have taken no rest till he had found a Druid able to discover the cause of that illness". They are spoken of as wearing cloaks of white, and in some cases as wearing bulls' hides, presumably after sacrifice. They also wore a tonsure which seems to have borne some relation to that used later by the Culdees. The Irish texts appear to have been re-edited with special relation to the omission of all material relating to the Druids, but in most accounts of the salient occurrences in Irish history they are referred to in such a manner as makes it impossible to doubt their great influence in political and public affairs. The Irish deities known as the Tuatha De Danann are alluded to as masters of Druidic lore. Female Druids functioned as priestesses or guardians of the sacred fires at Kildare and elsewhere, and to them Christian nuns duly succeeded.

In the Irish popular tales and sagas Druidism is mentioned so frequently as to prove beyond doubt that it was the ancient religion of Erin. In these "Druidism" stands for magic, and *slat na draoichta* or "the rod of druidism" for the magic wand. Of their feats in the mysterious arts the sagas are eloquent. They flooded plains, produced blizzards and fiery hail-storms, overcast mountains, and turned stones into armed men. They assumed what shapes they pleased, or made others assume them. They could cause forgetfulness by a magic draught, and seem to have possessed hypnotic powers. Their training included memorizing long incantations and spells, and these descended to the *filid*, or poets, their successors. The very earliest written records of Ireland refer to "the Science of Goibniu", a master of Druidic magic, and to "the healing of Diancecht", and these are to be found in manuscripts of the eighth or ninth century still in use magically in Christian times.

"When we recall the fact," says Mr. Kendrick, "that there most certainly were important assemblies held in Ireland, taking place at fixed intervals and attended by delegates from distant parts, it will be seen that we cannot fairly assume that Irish Druidism lacked that co-ordination of its members such as obtained in Gaul." And again : "It is significant that the Druids of Ireland were servants of the primitive Keltic festival-system in its central European form."

The evidence for the existence of Druidism in Wales is even more abundant, and exhibits more positive proofs of the continuance of the cult in the Principality until a relatively late date. There is every reason to believe that on the arrival of the Saxons and the consequent withdrawal of the Kelts of South Britain to what is now called Wales, whence large numbers of them certainly sought refuge, the cult of Druidism found a haven among the Welsh mountains. I am aware that several writers of authority have questioned both the emigration and the religious revival which accompanied it, but they have done so not on acceptable historical evidence, but on "reasonable" grounds alone. However, no arguments are reasonable which do not rest on solid proof, and these certainly do not.

That Druidism did not die out in Wales after the Roman period is clear enough, although the point has been hotly contested. Not only do the Triads conserve notices of its survival until at least the sixth century of our era, but the memorials of folklore prove it to have lasted much longer in a more or less corrupted form. Indeed, the Bards of Wales pretended to a knowledge of the mystical lore of the Druids. The bard Gwalchmai (1150-1190) says, in his elegy on the death of Madog, Prince of Powys : " Would to God the day of doom were arrived, since Druids are come bringing the news of woe."

We find the position of the Bard laid down clearly enough by Cynddelw, a contemporary of Gwalchmai, in his panegyric on Owen Gwynedd, in which he says : " Bards are constituted the judges of excellence, and bards will praise thee, even Druids of the circle, of four dialects, coming from the four regions." Elsewhere in a poem recited at a poetic contest, he speaks of "Druids of the splendid race, wearers of the gold chains", as if they were still existing. In another poem addressed to Owen Cyveilcawg, Prince of Powys, he makes repeated mention of the Druids : " It is commanded by Druids of the land . . . let songs be prepared", and in his elegy on the death of Rhiryd, he calls himself "a bard of Keridwen, the mystic goddess", and alludes to the poems of Taliesin as follows : " From the mouth of Taliesin is the Bardic mystery, concealed by the Bards". Llywarch ab Llewelyn (1160-1220) also alludes to "the order of the primitive Bards", and speaks of the prophecies of the Druids as if they were his contemporaries. Philip Brydydd, president of the Bards (1200-1250), alludes to the Bardic contests and to aspirants to the chair he holds, saying that none in the presence of the grave Druids of Britain could aspire to it without distinction in their art ; thus also mentioning the Druids as his contemporaries.

There is, indeed, little doubt that some more or less corrupted survival of Druidism was known in Wales even so late as the thirteenth century, as we shall see in the ensuing chapters.

NOTE : Davies in his *Mythology of the British Druids*[1] rather elaborately outlines the evidence for the existence of Druidism in North Britain in the sixth century A.D. In the story of Coll, "the great mystagogue" of Cornwall, he says, it is stated that this magician gave to Brynach, prince of the Northern Gwyddelians of Strathclyde, in Scotland, a present of the Eaglet which was deposited by the mystical sow whose symbolical progeny was farrowed nearly over the entire length of Britain. The young of this eagle were the "two dusky birds of Gwenddoleu, prince of the Strathclyde Britons, who lived about 593, and who was defeated and slain by the Saxon prince of Deira and Bernicia, the defeat of a Druidic prince and mystic, Davies believed, by a Christian Saxon ruler. Merlin, he states, was a priest of Gwenddoleu, as is mentioned in the poem called "Avallenau", and to him the prince presented a hundred and forty-seven apple trees, which Davies thought were the mystical letters enshrining the secrets of Druidism. " Gwenddoleu," he writes, " was the head of an ancient Druidical establishment in North Britain."

Continuing his description of Merlin, he writes :

[1] p. 462 ff.

Merddin is styled supreme judge of the North; that is, of the regions beyond the little kingdom of Strath Clwyd; and the *Syw*, or diviner, of every region: and in virtue of this office he was *Cerddglud Clyd Lliant*, president of Bardic lore, about the waters of Clyde.   He was companion of *Canawon Cynllaith*, the offspring of the goddess of slaughter, whom Aneurin thus commemorates, in the songs of the Gododin: " If, in the banquet of mead and wine, the Saxons sacrificed to Slaughter, the mother of Spoliation; the energetic Eidiol also honoured her before the mount, in the presence of the god of victory, the king who rises in light, and ascends the sky."   And this connection between the British divinities of slaughter and victory is marked in the character of Merddin, or Merlin, who is styled: *Allwedd byddin Budd Ner*—the key or interpreter of the army of the god of victory.

He was the brother of *Gwenddydd Wen, Adlam Cerddeu*—the fair lady of the day, the refuge of Bardic lore—a mythological character; and this lady addresses the venerable priest in the following terms: "Arise from thy secret place, and unfold the books of the *Awen* (Bardic spirit), the object of general dread, and the speech of *Bun* (Proserpine) and the visions of sleep."

These are some of the qualifications of Merddin, as recorded by a *Northern*, but unknown Bard, who wrote in his name and character about the year 948.   He was a supreme judge, a priest, and a prophet—and he was conversant in the mysteries of the very same divinities, *Cynllaith, Budd, Awen,* and *Bun,* which were revered at the great temple of Stonehenge.

Stephens, however, in his *Literature of the Kymry*[1] does not believe these poems to be earlier than the reign of Owen Gwynedd (1160), and points to a circumstance of anachronism in that the poet has made Merlin a devout Christian !   It is difficult, therefore, to regard this "evidence" seriously, and it is only given here for the sake of completeness. At the same time it is certainly partially authenticated by other more trustworthy MSS., and there can be no doubt that Druidism did survive in the Cymric portion of Southern Scotland for centuries.

[1] p. 233 ff.

CHAPTER III

THE MYSTERY OF KELTIC PHILOSOPHY

THE mystery of Keltic thought has been the despair of generations of philosophers and æsthetes. The debate concerning it has been scarcely less amazing in its vehemence than that other and allied controversy on the origin of the Keltic race. Renan and Arnold manifestly wrestled with it much in the same primitive manner as the astrologers of Chaldea strove with the science of the stars. But an abyss so profound is scarcely to be plumbed by the discernment of the polite essayist, or measured by the logical processes of the student of Comparative Religion. It is a task for the prophet or the seer, for a Blake or a Brahan Seer. To the man who has no magic in his blood the cavern of Keltic profundity is for ever sealed. He who approaches it must, I feel, not alone be of the ancient stock of the first culture-bringers of this island, but he must also have heard since childhood the deep and repeated call of ancestral voices urging him to the task of the exploration of the mysteries of his people.

The Kelts, that race of artists, poets, and aristocrats, appear originally to have formed themselves into a nation in the region betwixt France and Hungary, in all likelihood in the South German plain between Switzerland and Bohemia, and probably developed slowly as a nation from a race known as the "Urn-Field people", a Bronze Age folk. In the course of generations they became welded into a nation, and as such they were known to the Greeks at least 500 years before our era, their country being spoken of by Hellenic writers as Keltica.   They introduced the iron civilization of La Tène into Gaul and Britain, and in doing so mingled with races of older occupancy, losing some of their racial characteristics in the process, perhaps.   But their cultural and æsthetic outlook, their peculiar philosophy, they did not lose, notwithstanding that this must have been powerfully affected by the beliefs and customs of the peoples with whom they intermixed, so that even to-day, although the name Kelt is rather confusedly applied to mixed races of almost wholly different physical appearance, to Welsh, Irish, Scots, and Bretons alike, there still remains among these dissimilar types a mental habitude and a similarity of opinion and outlook which reveal the previous existence of a common philosophy and a common tradition.

The Kelt, tall or short, long- or round-skulled, dark, fair or rufous, is nevertheless scarcely to be mistaken so far as his mental qualities are concerned. He was labelled by the older School of Anthropologists, by Broca, and others, as "sanguine-bilious", and one can see no good reason to doubt or discard the psychological diagnosis.   He reveals himself normally as a man frequently gloomy and irritable, prone to the sudden illumination of enthusiasm, a man of prolonged silences, suddenly garrulous, dreamy, but passing from repose to violent but usually short-lived action.   Conservative and superstitious, fatalist, fearless, he is all these things. Yet he is as various individually as the men of other races, in some cases highly emotional, in others strangely passive.   In all probability the general type of man we now call the Kelt displays the several psychological facets of the various races with whom his primal stock originally mingled, and, according to the law of miscegenation, these assume a different form with each individual, as he throws back to Iberian, Teutonic, or other ancestors. But, despite the intermixture, the ancient leaven of Kelticism triumphs and the peculiar genius of the ancient race —strong because so ancient and so perfectly moulded in the matrix of its origin—shines with an almost superhuman radiance through the veils of alien character or idiosyncracy which in some cases even seem at first sight to have obliterated it. One must often wait long and patiently to behold the illumination. But some day under stress of passion or triumph or sorrow it will manifest itself in such a way that it cannot be mistaken, in the sad, low, characteristic laugh, the gloomy and ominous scowl, in a quick exasperation and fierce resentment which will surprise or amuse men of slower blood, or in the proud and haughty scorn to which the finer and more purely-bred scions of this race of Europe's aristocrats are so disconcertingly prone.

What is the mystical secret of the Kelt, poet, prophet, warrior, aristocrat among aristocrats? It is the memory, the soul-recollection of a former moral and intellectual pre-eminence which he has not lost, for its gifts remain within him, but the arcanum of which he cannot discover. He is like a man with a chest of treasure who has lost the key.

In this repository lie the Books of the Secrets of Britain, those most ancient and mysterious volumes containing the lore of the civilizing race of this island in its pristine days. The secrets it holds are of inestimable spiritual concern and importance to the people of a land still overwhelmingly Keltic in thought and character. That Britain, to which the whole world looks for guidance in science and political thought, which governs almost one quarter of the globe, which has achieved triumphs unparalleled in the fields of scholarship, invention, and government, whose light burns above those of all nations, should yet not be enabled to boast a native mysticism of her own, but be compelled to borrow from Eastern sources to supply this deficiency, is humiliating indeed. It is not that that native mystical tradition does not exist. It lies almost undisturbed in the cavern of the Keltic past, whence it is still possible to regain it for the behoof of our race.

The first task before us in seeking to recover the secret of the Keltic Grail is, naturally, to review briefly the material, documentary and otherwise, which may help us to a just understanding of the mystical literature of the British Kelt. It is from this and from the relics of early British faith and philosophy as evinced in popular rites of immemorial tradition that we hope to glean the broken sherds of the vessel of British native mysticism, and to piece them into a recovered and restored whole.

The mystical and occult literature of the Brythonic Kelts of South Britain is partly derived from the collection of tales known as the *Mabinogion*, which, though existing in a MS. of the fourteenth century, was obviously composed at a much earlier date, as its mythological character proves. The Welsh Triads likewise enshrine similar material, dating, probably, from the twelfth century, but embalming mystical lore greatly more ancient. The so-called *Book of Taliesin*, written, or more probably re-written, at some time during the fifteenth century, is on the same footing. The many efforts to disprove the authentic and ancient character of the mythological material contained in these MSS. have signally failed, made as they were by literary persons for the most part unacquainted with mythological science.

The question of the survival of Druidical knowledge in the bardic poetry of Wales is one which has been debated with unusual heat. One of the earliest protagonists of the theory of its continuity was the Rev. Edward Davies, who, in his *Mythology of the British Druids*, uncompromisingly and wholeheartedly addressed himself to its affirmation. It has been proved amply enough by Nash and others[1] that his translations of the ancient Welsh poems were somewhat inexact and garbled, and that his mythological notions of the existence of a "Helio-Arkite" religion in Wales until a late date were sufficiently absurd. But as the "translations" of his critics were equally bad and their views equally unsound, allowances must be made for him. His theories were further elaborated by the Hon. Algernon Herbert in his anonymous works : *Britannia after the Romans* (1836) and *The Neo-Druidic Heresy* (1838), in which he gave it as his belief that the adherence to the old paganism of the Druids had caused a schism in the British Church, and encouraged the maintenance of a Neo-Druidic heresy therein.

Their opponents indicated not only that the majority of their translations were inexact, but that many of the passages believed to be of a mystical or mythological nature were in reality of Christian origin. But in doing so, they went too far—as far, indeed, as Davies and Herbert had gone in the other direction. The truth is that when the Welsh poems in *The Book of Taliesin, The Red Book of Hergest, The Black Book of Caermarthen*, and in the tales in the *Mabinogion* are sifted and examined scientifically, they still contain a residuum of mystical

[1] See his *Taliesin*, 1858.

and mythological material not to be accounted for by the methods of their critics.

These were not practical mythologists or mystics, and most of them (Nash, in particular, as Skene has shown) had a very short way of dismissing evidence which ran counter to their ideas. They stressed the notion that the bards of Wales, Taliesin, Llywarch Hên, and Aneurin referred to the deities of ancient Britain æsthetically, as might the Augustan poets to the gods of classical mythology. But the direct and personal manner in which the allusions are often made renders such an idea quite untenable.

Moreover, as will be shown, there is nothing inherently impossible in the idea that the ancient British religion and mysticism lingered in Wales and other distant parts of the island for many centuries after the departure of the Romans. Those who adopt the negative positive have to explain the presence of hundreds of surviving superstitions in Britain at the present time, the burning of a Welsh Druidic idol along with its priest in London in the reign of Henry VIII, the comparatively recent sacrifice of bulls in the Highlands of Scotland in connection with primitive rites, the existence of such celebrations as the worship of Shoney in the North of Scotland, and many other similar festivals which will be adduced in their proper place, the late observance of witchcraft, a broken-down survival of Iberian-Keltic religion, and a host of other evidences. They have also to account satisfactorily for the survival of antique faiths elsewhere in lands where paganism has, to all intents, seemingly been rooted out for centuries, for the Nagualism of Mexico and Central America, for the Antiche Religione or the worship of Diana in modern Italy, and for similar beliefs and practices in the Balkans and Russia.

This is not the place for a full-dress discussion on the authenticity of the ancient Welsh literature as a whole. Yet the present writer cannot but subscribe to its partial witness for the preservation of a very considerable body of authentic British lore of Druidic and Keltic origin. That being so, he will endeavour to employ only such evidences of it as appear to him safe and reasonable to make use of, and will do so without further apology for its witness unless where such appears essential to the course of reasonable proof.

Before proceeding to examine the mystical material they contain, it will be well to summarize briefly such information as we possess regarding the principal divinities of whom these tales and poems recount the adventures. Some of them have been identified with the gods of the Gaels, but the majority of them have a local and strictly "Welsh" character. It is safe to say, however, that they are of both Brythonic and Goidelic origin, the results of a mingling of beliefs and tales common to both branches of the Keltic family, as is admitted by the majority of standard authorities.

The first group to attract our attention, and perhaps the most outstanding, is that of Llyr, as alluded to in the *Mabinogion*. Llyr is god of the sea, and the histories of his sons Bran and Manawydden, his daughter Branwen, and the half-brothers Nissyen and Evanissyen are recounted in the stories of Branwen and Manawydden. These allude to the invasion of Ireland, to whose king Branwen had been married. Manawydden is Lord of Elysium, and a craftsman and agriculturist. Bran is chiefly famous as the possessor of a magical head which, after death, prophesied and protected the island of Britain from invasion. He presided over poetry and bardic music, and was of titan mould. He seems to have been associated with the world of the hereafter, or rather the underworld of fertility, as is his sister Branwen, as her possession of a magic cauldron reveals.

The children of Don, another Brythonic group, are Gwydion, Gilvæthwy, Amæthon, Govannon, and Arianrhod, with her sons Dylan and Llew. They resemble the Irish Tuatha De Danaan, and their adventures are described in the *mabinogi* of Math, which recounts the passion of Gilvæthwy for Math's handmaiden Goewin, and the manner in which Gwydion procures the magical swine of Pryderi, which had been gifted him by Arawn Lord of Annwn or Hades. Math is obviously a territorial and local god of Gwynedd in Wales, a magician *par excellence*, a "god of Druidism". Gwydion is the patron of poetry, divination, and prophecy, the ideal bard, as well as a philosopher and culture-bringer. Amæthon is a husbandman, and Govannon a "smith" or artificer, a species of Keltic Vulcan. Arianrhod, or "Silver Wheel", represented the constellation Corona Borealis, but is also associated with the earth's fertility.

Another group found in the *Mabinogion* is that of Pwyll, Prince of Dyved, his wife Rhiannon, and their son Pryderi. Pwyll changes places for a year with Arawn, King of *Annwn*, or Hades, and makes war on his rival Havgan. Still another group is that of Beli and his sons Llud, Caswallawn, and Llevelys.

In *The Book of Taliesin* we encounter a group still more important from the mystical point of view, that of Keridwen, her hideous son Avagddu, his sister Creirwy, and his brother Morvran. So that Avagddu, the ugly, may be compensated by the possession of supernatural knowledge, Keridwen prepares a cauldron of inspiration which must be brewed for a year, and which will produce three drops of divine fluid. She sets a servant, Gwion, to watch it, and the three drops falling on his finger, he conveys it to his mouth and becomes inspired. Keridwen, in her anger, pursues him, and as he assumes various forms, a hare, a fish, and a grain of wheat, in his flight, she takes on the shape of a greyhound, an otter, and at last a hen, in which guise she swallows the grain, later bearing Gwion as a child, whom she abandons to the sea in a coracle. As we shall see, this myth is all-important to an understanding of British mystical lore. The child she abandons to the waves becomes, later, Taliesin, the magical bard.

The Druidic bards who lived and sang under the Welsh princes unanimously represent Keridwen as presiding over the hidden mysteries of their ancient cult. Cynddelw, who flourished about the middle of the twelfth century, sings : " How mysterious were the ways of the songs of Keridwen ! How necessary to understand them in their *true sense* !" Llywarch ap Llywelyn, who wrote between 1160 and 1220, asks for "inspiration as if it were from the Cauldron of Keridwen", and says that he will address his lord "with the dowry of Keridwen, the Ruler of Bardism". It was essential for those bards who aspired to the Chair of Song to have tasted the waters of inspiration from her cauldron, to have been initiated into her mysteries. That the myth of Keridwen of the Lake of Tegid, the god or genius of which was the husband of this deity, is all-important in our quest may be gathered from a passage in *The Book of Taliesin*.

Then she (Keridwen) determined, agreeably to the mystery of the books of Pheryllt, to prepare for her son a cauldron of water of inspiration and knowledge. . . .
In the meantime Keridwen, with due attention to the books of astronomy, and to the hours of the planets,

employed herself daily in collecting plants of every species, which preserved any rare virtues. . . . She stationed Gwion the Little, the son of Gwreany the Herald of Llanvair, in Powys, the land of rest, to superintend the preparation of the cauldron.

The Pheryllt, according to whose ritual she proceeded, are frequently mentioned by the bards of Wales, and an old chronicle, quoted by Dr. Thomas Williams, states that the Pheryllt had a college at Oxford prior to the foundation of that University. These Pheryllt appear to have been a section of the Druidic brotherhood, teachers and scientists, skilled in all that required the agency of fire, hence the name has frequently been translated "alchemists" or "metallurgists". Indeed, chemistry and metallurgy are known as *Celvyddydan Pheryllt*, or "the arts of the Pheryllt", who would seem to have had as their headquarters the city of Emrys in the district of Snowdon, famous for its magical associations, the city of the dragons of Beli.[1]

Somewhere in the district of Snowdon lie the remains of this ancient British city of Emrys, or "the ambrosial city", also known in Welsh tradition as the city of Dinas Affaraon, or "the higher powers". To this mysterious community the poems of the Welsh bards allude so frequently as to place its actual existence beyond all question. Not only is it mentioned in *The Black Book of Caermarthen* and other Cymric manuscripts as the centre of mystical rites, but it is alluded to by one of Camden's commentators as occupying the summit of "the panting cliff" on Snowdon itself. Davies says that it stood "upon the road from the promontory of Lleyn to that part of the coast which is opposite Mona" (Anglesey), and Gibson, in his work on Camden, identifies it with the ruins of an exceedingly strong fortification encompassed by a triple wall on an eminence called Broich y Ddinas, "the ridge of the city", which forms part of the summit of Penmaen. Within each wall the foundation of at least a hundred towers of about six yards' diameter remain, and the defences themselves were at least six feet in thickness. " The greatness of this work," he says, " shows that it was a princely fortification, strengthened by Nature and workmanship, seated on the top of one of the highest mountains of that part of Snowdon which lie toward the sea."

In Emrys were concealed in the time of Bilé the solar deity, and in the time of Prydain the son of Ædd the Great, the dragons which are so frequently referred to as harnessed to the car of Keridwen, so it appears not improbable that the city was in some manner associated with her mysteries. Davies believed that the Pheryllt were priests of those mysteries in the ambrosial city of Emrys.

Now what, precisely, is the significance of the goddess Keridwen and her mystical cauldron? Mythically speaking, the vessel in question was designed for the preparation of a brew which induced inspiration and awoke the prophetic and bardic faculties. The myth is obviously an allegory of initiation, of which the tasting of the water was an essential rite.

In the poem known as "The Chair of Taliesin" in *The Book of Taliesin* (No. XIII) a number of ingredients are enumerated which went to compose the mystical elixir brewed in the Cauldron of Keridwen, the Pair Pumwydd, the "Cauldron of the Five Trees", so-called in allusion to the five particular trees or plants requisite to the preparation. Certain Cymric legends represent this Pair as a bath, the water of which conferred immortality, but deprived the bather of utterance—an allusion, perhaps, to the oath of secrecy administered prior to initiation. Elsewhere Taliesin alludes to it as "the Cauldron of the ruler of the deep", and states that it will not boil the food of him who is not bound by his oath.

It is thus clear enough that the Welsh Bards made use in their initiatory rites of a decoction of plants or herbs which they believed could bestow certain powers of inspiration, eloquence, prophecy, and song upon the votary who partook of it. The use of such purificatory or lustrational water was not unknown in the mysteries of Greece and Rome. In connection with the mysteries of Ceres a decoction of laurel, salt, barley, sea-water, and crowns of flowers was employed, and this appears as similar to the ingredients of Keridwen's cauldron, which, according to Taliesin, contained berries, the foam of the ocean, cresses, wort and vervain which had been borne aloft and kept apart from the influence of the moon. A part of this potion was also added to the Gwin, or Bragwod, or sacred drink used commonly by the British initiates, which was made from wine, honey, water, and malt, and which thus resembles the liquor of the devotees of Ceres, a concoction of wine, barley, water, and meal.

The residue of the water in the cauldron of Keridwen was, as we have seen, poisonous and accursed, that is, it was symbolically supposed to contain the sins and pollutions of the novitiates, and was cast out, precisely as was the residue of the water employed in the mysteries of Ceres.[1]

The mysterious cauldron is alluded to by Taliesin as having been instituted by nine maidens who "warmed it with their breath". Davies[2] believes

[1] *Athenæus*, Lib. XI, Ch. 15.
[2] *British Druids*, p. 223.

them to have been the Gwyllion, or "fairies", prophetic damsels who bore a resemblance to the nine muses of classical lore. They are mentioned by Taliesin as preparing their cauldron in a "quadrangular caer" or sanctuary in "the island of the strong door". This seems to refer to the island of Seon mentioned in the same poem, and which must surely be one and the same with the Sena or Ile de Sein, not far from Brest, mentioned by Pomponius Mela[1] as the "abode of priestesses holy in perpetual virginity, and nine in number. They are," he proceeds, " called Gallicenæ, and are thought to be endowed with singular powers. By their charms they are able to raise the winds and seas, to turn themselves into what animals they will, to cure wounds and diseases incurable by others, to know and predict the future." In a word, they were Druidesses, as modern authorities have admitted. Once a year they unroofed their temple, and if, in the task of re-thatching it, one of them stumbled, she was immediately torn in pieces by the others.

Strabo likewise mentions these priestesses of Sena as the devotees of "Bacchus", "possessed of Dionysius". This is, of course, merely another way of saying that these women were the hierophants of a Keltic deity whose rites and mysteries resembled those of Bacchus, the orgiastic celebrations which preceded the deity's gifts of inspiration and prophecy. M. Salmon Reinach dismisses the stories of Strabo and Mela as a fable based on the myth of Circe, but, as Canon MacCulloch reasonably remarks, " even if they are garbled, they seem to be based on actual observation and are paralleled from other regions. . . . The facts that the rites were called Dionysiac is no reason for denying the fact that some orgiastic rites were practised. Classical writers usually reported all barbaric rites in terms of their own religion."[1]   Says Mr. Kendrick : " Although it is quite possible the authors were tempted to interpret the reputed existence of Keltic island-communication in the terms of classical mythology, with its tales of the Isle of Circe and so on, yet, since there is abundant evidence that the Gauls, like many other ancient peoples, felt that some peculiar holiness was attached to lonely islands, it is almost an inevitable consequence that the quality of sacredness should be translated to those who lived upon them."

It is obviously to some such orgiastic ceremony that the bard Aneurin alludes in a poem cited by Davies.[2]

> In the presence of the blessed ones, before the great assembly, before the occupiers of the holme, when the house was recovered from the swamp, surrounded with crooked horns and crooked swords, in honour of the mighty king of the plains, the king with open countenance : I saw dark gore arising on the stalks of plants, on the clasp of the chain, on the bunches on the sovereign, on the bush and spear. Ruddy was the sea-beach, whilst the circular revolution was performed by the attendants, and the white bands, in graceful extravagance.
>
> The assembled train were dancing, after the manner, and singing in cadence, with garlands on their brows; loud was the clattering of shields round the ancient cauldron in frantic mirth, and lively was the aspect of him, who, in his prowess, had snatched over the ford that involved ball which cast its rays to a distance, the splendid product of the adder, shot forth by serpents.
>
> But wounded art thou, severely wounded, thou delight of princesses, thou who lovedst the living herd! It was my earnest wish that thou mightest live, O thou of victorious energy! Alas, thou Bull, wrongfully oppressed, thy death I deplore. Thou hast been a friend of tranquillity!

[1] op. cit. p. 139.
[2] op. cit. appendix, p. 574.

In view of the sea, in the front of the assembled men, and near the pit of conflict, the raven has pierced thee in wrath!

That these Druidesses of Sena were identified with the nine guardians of the Cauldron of Keridwen, shows that they were the hereditary priestesses of her cult, like the priestesses of Galatian Artemis or the goddesses of Gaul with their female votaries. But the allusion of Aneurin to the "involved ball" introduces us to another phase of the Keltic mysteries.

The ball in question is, of course, the celebrated serpent's egg of Druidic lore. The *locus classicus* of its allusion is the well-known statement of Pliny[1] who says of it:

There is also another kind of egg, of much renown in the Gallic provinces, but ignored by the Greeks. In the summer, numberless snakes entwine themselves into a ball, held together by a secretion from their bodies and by the spittle. This is called *anguinum*. The Druids say that hissing serpents throw this up into the air, and that it must be caught in a cloak, and not allowed to touch the ground; and that one must instantly take to flight on horseback, as the serpents will pursue until some stream cuts them off. It may be tested, they say, by seeing if it floats against the current of a river, even though it be set in gold. But as it is the way of magicians to cast a cunning veil about their frauds, they pretend that these eggs can only be taken on a certain day of the moon, as though it rested with mankind to make the moon and the serpents accord as to the moment of the operation. I myself, however, have seen one of these eggs; it was round, and about as large as a smallish apple; the shell was cartalaginous, and pocked like the arms of a polypus. The Druids esteem it highly. It is said to ensure success in lawsuits and a favourable reception with princes; but this is false, because a man of the Vocontii, who was also a Roman knight, kept one of these eggs in his bosom during a trial, and was put to death by the Emperor Claudius, as far as I can see, for that reason alone.

[1] *Nat. Hist.*, XXIX, 52.

Regarding the precise nature of this "snakes' egg" there is considerable conflict of opinion. Certain prehistoric beads of blue and green glass, sometimes carved and inlaid with white paste, are known in Cornwall, Wales, and Scotland as "snakestones" and in Ireland as "Druids' Glass." These appear to date from the early centuries before the Christian era, and, as the Druids must have been familiar with them, it is improbable that they would have regarded them as natural formations. Nor do they fit in with the description of Pliny, who represents the *anguinum* as about the size of an apple, and its shell or husk as horny.

Some authorities believe the "serpent's egg" to have been a fossil echidnus or ammonite. But when we recall the circumstance that the Druids were known to the Welsh bards as *Naddred,* or Adders, in allusion probably to their supposed regeneration as initiates, an allegorical reference to the serpent which casts its skin, it will be seen that the statement of Pliny is merely a confused account of the manner in which the Druids or "Adders" assembled and manufactured these emblems, which were probably glass balls covered with skin, and known to the Kymry as *Gleiniau Nadredd*. That they were supposed to ensure good fortune in lawsuits seems to indicate their probable significance as amulets radiating "rightness" or justice, and perhaps bestowing eloquence in advocacy.

We now approach another and most important avenue of possible proof that the philosophic ideas of the Druids actually did survive in Wales by the aid of the Bards. In the first place it may be interesting, if nothing more, to quote from the "Advertisement" of *Poems, Lyrical and Pastoral,* published in 1794, by Edward

Williams, who afterwards edited the *Myvyrian Archæology*.

He maintained [says Skene[1]] that there had existed at an early period, when bardism flourished as an institution of the country, four chairs or schools of bards, and that one of these chairs still remained—the chair of Glamorgan . . . that the succession of bards and bardic presidents could be traced back to 1300 . . . that Llywelyn Sion, who was bardic president in 1580 and died in 1616, had reduced this system to writing under the title of the *Book of Bardism, or the Druidism of the Bards of the Isle of Britain*, which he professed to have compiled from old books in the collection of MSS. at Raglan Castle.

The "Advertisement" is as follows :

The patriarchal religion of Ancient Britain, called Druidism, but by the Welsh most commonly Barddas, Bardism, though they also term it Derwyddoniaeth, Druidism, is no more inimical to Christianity than the religion of Noah, Job, or Abraham; it has never, as some imagine, been quite extinct in Britain; the Welsh Bards have, through all ages *down to the present*, kept it alive. There is in my possession a manuscript synopsis of it by Llewelyn Sion, a Bard, written about the year 1560 : its truth and accuracy are corroborated by innumerable notices and allusions in our Bardic manuscripts of every age up to Taliesin in the sixth century, whose poems exhibit a complete system of Druidism. By these (undoubtedly authentic) writings it will appear that the Ancient British Christianity was strongly tinctured with Druidism.

Sharon Turner, the celebrated antiquary, addressed himself to the consideration of Williams's presentation of Sion's work, and wrote :

These triads, of course, only prove that the bards of the middle ages had these notions, but it is highly probable that what they believed on this point they derived from their ancestors.

They mention three circles of existence :—1, The *Cylch y Ceugant*, or all-enclosing circle, which contains the Deity alone. 2, The circle of *Gwynvydd* or Felicity, the abode of good men who have passed through their

[1] *Four Ancient Books of Wales*, I, 29.

terrestrial changes. 3, The circle of *Abred* or Evil, that in which mankind pass through their various stages of existence before being qualified to enter the circle of felicity.

All animated beings have three stages of existence to pass through—the state of *Abred* or evil, in *Annwn* or the Great Deep; the state of freedom in the human form, and the state of love, which is happiness in the *Nef* or heaven. All beings but God must undergo three *angen* or necessities; they must have a beginning in *Annwn* or the great deep, a progression in *Abred* or the state of evil, and a completion in the circle of felicity in heaven.

In passing through the changes of being, attached to the state of *Abred*, it is possible for man by misconduct to fall retrograde into the lowest state from which he had emerged. There are three things which will inevitably plunge him back into the changes of *Abred*—1, Pride; for this he will fall to *Annwn*, which is the lowest point at which existence begins. 2, Falsehood, which will re-plunge him in *Obryn*, or a transmigration into some degrading form. 3, Cruelty, which will consign him to *Cydvil*, or a transmigration into some ferocious beast. From these he must proceed again in due course through changes of being, up to humanity.

Humanity was the limit of degrading transmigrations; all the changes above humanity were felicitating, and they were to be perpetual, with ever-increasing acquisitions of knowledge and happiness.

Now Nash, as he is bound to do in view of his thesis of the dubious character of all Welsh Bardic literature, tries to throw cold water upon the authentic nature of Sion's writings. He says :

The MS. of Llywelyn Sion was, according to the statement of Dr. Owen Pughe, last transcribed and revised by Edward Davydd of Margam, who died in 1690. The latter says, in his preface, that he compiled it from the books of bards and learned teachers, lest the materials should become lost, and more particularly from the books of Meyrig Davydd, Davydd Llwyd Mathew, Davydd Benwyn, and Llywelyn Sion, who were Bardic presidents of the Glamorgan chair from 1560 to 1580. . . . Llywelyn Sion, who died in 1616, says that the authors, teachers, and judges, who sanctioned this system and code, were the Druids and Bards after they had come to the faith in Christ.

" The original manuscript of Edward Davydd is (wrote Turner in 1803) yet extant in the library of Llan Haran, in Glamorganshire."

What, one asks, is there of the improbable in all this? " It does not follow," says Skene, " because the poems are not what Davies and Herbert represent them to be that they are therefore not genuine." Have the literatures of other countries not been handed down by means more devious than we find recorded by Sion? What of the Central American " Popol Vuh ", the Kabbala, the Scriptures themselves, the works of the classical era? Are the evidences of their antiquity in manuscript any more "respectable"?

And did Llywelyn Sion actually invent the mystic cycles of which he speaks? If he did, it is surprising that they so closely resemble those of other mythologies, and that one of these cycles at least is mentioned in several of the old lays and in the *Mabinogion*. It seems to me, indeed, highly improbable that Sion "invented" this mystical progression for the following reasons : (1) That, as I shall show later, it agrees with the circumstances of other and similar systems ; (2) that similar mystical cosmologies have come down to us unimpaired from an even greater antiquity than we are here dealing with ; and (3) that the system bears the impress of authority and tradition on the face of it.

But Davies, the extreme protagonist of Neo-Druidism, would have none of Sion's system, and attributed a later French origin to it. " It is not," he says, " the Druidism of History, or of the British Bards." In this estimate Nash agrees with him. But he seems to have been carried away by the fact that Edward Williams's son, Taliesin Williams, published a version of the *Book of Bardism* which did not contain any reference to the mysteries, and that the *Book* containing the material of Sion remained unpublished at the time of Edward Williams's death, although it was later published, under the title of *Barddas*, for the Welsh Society in 1862.

Before dealing with the extraordinary material contained in *Barddas*—material which entirely shatters the contentions of the critics of the authentic character of the Druidic tradition in Wales—let me remark that it is amazing to a modern student of myth and folklore that the antagonists of the Bardic and Druidic tradition should have utterly denied the mythological authenticity of many of the poems and even of the incidents in the *Mabinogion*. These are now, especially the latter, fully recognized by standard authorities as the veritable remains of Brythonic myth. And if the mythology of the Keltic race, whose priests were the Druids, should have been handed down almost unimpaired, why may not the philosophy of the Druids have been preserved by similar means? That this was actually achieved I hope to demonstrate in the succeeding chapter.

CHAPTER IV

"BARDDAS"

"BARDDAS," the volume containing the material the existence of which Nash had denied, was published under the auspices of the Welsh Manuscript Society at Llandovery in 1862, with translations and notes by the Rev. J. Williams ab Ithel, rector of Llanyomowddwy, Merionethshire. In its title it purported to be " a collection of original documents illustrative of the theology, wisdom and usages of the Bardo-Druidic system of the Isle of Britain."[1]

In the preface it is stated that the promoters of the National Eisteddfod held at Llangollen in 1858, desirous of rescuing the traditions of the bards from oblivion, offered a prize for " the fullest illustration from original sources of the theology, discipline and usages of the Bardo-Druidic system of the Isle of Britain." Only one composition was received, bearing the anonymous signature of "Plennydd." With respect to its authenticity, the judges stated that the manuscripts it contained were genuine, " though their authors cannot in many instances be named, any more than we can name the authors of the Common Law of England, yet the existence of the peculiar dogmas and usages which they represent may be proved from the compositions of the Bards, from the era of Taliesin down to the present time . . . it is among the remains of Bardism . . . we may hope to discover, if at all, that Golden

[1] The word "Barddas" means "Bardism".

Key, concealed and secured, which can open the mysteries or esoteric doctrine of ancient nations.''

With few exceptions, we are told, the documents included in the collection were gathered from the manuscripts of the late Iolo Morganwg, frequently mentioned in the preceding chapter as Edward Williams. They were in his handwriting, and the judges had every reason to believe that they were transcripts from older manuscripts. He made them in the first instance on the backs of old letters and bills, in which state they were discovered after his death. The Editor, writing of these, says : '' We have had an opportunity of examining fully and carefully those papers . . . and unhesitatingly pronounce him to be incapable of perpetrating literary deceit or forgery.'' Indeed, the style is in general too archaic for the eighteenth century, and it appears that Iolo Morganwg himself did not fully understand certain of the documents, nor did he correct the errors they obviously contained. It is clear, too, that in making his transcripts he had frequently more than one original to found upon, and the lack of uniformity in some of the details conclusively proves that he was merely a copyist and nothing more.

Again, he refers to the actual existence of some of the documents which he has copied, and gives with great minuteness the names and addresses of the owners. He further states : '' The Triades that are here selected are from a manuscript collection by Llywelyn Sion, a Bard of Glamorgan, about the year 1560. Of this manuscript I have a transcript ; the original is in the possession of Mr. Richard Bradford of Bettws, near Bridgend, in Glamorgan, son of the late Mr. John Bradford, who, for skill in ancient British Bardism, left not his equal behind.'' This statement must have been penned nearly a century

before the publication of *Barddas* and was printed
in Williams's *Poems, Lyrical and Pastoral* already
alluded to. Had the reference been a false one it
would certainly have been refuted at the time.

Other critics attempted to refer the material of
Barddas to the Eisteddvoddau held subsequently
to the beginning of the fifteenth century, when certain
bardic rites were authorized which were handed
down through the medium of the bardic chair of
Glamorgan. These were said to be the invention
of the bards of the fifteenth, sixteenth and
seventeenth centuries, simply because the code had
not been reduced to writing before their time. Some
actually said that they derived it from the Brahmins
of India ! This notwithstanding, it bears the stamp
of authenticity in every line, and that it could have
been "invented" by Welsh bards who lived centuries
apart and had not a scintilla of knowledge regarding
Brahminism or any other esoteric religion is a
suggestion of the most jejune description. Indeed,
one is forced to agree with the editor of *Barddas*
when he says : " We believe that the bards of the
fifteenth and sixteenth centuries were, to some
extent, acquainted with the poetical productions of
their predecessors," even if they did not agree upon
any system drawn from their writings. Many
passages in the volume may be paralleled from the
works of the Welsh bards. The material of
Barddas, its editor believed, had been collected
chiefly from the works of bards who flourished from
the fourteenth to the seventeenth century, by
Llywelyn Sion, who copied them in the library of
Raglan Castle.

" There is no doubt," says the editor, " that these
bards viewed the traditions of the Gorsedd as the
genuine remains of Ancient Druidism ; *and there is*

reason to believe that in their main features they were so.[1] The variations observable in minor points would indicate in what direction, and to what extent, they suffered in their passage from the Christian era downwards.''

That the introduction of Christianity did not mean the abandonment of the Druidic philosophy is clear enough from certain passages in the works of the Welsh bards. One of the triads refers especially to this when it says : ''There are three special doctrines that have been obtained by the nation of the Cymry : the first, from the age of ages, was that of the Gwyddoniaid, prior to the time of Prydain, son of Aedd the Great ; the second was Bardism, as taught by the Bards, after they had been instituted ; the third was the Faith in Christ, being THE BEST OF THE THREE.''

Indeed, Christianity seems to have been regarded by the Kelts as the fulfilment of Druidism, a creed attuned so closely to the nobler aspirations of the Keltic spirit that it was easy of assumption by it. What has been said concerning the Culdee caste obviously aids this reflection, and it is known that many Druids actually became Christian priests. The famous bull of Pope Gregory I (A.D. 540—604) permitted a fusion between Keltic and Christian belief which rendered the latter easier of acceptance without altogether destroying the former.

We come now to the material in *Barddas* itself.

The first book is entitled ''Symbol'' and deals with the origin of letters, the alphabet and the secret writing of the Bards. Letters, says the Bardic tradition, were invented by Einiged the Giant, son of Alser, for the purpose of recording praiseworthy actions, and the wooden blocks on which they were

[1] Italics are mine.—L.S.

inscribed were known as *coelbren*.[1] Bran the Blessed it was who brought the art of dressing goat-skin as parchment from Rome. The three original letters were obtained by Menw the Aged from the voice of God Himself, which manifested itself in rays of light, thus $\mid\mid\backslash$ in three columns. The sense of O was given to the first column, I to the second or middle, and V to the third, whence the word OIV, which may not be pronounced. As a bardic poem says :

> The Eternal, Origin, Self-existent Distributor.
> Holy be the lips that canonically pronounce them;
> Another name in full word,
> Is OI and OIV the word—Ieuan Rudd sang it.

By this name the Universe calls God inwardly—the sea, the land, earth and air, and all the visibles and invisibles of the world, all the worlds of all the Celestials and Terrestrials, every thing animate and inanimate. The three mystic letters signify the three attributes of God : love, knowledge and truth. It was because of this principle that three degrees were conferred upon the Bards of the Isle of Britain.

Out of the knowledge of the vocalization of language and speech received from these three principal letters sixteen letters were formed ; all letters employed by the Bards were developed from them, and formed the Abcedilros, a word composed of the ten primary letters. Later other letters were formed, to the number of twenty-four.

But only a Bard of thorough secrecy knows how the name of God is to be spoken audibly by means of the three principal columns of letters, because only he knows their meaning, accent and powers. This

---

[1] At least a dozen passages in the bardic poems written between 1160 and 1600 allude to this tradition.

secret must not be divulged save to him who is warranted as having *Awen*[1] from God, for God alone can pronounce His name perfectly.   He who reasons and meditates will comprehend the meaning of the primitive system of sixteen letters and will perceive and understand the Name of God and the just reverence due to Him.   The three letters O.I.V. were originally and authoritatively written ◇ | V, and without the violation of secrecy there cannot be another system arising from these letters.

From this trinity of letters arose the custom of casting knowledge into Triads, and the three rays of light were regarded as the three principal signs of the sciences, and from them were obtained fixity and authority for the arts and sciences.

After a dissertation on the traditions of the manner in which Bardism and the Gorsedd were established, we receive enlightenment on the principal elements of things.   These are power, matter and mode. The elements of Science are life, intellect and affection ; of Wisdom, object, mode and benefit ; and of Memorials, understanding from affection, distinctive sign and reverence for the better.

The three foundations of *Awen* from God are : to understand the truth, to love the truth and to maintain the truth.

A long description of Cymric arithmetic follows, and of the technical making of books or *coelbren*, neither of which is germane to our subject.   But we may quote the following :

> The mysteries of the Bards, that is to say, the secret *coelbrens*, are small *ebillion*, a finger long, having notches, so that they may be used by two persons or more, who are confidants.   It is by placing and joining them together, with reference to what is secret, that words and phrases are formed ; and by bundling them into words according

[1] Genius, or inspiration.

to secrecy, missive epistles and secret books are constructed, the meaning of which no one knows but confidants; nor is it right, according to usage and troth, to divulge the same. They are called the Charms of the Bards, or Bardic Mystery.

Secret *coelvains* are similar, made of small stones bearing the marks of mystery; and it is by disposing them, according to the arrangement and art of the secret, that necessary sciences are demonstrated. And where such *coelbrens* exhibit the number of the letters of the Historical *coelbren*, let them be made secret by changing one letter for another, so that it be not ascertained, except from the necessity and declination of the same letter twice in the same meaning and power.

That is, they are to be cast in cipher.

The last entry in the *Book of Symbols* is the following questionary :[1]

Question—What is the *Dasgubell Rodd?*
Answer—The keys of the primitive *coelbren.*
Q.—What is it that explains the primitive *coelbren?*
A.—The *Dasgubell Rodd.*
Q.—What else?
A.—The secret of the *Dasgubell Rodd.*
Q.—What secret?
A.—The secret of the Bards of the Isle of Britain.
Q.—What will divulge the secret of the Bards of the Isle of Britain?
A.—Instruction by a master in virtue of a vow.
Q.—What kind of vow?
A.—A vow made with God.

For us the second book, entitled "Dwy-ffyddiaeth", or "Theology", is of greatly more importance, for in it are enshrined the mystical teachings of Bardism. It opens with a large number of theological triads, which need not be quoted at this juncture. But farther on we encounter the caption "Druidism", in which document we are informed of the Druidical ideas concerning the nature of godhead. God is goodness and power, and is opposed in duality to *Cythraul,* darkness and powerless

[1] The Dasgubell Rod is the "gift besom", which is supposed to sweep away what hides the truth.

inability. God mercifully united Himself with this lifelessness or evil with the intention of subduing it unto life or goodness, and from this intellectual existences and animations first sprang.

These began in the depths of *Annwn*, or the abyss, the lowest and least grade, for there can be no intellectual existence without gradation, and in respect of gradation there cannot but be a beginning, a middle, an end or extremity—first, augmentation and ultimate or conclusion. "Thus animations in *Annwn* are partakers of life and goodness in the lowest possible degree and of death and evil in the highest degree.   Therefore they are necessarily evil, because of the preponderance of evil over the good. Their duration is necessarily short, but by dissolution and death they are removed gradually to a higher degree, where they receive an accumulation of life and goodness, and thus they progress from grade to grade, nearer and nearer to the extremity of life and goodness, God, of his merciful affection for animated beings, preparing the ways along *Abred*, out of pure love to them, until they arrive at the state and point of human existence, where goodness and evil equiponderate, neither weighing down the other. From this sprang liberty and choice and elective power in man, so that he can perform whichever he likes of any two things, as of good and evil ; and thus is it seen that the state of humanity is a state of probation and instruction, where the good and evil equiponderate, and animated beings are left to their own will and pleasure."

There are three circles of spiritual evolution, the Circle of *Abred*, in which are all corporal and dead existences, the Circle of *Gwynvyd*, in which are all animated and immortal beings, and the Circle of *Ceugant*, where there is only God. *Abred* thus includes humanity, and all below it. But, necessarily evil as its condition is, God does not hate the lower things existing in it, knowing that they cannot be otherwise. But when life arrives at the point of humanity in *Abred,* where good and evil equiponderate, man is free from all obligation, and his state is one of will and freedom and ability, where every act is one of consent and choice. Whatever he does he could do differently, therefore it is right that he should receive punishment or reward as his works require.

The enigma of the Bards is posited thus :

'' There is nothing truly hidden but what is not conceivable ;

There is nothing not conceivable but what is immeasurable ;

There is nothing immeasurable but God ;

There is no God but that which is not conceivable ;

There is nothing not conceivable but that which is truly hidden ;

There is nothing truly hidden but God.''

Its solution is as follows :

What is not conceivable is the greatest of all, and the immeasurable of what is not in place ;

God is the greatest of all, and the immeasurable of intelligence ;

And there can be no existence to any thing but from intelligence ;

And the non-existence of all things comes from what is not in place.

God the Father, we are informed, is called by some Hên Ddihenydd, that is '' Ancient and Unoriginated One,'' '' the original lifespring, or springing into life at the lowest point of animated

existence, or out of the chaotic mass of matter in its
utmost state of decomposition," according to a note
or gloss of Iolo Morganwg. God the Son is called
Iau, that is the Younger, the last manifestation of the
Deity or God under a finite form and corporeity.
" And when He became man in this world, he was
called Jesus Christ," or God the Dovydd, that is
" God the Tower". And he had other names, such
as Perydd or " the First Cause," and " God the
Ner " or "Energy", and " God the Nav," or
Creator. He is also called "Hu the Mighty," or
" the Pervader."[1]

The next manuscript in the "Book of Theology",
as this department of *Barddas* may be called, is
"The Book of Bardism", by Llywelyn Sion himself.
This he professes to have extracted from old books,
"namely the books of Einion the Priest, Taliesin the
Chief of Bards, Davydd Ddu of Hiraddug, Cwtta
Cyvarwydd, Jonas of Menevia, Ederyn the Golden-
tongued, Sion Cent, Rhys Goch, and others in the
Library of Raglan, by permission of the lord William
Herbert, earl of Pembroke, to whom God grant that
I may prove thankful as long as I live. The first is
a Treatise in the form of Question and Answer, by
a Bard and his Disciple—the work of Sion Cent,
which contains many of the principal subjects of the
primitive wisdom, as it existed among the Bards of
the Isle of Britain from the age of ages."[2]

It is couched in the form of question and answer
between the Bard and his disciple.

The Bard first informs the novice that he "came

[1] He is probably one and the same with that Hesus, described
by Lucan as a god of the Gauls, and may later have been
confounded with Jesus.

[2] It should be mentioned here that the existence of every one
of the bards alluded to has been authenticated, and that the
works of most of them have been published in *The Myvyrian
Archæology* and elsewhere. See notes to *Barddas,* pp. 224-5.

from the Great World" and had his beginning in *Annwn*, but that he is now in the Little World, having traversed the circle of *Abred*, and is a man at its termination and extreme limits. Before that, he was in *Annwn* "the least possible that was capable of life", and he has come through every form capable of body and life to the state of man along the circle of *Abred*.

Gwynvyd, he assures the novice, "cannot be obtained without seeing and knowing everything, but it is not possible to see and to know everything without suffering everything. And there can be no full and perfect love that does not produce those things which are necessary to lead to the knowledge that causes *Gwynvyd*, for there can be no *Gwynvyd* without the complete knowledge of every form of existence, and of every evil and good, and of every operation and power and condition of evil and good. And this knowledge cannot be obtained without experience in every form of life, in every incident, in every suffering, in every evil and in every good, so that they may be respectively known one from the other. All this is necessary before there can be *Gwynvyd*, and there is need of them all before there can be perfect love of God, and there must be perfect love of God before there can be *Gwynvyd*."

Every living being shall attain at last to the circle of *Gwynvyd*, traversing the circle of *Abred* from the depth of *Annwn*, and passing through death to the circle of *Gwynvyd*, so that at length the *Abred* will end for ever, " and there shall be no migrating through every form of existence after that." But God alone can traverse the circle of *Ceugant*. But none shall go at death to *Gwynvyd* who in life did not attach himself to goodness and godliness and every act of wisdom, justice and love. It is a preponderance of these qualities which open to the human soul the gates of *Gwynvyd*.   But he who does not follow goodness "shall fall in *Abred* to a corresponding form and species of existence of the same nature as himself, whence he shall return to the state of man as before. . . . And thus shall he fall for ever until he seeks godliness."   One may fall many times in *Abred*, and the migration of most through it is long. Even the angels who reached *Gwynvyd* fell once more in *Abred* through attempting to reach *Ceugant*, the sphere inhabited by God alone.

When the Cymry were converted to the faith of Christ, says Sion, their Bards obtained a clearer *Awen*, or inspirational vision, from God.   *Awen* is to be obtained by habituating oneself to a holy life, to love, justice and mercy and the practice of good sciences, and the avoidance of all hatred and cruelty.

That transmigration of a kind is implied in the bardic writings may be observed from the following passage : " When a wicked man dies and his soul enters the meanest worm in existence, he becomes better and ascends on the migration of *Abred*." The bard Casnodyn (A.D. 1290-1340) seems to allude to this belief when he says :

Thou didst prepare the slough of hell suitable for Satan,
The habitation for worms, where they will be in mortal strife.

There follows a quaint myth of the creation, in which Hebrew and Cymric ideas are strangely associated, and in which we are informed that the first man was Menyw the Aged.[1]   The world, it is said, was formed out of the *manred*, atoms collected out of the infinite expanse in the circle of *Ceugant* and arranged in order in the circle of *Gwynvyd* "as

[1] Cf. the Egyptian Mena, or Menes.

worlds and lives and creatures, without number, weight or measure. And *Annwn,* the abyss, was created in the extreme limits of the circle of *Gwynvyd*".

We have next to traverse an immense tract of long and rather sententious triads which need not detain us here, such as "The three indispensables of godliness : love ; truth ; and prudence." But we return to essentials when we encounter the doctrine of *Eneidvaddeu.*

In the Laws of Dyvnwal Moelmud we read : "There are three strong punishments : *eneidvaddeu* ; cutting off a limb ; and banishment from the country, by the cry and pursuit of men and dogs ; and it is for the king to direct which he willeth to be inflicted." This makes the doctrine in question as old at least as 430 B.C., says the commentator of *Barddas,* and it is plain that the significance of the word is "reparation". As the passages in relation to it are somewhat obscure I prefer to quote them :

In three ways a man may happen to become *eneidvaddeu*; one is punishment due, by the verdict of country and law, for injurious evil—an injurious evil being killing and burning, murder and waylaying, and the betraying of country and nation. That is to say, he who commits those evils ought to be executed; and every execution takes place either by the judgment of a court of law, or in war by the verdict of country and nation. The second is the man who surrenders himself, at the demand of justice which he feels in his conscience, to execution for an injurious and punishable evil, which he confesses to have committed, and where he cannot render compensation and satisfaction for the injury he has done, otherwise than by submitting voluntarily to the punishment due for what he has done. The third is the man who undergoes the danger and chance of execution in behalf of truth and justice, at the call of peace and mercy, and is slain. Such a man is adjudged to be slain for the good which he has done; and on that account he ascends to the circle of *Gwynvyd*. In any other than these three ways, a man cannot be adjudged as *eneidvaddeu* by man, for it is God alone who knows how to judge what is otherwise. The first of them will remain in *Abred*, in the state and nature of man, without falling lower; and the other two will ascend to the circle of *Gwynvyd*.

The three accelerations of the end of *Abred*: diseases; fighting; and becoming *eneidvaddeu*, justly, reasonably, and necessarily, from doing good; for without them there would be no release from *Abred*, but at a much later period. Herein is seen that it was for the benefit of, and mercy to, living beings, God ordained the mutual fighting and mutual slaughter which take place among them.

We now come to the third book, "The Book of Wisdom", in which we are first attracted by the doctrines of the elements : "*Manred*, the original form of all the materials, or all the constituents, that is, the elements, of which the first four of the five were dead, namely, *calas,* fluidity, breath, and fire, until God agitated them by uttering His Name, when instantly they became alive and in one triumphant song, and manifested their condition.

"The three materials of every being and existence : *calas*, and hence every motionless body and solidity, and every hardness and concretion ; fluidity, and hence every cessation, migration, and return ; and *nwyvre,* hence every animation and life, and every strength, understanding and knowledge, and the same is God, without Whom there can be no life and vitality.

Others say :

There are three materials of everything, namely : *calas,* and hence every corporeity ; fluidity, and hence every colour and form, and every course and return ; and *nwyvre,* and hence every life, being God, from Whom proceeds every soul, animation, strength and understanding, for where He is not, neither one nor another of these things can exist."

According to another mode, as other teachers say from an old account :

Earth, water, firmament, fire and *nyv* ; and the *nyv* is God, and life, and intellect. From the first four are all death and mortality ; and from the fifth are all life and animation, all power, knowledge, and motion.

We next come to statements regarding the Materials of Man. These are attributed to the Bard Taliesin, are taken from *The Book of Llanwrst* and are as follows :

> There are eight parts in man: the first is the earth, which is inert and heavy, and from it proceeds the flesh; the second are the stones, which are hard, and are the substance of the bones; the third is the water, which is moist and cold, and is the substance of the blood; the fourth is the salt, which is briny and sharp, and from it are the nerves, and the temperament of feeling, as regards bodily sense and faculty; the fifth is the firmament, or wind, out of which proceeds the breathing; the sixth is the sun, which is clear and fair, and from it proceed the fire, or bodily heat, the light and colour; the seventh is the Holy Ghost, from Whom issue the soul and life; and the eighth is Christ, that is the intellect, wisdom, and the light of soul and life.

> If the preponderating part of man is from the earth, he will be foolish, sluggish and very heavy; also a short, little, and slender dwarf, in a great or small degree, according to the preponderance. If it should be from the firmament, he will be light, unsteady, garrulous, and fond of gossip. If from the stones, his heart, understanding and judgment will be hard, and he will be a miser and a thief. If from the sun, he will be genial, affectionate, active, docile, and poetic. If from the Holy Ghost, then he will be godly, amiable, and merciful, with a just and gentle judgment, and abounding in arts. And being thus, he cannot but equiponderate with Christ, and divine sonship.

The parts of the human body in which the faculties lie are enumerated as follow :

1. In the forehead are the sense and intellect :
2. In the nape is the memory ;

3. In the pate are discretion and reason ;
4. In the breast is lust ;
5. In the heart is love ;
6. In the bile are anger and wrath ;
7. In the lungs is the breath ;
8. In the spleen is joyousness ;
9. In the body is the blood ;
10. In the liver is the heat ;
11. In the spirit is the mind ;
12. In the soul is faith.

We are then introduced to a long series of dissertations on the cycle of the year, and the months, and later to the "Book of Privilege and Usage", which deals with the laws and regulations of Bardism.

The surprising resemblance of the ideas discovered in *Barddas* to certain systems of Eastern philosophy and theology cannot but have struck the reader. Indeed, it must be clear that it enshrines the remains of a world-system of thought probably greatly more ancient than Druidism itself, and containing ideas common to Egyptian, Brahmin and Buddhist philosophy.

But that it was copied from any of these at first-hand it is ludicrous to suppose. There was, indeed, no opportunity for a Welsh bard or bards of the thirteenth or any century up to the seventeenth deliberately borrowing from the sacred systems of the East. True, in Roman times a great deal of Oriental philosophy found its way to Britain, and it is possible that this may have coloured Druidism to some extent. But the main beliefs set forth in the system appearing in *Barddas* are already indicated, if roughly, in what Cæsar and other classical writers have to say regarding Druidism.

It seems, indeed, much more probable that the system appearing in *Barddas* had its primal origin in that North-West African centre whence came the Iberian race, than in the East. That it had absorbed Christian elements as well is obvious, but in the course of centuries of Christianity it was impossible that it should not be so. But this renders it no more "Christian" than certain American Indian legends have become Christian through European sophistication.

Let us briefly review the "theological" material drawn from *Barddas*. First, we have in God and *Cythraul*, light and darkness, an evidence of that duality visible in most religions which have passed the primary stage. Only, we do not find *Cythraul*, which is described as "darkness" and "powerless inability", as an active force of evil, like Satan, or the Persian Ahriman. Indeed, this "inability" is so little harmful that God actually unites with it to "subdue it unto life."

Annwn, the abyss, is a region by no means exotic, for it enters into the *mabinogi* of "Pwyll, Prince of Dyfed." Its ruler is Arawn, who takes Pwyll's place on earth for a year while the Prince of Dyfed sets the affairs of his dark realm to rights. It is also mentioned in the ancient poem called "The Spoils of *Annwn*" in *The Book of Taliesin*, and the name may even have been applied in a mocking sense to that part of Britain north of the Wall.

But the earliest type of *Annwn* was rather a place of Elysium than an abyss of death, or it may be, conversely, that it was the idea of a grim gulf which was transformed to the notion of a place of delight. In any case, early ideas of the Otherworld are usually sufficiently vague, but it certainly looks as if the word had been utilized in the Bardic writings as a specific name for a pit of matter awaiting the vivifying influence of soul-force to spring into life.   In this it bears a resemblance to certain American Indian mythic centres, especially to that of the Zuñi of New Mexico, and it is similar to the state alluded to in a hymn in the Hindu Rig-Veda, when there was neither entity nor non-entity, when the Universe was undistinguishable water enveloped in darkness. "The desire (Karma) arose in it, which was the primal germ of mind . . . the bond between entity and non-entity." This is certainly a most curious correspondence, but to argue that those from whose writings the materials in *Barddas* was taken knew of this somewhat obscure hymn, is absurd. We find much the same state of things alluded to in the Egyptian myth of Ra, in his form of Khepera. "Heaven," says Ra, " did not exist, and earth had not come into being, and the things of the earth and creeping things had not come into existence in that place, and I raised them from out of Nu, from a state of inactivity."   This Nu was a watery abyss, similar to *Annwn* (pronounced "Anoon").   When the myth was affixed to the theology of the Osirian religion we read that Osiris gave the primeval abyss a soul of its own.

From *Annwn*, life crawls out to *Abred*, the circle of trial, the material world. *Abred* is, indeed, the earth-plane, which cannot but be evil, but from which the rise to *Gwynvyd* is certain, sooner or later, although many relapses into *Abred* may take place before its consummation.   But we shall return to the consideration of the theology of *Barddas* in a subsequent chapter after dealing with matters which may throw considerable light upon it.

CHAPTER V

THE ARCANE TRADITION IN BRITISH MEDIÆVAL LITERATURE

WE have now to pursue our quest for the evidences of the survival of native arcane belief in the mediæval literature of Britain. Geoffrey of Monmouth's *Historia Regum Britanniæ* has been so canvassed by the critics that I do not propose to enter the welter of controversy concerning the authenticity of its sources. I will only say that from the first I almost instinctively adopted the theory of its derivation from ancient Cambrian and Breton sources. Subsequent study of the work has not shaken that early impression, but I may perhaps briefly justify it here.

Geoffrey's proper name was Grufydd ab Arthur, he was a Welshman and Archdeacon of Monmouth, therefore had exceptional opportunities of gleaning the traditions of his race as current during the twelfth century. He states clearly in the preface of one of the earliest manuscript copies of his work that he "turned this book from Kymraeg to Latin and in my old age retranslated it from Latin to Kymraeg." It was, therefore, first written in the Welsh tongue. A later version of the manner in which it was composed states that Walter Mapes, Archdeacon of Oxford, brought a book from Brittany, written in the British language, which could only be translated by one who had a knowledge of Kymric, and that this is the basis of Geoffrey's history.

There seems to be nothing inharmonious in the two statements. Geoffrey might well have drawn the materials of his history from Welsh tradition and from such a Breton book, and I have never felt constrained to credit for a moment that his work is "one of the great literary ruses of all time." His facts differ materially from those of Nennius and the Cymric chronicles by being more diffusive in parts, defective in others and less particular in all. I do not for a moment suggest that much of it is not fabulous, but this does not at all detract from the probability that it was drawn from such sources as I believe it to have been. Moreover, many of the allusions to the Arthurian story are such as were almost certainly derived from a Breton source. Arthur's residence is invariably given as Caerleon, while the British chronicles as constantly refer it to Cornwall. Moreover the Roman wars of that hero are altogether unknown to the native legends, and the descriptions of Paris, Burgundy, the Alps and Italy could certainly not have been written in the first instance by a contemporary Briton. Again, Geoffrey displays an almost complete ignorance of Kymric incidents in Arthur's career, and the discrepancies between his work and that of Nennius as regards early British chronicles are so salient as to render it positive that he followed some alien source in the main. The mere fact, too, that the Breton book is associated with the name of Walter Mapes, the great introducer of Cymric romance in Norman dress, is sufficient to justify Geoffrey's statement that he procured it from Mapes, who never at any time denied the circumstance.

But this is not to say that Geoffrey had not access to certain Welsh manuscripts and traditions, or that he did not make use of them. That he did, is, I think, obvious enough, from the fact that he was also the author of the *Vita Merlini*, the prophecies of Merlin.

Now, Mr. Kendrick says that in his history and his *Vita* Geoffrey mentions not a word about Druidical training or practice. But that is surely beside the question. He alludes to Merlin, for example, as "rex erat et vates", a king and a prophet. But as we do not have the Welsh version of his history to guide us, we cannot say from what word the expression "vates" was translated.

In Geoffrey's history, then, I believe we have a mingling of British and Armorican traditions. What light, precisely, does it cast on the early British tradition of arcane belief, if any at all?

In Chapter X we read how Bladud kept fires in the Temple of Minerva which never went out, and how he taught necromancy in his kingdom, "nor did he leave off practising his magical operations till he attempted to fly to the upper region of the air with wings which he had prepared, and fell down upon the Temple of Apollo in the city of Trinovantum, where he was dashed to pieces." This is precisely what we find certain Irish Druids practising.

Then we read of King Leir, who partitioned the kingdom between his daughters, and of the manner in which he was buried in a tomb under the River Sore at Leicester, "which had been built originally underground to the honour of the god Janus". Janus here undoubtedly stands for Bran "the Blessed", whose triple-faced head, like that of the Roman god, had magical properties of guardianship, and Leir himself is merely the British sea-god Llyr, the father of Manannan. Belinus, who follows in the chronicle, is another Druidical god disguised as a British king.

Searching for other reminiscences of the survivals of Druidic belief, we encounter a reference to Lud, who rebuilt the walls of Trinovantum, or London, who is the Keltic deity Llud or Nodens. A little farther on, we read of a great sacrifice of animals offered up by Cassibelaun to "the tutelary gods" in token of victory. "At this solemnity they offered forty thousand cows and a hundred thousand sheep, and also fowls of several kinds without number, besides thirty thousand wild beasts of several kinds. As soon as they had performed these solemn honours to their gods, they feasted themselves on the remainder, as was usual at such sacrifices." The description of the animals thus slaughtered is precisely in line with Druidic practice, especially with regard to the wild beasts, of which many thousands were annually sacrificed at the Druidic festivals.

In the nineteenth chapter of the fourth book an account is given of the manner in which Lucius, King of Britain, embraced Christianity. The passage reads :

> The holy doctors, after they had almost extinguished paganism over the whole island, dedicated the temples, that had been founded in honour of many gods, to the one only God and His saints, and filled them with congregations of Christians. There were then in Britain eight and twenty flamens, as also three archflamens, to whose jurisdiction the other judges and enthusiasts were subject. These also, according to the apostolic command, they delivered from idolatry, and where they were flamens made them bishops, where archflamens, archbishops. The seats of the archflamens were at the three noblest cities, viz., London, York, and the City of Legions, which its old walls and buildings show to have been situated upon the River Uske in Glamorganshire. To these three, now purified from superstition, were made subject twenty-eight bishops, with their dioceses.

This account is usually regarded as entirely fabulous. But when one recalls what has already been said regarding the Culdees and the existence in the early British Church for many centuries of a caste which in many ways differed from the orthodox clergy, it seems not altogether improbable that it may be based on fact, if it is not altogether accurate.

The next reference of interest is that concerning Merlin, who was consulted by Vortigern regarding the building of a tower in which he might successfully defend himself from the fury of the Saxons. Hearing that Merlin is a man who never had a father, and being advised by his magicians to seek for such an one and to sprinkle the foundations of the tower with his blood, in order to put a finish to an earthquake which constantly overthrows it, Vortigern sends for him. He confutes the magicians, and tells the king that his tower will not stand because of two dragons, red and white, which lie beneath it in a pool. Merlin then prophesies concerning the future of Britain in a strain which indubitably must have been borrowed from native Cambrian sources.

Later, Aurelius, King of Britain, desirous of erecting a monument to those British nobles who had been slaughtered by the Saxons, once more consults Merlin as to the nature it should take, and the enchanter advises him to send to Ireland for the Giants' Dance (Stonehenge), and to erect it in Britain as a lasting memorial to the dead heroes. At this Aurelius laughed, and Merlin, rebuking him, answered :

> I entreat your majesty to forbear vain laughter, for what I say is without vanity. They are mystical stones, and of a medicinal virtue. The giants of old brought them from the farthest coast of Africa, and placed them in Ireland, while they inhabited that country. Their design in this was to make baths in them when they should be taken with any illness. For their method was to wash the stones, and put their sick into the water, which infallibly cured them. With the like success they cured wounds also, adding only the application of some herbs. There is not a stone there which has not some healing virtue.

H

The stones were accordingly taken down and conveyed to Britain, where they were re-erected.

I submit that this account is a broken and hazy tradition of the actual carriage of certain of the stones of Stonehenge to Salisbury Plain. I do not for a moment mean to convey the impression that Stonehenge was erected by the Druids, for there is the best possible evidence that it was built 1700-1800 years B.C., although it was certainly utilized by the Druids in their time. But I wish to indicate the African association of the cult connected with Stonehenge, as mentioned in the legend, and to point out that certain of the stones or lesser uprights are actually of non-local origin, having been brought, according to Dr. Thomas, of H.M. Geological Survey, from the Prescelly Range in Pembrokeshire. That they were erected a little later than the large outer stones is certain. Their "alien" origin is thus soundly proven, and I believe Geoffrey's account of the business to be a distorted and time-worn memory of the manner in which they were conveyed from west to east. His history is thus justified to a great extent as a record of traditions extraordinarily venerable and important.[1]

But was Merlin really a "Druid"? Indeed, are there any grounds for believing that he ever existed? Says Mr. Kendrick:

> Actually the Merlin stories form a group that originally concerned two distinct persons, one a sixth century Welsh prince, Myrddin ab Morfryn, and the other Vortigern's prophet Ambrosius, who figures in the *Historia Britonum* of Nennius. Geoffrey used the name Merlinus for both these persons, and then proceeded to combine the stories about them as though they referred to a single individual. The Welsh prince is certainly the hero of his later *Vita Merlini*, but in the earlier *Historia*

[1] On the whole question of Stonehenge see F. Stevens's *Stonehenge To-day and Yesterday,* published by the Stationery Office.

Regum Britanniæ it is Ambrosius who is uppermost in his mind; in fact, in his first work he plainly says that Ambrosius was another name for Merlin.

Other authorities, however, have different explanations of the personality of Merlin. Canon MacCulloch regards him as "an ideal magician, possibly an old god, like the Irish 'god of Druidism'". Rhŷs believed him to be a description of Keltic Zeus, who was worshipped at Stonehenge.

It has been assumed by certain authorities, the Comte de Villemarqué among them,[1] that Myrddin ab Morfryn was a different personage from Merlin-Ambrosius, or Merlin Emrys, as he is sometimes called. But both appear to have lived in Strathclyde, both were enchanters and predicted the same events. Again Merlin-Ambrosius appears as a young man before Vortigern about the year 480, and Merlin ap Morfryn at the Court of Rydderch Hael is an old man in 570. Merlin ab Morfryn the prince was apparently the person whose character formed the nucleus from which the other was developed as a figure in later romance. At the Court of Rydderch Hael he was known as Lalockin, or "the twin", and in the dialogue between him and his sister Gwenddydd she alludes to him as "my world-famous twin brother". The Welsh bards of the twelfth century, too, put the predictions of Merlin-Ambrosius into the mouth of Merlin ab Morfryn, and this more than a century after Geoffrey's history had been written, therefore they must have believed them to be identical. It seems probable that Merlin-Ambrosius was so called because of his patronage by Aurelius Ambrosius, brother of Uther Pendragon, who was supposed to have destroyed the unpatriotic Vortigern, and to have transplanted Stonehenge. In all likelihood Merlin-Ambrosius is a mythological

[1] *Barzaz Breiz*, Intro., p. 12, Vol. I.

character engrafted on to Merlin ab Morfryn, who in his youth may have been associated with Aurelius Ambrosius. Indeed, there are several Welsh poems attributed to Merlin, and there is no good reason why he should not be regarded as a real man, a "bardic president about the Water of Clyde", as his sister calls him, renowned as an enchanter and wise man in the sixth century. I am aware that recent criticism absolutely denies the reality of Merlin, but that a Merlin actually existed is proved, and I cannot subscribe to decisions which are obviously based more on a mere affectation of contempt for tradition, and even fact, than on reasonable or historical grounds. To see the entire *corpus* of Arthurian literature rejected as an archæologist of the Tape-Measure School might reject an artifact because it had no "horizon", is painful indeed. When will historical critics learn that tradition, in the proper hands, can be as of much avail as written record? But the Welsh poems which presume to have been written by him are certainly much later than the actual Merlin's time. That Cymric tradition acknowledged Merlin as a Druid may be seen from the following verses from the Breton, given by Villemarqué :

Merlin! Merlin! where art thou going
So early in the day with thy black dog?
Oi! oi! oi! oi! oi!
Ioi! oi! oi! ioi! oi!

I have come here to search for the way,
To find the red egg;
The red egg of the marine serpent,
By the sea side in the hollow of the stone.
I am going to seek in the valley,
The green water cress, and the golden grass,
And the top branch of the oak,
In the wood by the side of the fountain.

Merlin! Merlin! retrace your steps;
Leave the branch on the oak,
And the green water cress in the valley,
As well as the golden grass;
And leave the red egg of the marine serpent,
In the foam by the hollow of the stone.
Merlin! Merlin! retrace thy steps,
There is no diviner but God.

Villemarqué, writing of the above poem, says:

This (the Herbe d'or, golden grass) is a medicinal plant, which the peasant Bretons hold in great estimation. They pretend that at a distance it shines like gold; and it is for this they give it the name. If one should happen to tread upon it, he will fall asleep, and come to understand the languages of birds, dogs and wolves. It is but rarely to be met with, and then only early in the morning; to gather it, it is necessary to go barefooted and in a shirt, and it should not be cut, but plucked out from the root. It is said that holy men only will be able to find it. It is no other than the Selage. Also, in going to gather it barefooted, and in a white robe, and fasting, no iron should be employed, the right hand should be passed under the left arm, and the linen should only be used once."[1]

It will thus be seen that Geoffrey's writings are perhaps more redolent of Druidism than certain critics may credit, that if he does not actually mention the word "Druid", his pages enshrine a goodly proportion of traditional material referring to Druidic customs and personages, proving that the tradition of Druidism, if concealed by the Bardic caste, was by no means popularly defunct in his day, as, indeed, we know from the material concerning Prince Hywel.

The value of the Arthurian literature in the conservation of ancient British mysticism is very considerable. That literature may for all practical purposes be divided into two sections: that which was the work of Welsh bards and arose out of Welsh tradition, and that which was probably derived therefrom and composed in Norman-French and English.

[1] It will be observed that the same procedure applies to the plucking of this plant as to that of the mandrake.

It is surprising what a hold the Arthurian saga seems to have taken on the British mind from first to last, and this can only be accounted for, I think, not only by the circumstances that it had a native origin, or that it appealed to the generations "when chivalry lifted up her lance on high", but that it was innately and instinctively felt that in these ancient British tales there resided not only the memory of brave and romantic things, but a mystical tradition much more profound and thought-compelling.

This occult tradition, indeed, emerged more clearly defined in the literature of the Grail, which, in some respects, is an appendix to the Arthurian saga. But the latter itself in its more separate form is our theme at the moment.

It would be fruitless here to deal at any length with the origins of the Arthurian saga. That it was Keltic and British there can be no reasonable doubt. It appears from a comparative study to have been common to both branches of the Keltic race in Britain, and the Normans, making conquests in South Wales, became familiar with it. As Rhŷs indicates, the names Arthur and Airem proceed from a common verbal root. Airem and Emer were, in Irish legend, the sons of Golam or Mil, and are the Keltic equivalents of Romulus and Remus, sons of Mars. Emer seems to have been the eponymous ancestor of the non-Keltic inhabitants of Ireland, and was slain by Airem, the progenitor of the conquering Kelts. Airem wedded Etain, daughter of Etar, King of the Echraidi or Faery, who was carried off by one Mider, in precisely the same manner as Guinevere was spirited away by Modred. Etain and Guinevere were both daughters of fairy kings. " Provided due allowance is made for the difference between the social settings of the respective stories," says Rhŷs, "the similarity becomes more unmistakable the more it is scanned". The names of both queens, too, can be traced etymologically to a similar root, implying "ghostly" or "shadowy". Thus not only the circumstances of the legends but the actual similarity of the names of their principal personages seem to show that the northern Goidelic Kelts possessed a body of myth almost precisely parallel with the Arthurian story of the Brythons. The high literary excellence and more formal shape of the Arthurian tradition, coming from the south, probably dictated the absorption of the similar Goidelic myth, and resulted in the final reunion of traditions which must have had a similar provenance in the misty past, when Goidel and Cymry were as yet undivided. The existence of a powerful British or Welsh-speaking state in Strathclyde in the south-west of Scotland and Cumberland probably did much to fuse the two Keltic legends into one, and the later migration of many of its inhabitants to North Wales must have assisted the process.

" The original machinery, so to say, of Welsh tales," says Rhŷs,[1] " was magic and the supernatural. . . . This was also probably the case with the stories about Arthur as they came from the mouths of the Brythonic Kelts." That they had their origin in mythological ideas associated with the religion of the Druids there can be no doubt. Says Canon MacCulloch : " We may postulate a local Arthur saga fusing an old Brythonic god with the historic sixth century Arthur. From this or from Geoffrey's handling of it sprang the great romantic cycle. In the ninth century Nennius's Arthur is the historic war-chief, possibly Count of Britain, but in the references to his hunting the *Porcus Troit* (the

[1] *Arthurian Legend*, p. 2.

Twrch Trwyth) the mythic Arthur momentarily appears. Geoffrey's Arthur differs from the later Arthur of romance, and he may have partially rationalized the saga, which was either of recent formation or else local and obscure, since there is no reference to Arthur in the *Mabinogion*. . . . In Geoffrey, Arthur is the fruit of Igerna's amour with Uther, to whom Merlin has given her husband's shape. Arthur conquers many hosts as well as giants, and his court is the resort of all valorous persons. But he is at last wounded by his wife's seducer, and carried to the Isle of Avallon to be cured of his wounds, and nothing more is ever heard of him. Some of these incidents occur also in the stories of Fionn and Mongan, and those of the mysterious begetting of a wonder child and his final disappearance into fairyland are local forms of a tale common to all branches of the Kelts. This was fitted to the history of the local god or hero Arthur, giving rise to the local saga to which were afterwards added events from the life of the historic Arthur. This complex saga must then have acquired a wider fame long before the romantic cycle took its place, as is suggested by the purely Welsh tales of Kulhwych and the *Dream of Rhonabwy*, in the former of which the personages (gods) of the *Mabinogion* figure in Arthur's train, though he is far from being the Arthur of the romances. Sporadic references to Arthur occur also in Welsh literature, and to the earlier saga belongs the Arthur who spoils Elysium of its cauldron in a Taliesin poem. . . . He may have been the object of a cult as these heroes (Fionn and Cuchulainn) perhaps were, or he may have been a god more and more idealized as a hero. If the earlier form of his name was Artor, 'a ploughman', but perhaps with a wider significance, and having an equivalent in Artaius, a Gaulish god equated with Mercury, he may have been a god of agriculture who became a war-god. But he was also regarded as a culture-hero, stealing a cauldron and also swine from the gods' land, the last incident euhemerized into the tale of an unsuccessful theft from March, son of Meirchion, while, like other culture-heroes, he is a bard."

This pretty well summarizes the question of Arthurian origins. In Arthur's saga nearly all the characters are reminiscent of ancient Brythonic deities, Kai, Peredur, and the rest. It remains for us to discover precisely how much of the mystical tradition is to be found remaining in (1) the native Welsh poems which allude to him and (2) in the Norman and English romances which deal with his story.

We have already dealt to some extent with the tradition of Arthur as alluded to in the pages of Geoffrey and Nennius. The early Welsh poems contain few references to Arthur, indeed only five mention him at all, and then it is rather the "historical" than the mythical Arthur. But there is one poem which merits our especial consideration. That is the poem generally known as "The Spoils of *Annwn*", credited to the bard Taliesin. Owing to its importance to our general thesis it is essential that the poem be here given in its entirety. The translation is that of Thomas Stephens.[1]

Praise to the Lord, Supreme Ruler of the high region,
Who hath extended his dominion to the shore of the world,
Complete was the prison of Gwair in Caer Sidi.
Through the permission of Pwyll and Pryderi
No one before him went to it;
A heavy blue chain firmly held the youth,
And for the spoils of *Annwn* gloomily he sings,
And till doom shall he continue his lay.
Thrice the fullness of Pridwen we went into it,
Except seven, none returned from Caer Sidi.

[1] See his *Literature of the Kymry*, p. 192 ff.

Am I not a candidate for fame, to be heard in the song,
In Caer Pedryvan four times revolving!
It will be my first word from the cauldron when it expresses;
By the breath of nine damsels it is gently warmed.
Is it not the cauldron of the chief of *Annwn* in its fashion?
With a ridge round its edge of pearls!

It will not boil the food of a coward not sworn,
A sword bright flashing to him will be brought,
And left in the hand of Llemynawg,
And before the portals of hell, the horns of light shall be
    burning.
And when we went with Arthur in his splendid labours,
Except seven, none returned from Caer Vediwid (or the
    inclosure of the perfect ones).

Am I not a candidate for fame, to be heard in the song,
In the quadrangular inclosure, in the island of the strong door,
Where the twilight and the jet of night moved together.
Bright wine was the beverage of the host,
Three times the fullness of Prydwen, we went on sea,
Except seven, none returned from Caer Rigor (or the
    inclosure of the Royal party).

I will not have merit, with the multitude in relating the
    hero's deeds,
Beyond Caer Wydr they beheld not the prowess of Arthur?
Three times twenty-hundred men stood on the wall,
It was difficult to converse with their sentinel.
Three times the fullness of Prydwen, we went with Arthur,
Except seven, none returned, from Caer Colur (or the
    gloomy inclosure).

I will not have merit from the multitude with trailing shields,
They know not on what day, or who caused it,
Nor what hour in the splendid day Cwy was born,
Nor who prevented him from going to the meanders of
    Devwy.
They know not the brindled ox, with his thick head-band,
And seven score knobs in his collar.
And when we went with Arthur of mournful memory,
Except seven, none returned from Caer Vandwy (or the
    inclosure resting on the height).

I will not have merit from men of drooping courage,
They know not what day the chief was caused,
Nor what hour in the splendid day the owner was born;
What animal they keep of silver head.
When we went with Arthur of mournful contention,
Except seven, none returned from Caer Ochren (or the
    inclosure of the shelving side).

Monks pack together like dogs in the choir
From their meetings with their witches;
Is there but one course to the wind, one to the water of
    the sea,
Is there but one spark to the fire of the unbounded tumult?
Monks pack together like wolves,
From their meetings with their witches,
They know not when the twilight and the dawn divide,
Nor what the course of the wind, nor who agitates it,
In what place it dies, on what region it roars.
The grave of the saint is vanishing from the foot of the
    altar.
I will pray to the Lord, the great Supreme,
That I be not wretched—may Christ be my portion.

The last line, as Davies surmised, is almost certainly a later addition. Critics have turned away from this most abstruse poem in despair. What is its purport, its hidden meaning? '' Could Lycophon or the sibyls,'' asks Turner, '' or any ancient oracle be more elaborately incomprehensible?'' Davies believed that it was associated with his ''Arkite'' mythology. It is obvious, however, that the Arthur with whom we have to do is not the Arthur of romance, but of myth, and that the expedition in which he sailed had for its object the exploration of the infernal regions. The poem is on the same lines as ''The Harrying of Hell'', the descent into the gulf, to cow its evil denizens and carry away its secrets and treasures. It is, indeed, part of the ritual of the candidate for adeptship into the British mysteries, resembling that for the neophyte into the Osirian, Cabiric or Orphean mysteries.

If the poem be analysed, the first verse will be found to refer to the Underworld region of *Annwn*. ''The prison of Gwair in Caer Sidi'' may be explained as follows: Gwair ap Geircin had attempted the journey, or essayed the adeptship, had failed, and had been imprisoned in Caer Sidi, which sometimes means the Zodiac, sometimes *Annwn* itself. He was known as "one of the three supreme prisoners of the isle of Britain", and was held in bondage by Pwyll, Prince of *Annwn* and Pryderi, his son. The intention of Arthur and his company was probably to rescue him or complete his initiation, and for that purpose three times a greater number of initiates than could be contained by Arthur's ship *Pridwen* essayed the task. *Annwn* is described in the Mabinogion of Pwyll as a palatial dwelling replete with every luxury rather than a darksome abyss, thus showing that the idea of it had become conventionalized.

The second verse alludes to the mystic cauldron of Keridwen, warmed by the breath of the nine damsels, the cauldron of inspiration already described, and "the island of the strong door" mentioned in the fourth verse has reference to some such mysterious island as Sena, where dwelt the nine damsels or Druidesses. The Caer Wydr spoken of in the fifth verse was Arthur's vessel of glass constructed for the especial purpose of the exploration of *Annwn,* and the bard says that he "will not have merit with the multitude in relating the hero's deeds, because they could not see his prowess after he had entered Caer Wydr, or the 'place' or vessel of glass". Merlin made a similar voyage in a similar ship or diving-bell, as did Alexander the Great, and indeed the latter story is mentioned by Taliesin. The allusion to "the brindled ox with his headband" is obviously to the sacred beast which figured in all such mysteries, the Osirian and the Mithraic as well as the British, the White Bull of the Sun. The place-names which conclude most of the stanzas appear to have reference to various regions in *Annwn.*

The last verse may be an addition, but in any case

it seems to cast aspersions on the knowledge of churchmen compared with that of the Druidic bards, especially as regards their ignorance of the regions or planes of Druidical cosmogony.

Taken as a whole, this mysterious poem seems to refer to a definite attempt on the part of the initiates of some mystical society to explore the underworld plane of *Annwn*. Attempts have been made to prove that it really has reference to an expedition of Arthur to Caledonia, which was euphemistically known as *Annwn* or Hades, probably by virtue of the old tradition mentioned by Procopius which alluded to the fatal conditions prevailing north of the Roman Wall. But the mystical allusions in the poem readily dispose of such a hypothesis.

Rhŷs, writing on the subject, says[1] :

> The principal treasure, which he and his men carried away thence, was the Cauldron of the Head of Hades, that is to say, of Pwyll. In that poem, xxx,[2] Pwyll and Pryderi are associated together, and the cauldron is found at a place called Caer Pedryvan, the Four-horned or Four-cornered Castle in Ynys Pybyrdor or the Isle of the Active Door, the dwellers of which are represented quaffing sparkling wine in a clime that blends the grey twilight of the evening with the jet-black darkness of night; so lamps burn in the front of the gates of Uffern or Hell. Besides the names Caer Pedryvan and Uffern, it has these others : Caer Vedwit, meaning probably the Castle of Revelry, in reference to the wine-drinking there; Caer Golud, or the Castle of Riches; Caer Ochren, Caer Rigor, and Caer Vandwy, all three of unknown interpretation.

Elsewhere Taliesin sings :

> Perfect is my chair in Caer Sidi :
> Plague and age hurt him not who's in it—
> They know, Manawydan and Pryderi.
> Three organs round a fire sing before it,
> And about its points are ocean's streams
> And the abundant well above it—
> Sweeter than white wine the drink in it.

[1] *The Arthurian Legend*, p. 300.
[2] " The Spoils of *Annwn*."

Rhŷs equates this with passages in the Welsh "Seint Greal" legend, and states with reference to Gweir that "he had only returned after a terrible imprisonment there (Caer Sidi), an initiation which made him for ever a bard". Farther on, once more referring to the cauldron, he says :

> With regard to that vessel, Taliessin, in poem xxx, mentions the following things respecting it : The Cauldron of the Head of Hades had a rim set with pearls adorning it ; the fire beneath it was kindled by the breath of nine maidens, utterances might be heard issuing from it ; and it would not boil food for a coward. The other poem does not mention the cauldron as being at Caer Sidi, but says that he who has his seat there has nought to fear from plague or old age. Compare with this what is said of the Grail in the romances, where Pelles and his brother figure. The Grail, when it comes, feeds those at the table with whatever kind of food each one desires. But those who are not worthy are not allowed by it to remain or to approach too near with impunity. Similarly those who worship at the Grail Chapel at King Peleur's remain young nor mark the lapse of time. Add to this that the Grail heals the sick and wounded. By means of accounts other than those in which the Grail belongs to Pelles or Peleur, the correspondence between it and the Cauldron of Pwyll, Head of Hades, might, perhaps, be more strikingly shown ; but the foregoing is sufficiently near for our purpose. Now, as the original identity of Pelles and Peleur with Pwyll and Pryderi has been shown to be probable, as has also the identity of Carbonek, where the Holy Grail was kept, with Caer Pedryvan, where Pwyll's Cauldron was found by Arthur and his men, the conclusion is all but inevitable, that the famous Cauldron served as a prototype of the far more famous Grail.

We see, therefore, that the visit to *Annwn*, the "Astral Plane", as we might call it, was for the purpose of seizing its spoils, its cauldron of mystical wisdom or inspiration. It is plain that a certain ritual must be gone through, a severe initiation, before its portals could be gained, and there was a risk of failure and "imprisonment", even of destruction. The prize was the Grail or cauldron of prophecy, which renewed life and gave health to the soul. That the *cultus* which guarded the secret was one of select initiates is obvious from the allusion to the multitude who "know not" the ritual of its mysteries.

But what of Arthur's connection with this myth or initiation and of the Harrying of Hades? It is plain that he, like Osiris, is the god of a mystical cult who must periodically take a journey through the underworld, not only for the purpose of subduing its evil inhabitants, but of learning their secrets and passwords in order that the souls of the just, the perfected initiates, will be enabled to journey through that plane unharmed. This Osiris did. By his agency, through the spells and passwords given in his books, the dead Osirian, the man of his cult, is franked safely through the gloomy region of Amenti, the Egyptian *Annwn*, to the golden realm of the divinity, so that he may live for ever.

That Arthur and Osiris are indeed figures originating in a common source must be reasonably clear to the student of myth. Druidism is only the cult of Osiris in another form, and Arthur seems to have a common origin with Ausar or Osiris. When Arthur is slain at the battle of Camelon by his treacherous nephew Modred, he is carried off in a barque by his sister to the mysterious Isle of Avallach or Avallon, an oversea or underworld locality, "the Place of Apples". There he remains, neither alive nor dead, awaiting the fateful day when Britain shall require his sword.

The history of Osiris has many points of resemblance with that of Arthur. When slain by his treacherous brother Set, the body of the Egyptian god was ferried in the sacred barque across the Nile, accompanied by his mourning sisters Isis and Nephthys, to the region of Aalu in the West, a place of plenteous fruits and grain.   There Osiris was supposed to rule as the god of the not-dead, awaiting a glorious resurrection.

Both Arthur and Osiris were associated with the cult of the bull.   Osiris, indeed, is referred to as a bull, the Apis bull was merely a form of him, and in the poem by Taliesin quoted previously, the sacred ox is alluded to in connection with Arthur's descent into *Annwn*.

Horus is probably the resurrected form of Osiris, and his myth bears a close resemblance to that of Arthur.   Like that monarch, he gathers round him a company of warriors who devote themselves to the destruction of evil monsters.   Horus was typified by the hawk, as Arthur was by the crow, for no Englishman in olden times would kill a crow lest it held the hero's spirit.   The name of Arthur's nephew Gwalchmei also means "hawk".

It will thus be seen that the points of resemblance between Arthur and Osiris are neither few nor unimportant, and that their myths appear to have arisen from a common source.   That Arthur was the god of a mystical cult, one of whose rites was associated with a real or allegorical passage through a lower plane from which mysterious secrets and treasures might be reft, seems certain enough.   Are there any evidences of the survival of that belief in British literature or tradition?

Let us first examine the Scottish legend of Thomas the Rymour, which survives in a very ancient ballad form.   Thomas meets with the Queen of Faerie at the Eildon Tree, near Ercildoune, and enters her mystic hill.   After a long journey through the Keltic Underworld, they reach a sphere which is unquestionably one and the same with the *Annwn* of Welsh legend.   It is, indeed, Avallon, for it is wealthy in apple-trees, which, however, must not be plucked. But that Thomas entered it as an initiate is clear from the fact that its queen instructs him in the art of prophecy, the very art, indeed, sought in *Annwn* or Avallon by Arthur and his followers. Moreover, the region in which Thomas actually lived was long before his day either a part of the Keltic and Welsh-speaking kingdom of Strathclyde or closely in cultural touch with it. The Keltic implications of the myth are not far to seek. His surname of Learmont, indeed, if it be actually historical, might be interpreted as signifying the Mount of Lêr or Llyr, the old British sea-god, father of Manannan, from whom the Isle of Man and Clackmannan take their names. But this is a mere walking upon the sands of surmise, and much surer footing is to be found in the known fact that he flourished in an environment which in his time was by no means yet dissociated from Keltic tradition, and in the assuredly Keltic colouring of the myth in which he appears. Not only is the name of Thomas Rymour traditionally connected with prophecies which contain a wealth of Keltic allusions, but something more than mere tradition associates his name with the authorship of a romance the setting and personnel of which are essentially Keltic—that *Sir Tristram*, which was cobbled and completed by a Wizard still more potent than he. There exist, too, excellent reasons for believing that even in the fourteenth century his countryside had not altogether cast off the memory and influences of that Brythonic civilization which had formerly flourished there. The etymology by which his sobriquet of "True Thomas" is explained as "Druid" Thomas may seem far-fetched enough, but has authority behind it at least equal in value to the evidence afforded by that tradition of prophetic practice which is said to have given him the title.

But even more valuable as a clue to the Keltic character of Thomas's legend is that portion of it which records his durance in a subterranean environment which recalls the underground dun of the *sidhe* or fairies of Scotland, Ireland, and Brittany. Not only is it the veritable Queen of Faerie herself who spirits Thomas away, but the description afforded of her and the *mise en scène* of her domain, no less than certain happenings therein, prove her to be of Keltic provenance.   She is attired in a manner which corresponds closely with the descriptions we have of the *sidhe* of Ireland, and is accompanied by the inevitable greyhounds so dear to these picturesque mound-dwellers.   Like the Loathly Lady of Arthurian story, she assumes a hag-like aspect on being kissed.   Once beneath Eildon Hill, Thomas beholds the orchard so characteristic of the Keltic Otherworld, but is warned that he must not partake of its fruit, a certain proof that this is no other than the food of the dead, of which if a man eat he may give up all hope of regaining upper earth.   He hears, too, the rushing of the great waters which separate the Keltic Otherworld from the land of the quick.

It is also noticeable that the names alluded to in the prophecies of Thomas are almost exclusively those of Keltic mages and scribes, Merlin and Gildas being chiefly quoted, and the legends relating to the first-mentioned being freely drawn upon.   The Arthurian character of many of the prophecies is, indeed, too marked to be ignored, and Scott, duly impressed by this, gave it as his opinion in his introduction to *Sir Tristram* that Thomas had collected his material from among the floating traditions of the British or Welsh-speaking people of Strathclyde, which still lingered in the southern counties during the fourteenth century.

Now it is apparent, although it has not so far been alluded to in any study of the subject, that Thomas's legend has many points of resemblance with that of Merlin himself, especially as detailed in Breton folklore. Like Thomas, Merlin was a soothsayer who fell a victim to the wiles of a fairy enchantress, Vivien, whom, according to one Breton form of the legend, he met in the glades of Broceliande. He dwelt with her in Joyous Garden, but in this case it was the man and not the "gay ladye" who exhibited signs of age once the troth was plighted. "It was foreseen long ago," says Merlin, "that a lady should lead me captive, and that I should become her prisoner for all time." For a season he leaves Joyous Garden, as Thomas and Tannhäuser leave their places of durance. But Vivien learns from him an enchantment which will keep him with her for ever, and employs it to retain him in her power. Waving her cloak round his head, she plunges him into a deep slumber, and transports him once more to Joyous Garden, where he is doomed to remain as the prisoner of love for ever.

But the important thing for us is that Thomas's myth relates the adventures of a man, and a man who once actually existed, in search of initiation in the Underworld. Here we have a Scotsman of the thirteenth century experiencing practically the same adventures in the Underworld, or astral plane, as did Arthur and his companions.

And this is only one of a number of accounts in which living men are said to have probed the secrets of the supernatural world and penetrated to some subterranean sphere in search of hidden knowledge

—sure evidence that the Cult of Druidic initiation survived well into modern times.

It will be germane to the argument if we examine one or two of the more modern of these explorations. Let us turn to *The Secret Commonwealth of Elves, Fauns, and Fairies,* written in 1691 by the Rev. Robert Kirk, M.A., Minister of Aberfoyle in Scotland, and edited by the late Andrew Lang in 1893. The MS. of the book seems to have been in the possession of Colin Kirk, Writer to the Signet, Edinburgh, and does not appear to have been printed before the issue of 1815 by Messrs. Longman, Scott's statement to the contrary notwithstanding.

The circumstances of Kirk's life are well enough authenticated. He was a student of theology at St. Andrews University, but took his Master of Arts degree at Edinburgh. He was the *seventh* and youngest son of James Kirk, who had also held the charge of Aberfoyle, and he originally ministered at Balquidder. A Keltic scholar, he translated the Bible and Psalter into Gaelic, publishing the latter in 1684. He was twice married, first to Isobel, daughter of Sir Colin Campbell of Mochester, and secondly to the daughter of Campbell of Forday, who survived him. I mention these facts merely to show that he was not apochryphal. He died in 1692, at the age of 51, and his tomb is inscribed " Robertus Kirk, B.M., Linguæ Hiberniæ Lumen." " In Scott's time," says Lang, " the tomb was to be seen in the east end of the Churchyard of Aberfoyle ; but the ashes of Mr. Kirk *are not there*. His successor, the Rev. Dr. Cochrane, in his *Sketches of Picturesque Scenery*, informs us that, as Mr. Kirk was walking on a dunshi, or fairy-hill, in his neighbourhood, he sunk down in a swoon, which was taken for death." " After the ceremony of a seeming funeral," writes Scott, "the form of the Rev. Robert Kirk appeared to a relation, and commanded him to go to Grahame of Duchray. 'Say to Duchray, who is my cousin as well as your own, that I am not dead, but a captive in Fairyland; and only one chance remains for my liberation. When the posthumous child, of which my wife has been delivered since my disappearance, shall be brought to baptism, I will appear in the room, when, if Duchray shall throw over my head the knife or dirk which he holds in his hand, I may be restored to society; but if this is neglected, I am lost for ever'. True to his tryst, Mr. Kirk did appear at the christening and 'was visibly seen'; but Duchray was so astonished that he did not throw his dirk over the head of the appearance, and to society Mr. Kirk has not yet been restored." It is still believed in the neighbourhood that Kirk was spirited away by the fairies.

Kirk, as Lang points out, treated the world of faery as "a mere fact in nature", his Presbyterianism notwithstanding. He did not believe the dwellers in fairyland to be the dead, but aery spirits, "an abstruse people," the forerunners of our more substantial race. Indeed, he speaks of the Elves as though he were describing the denizens of the Astral Plane, and their Kingdom as that plane itself. But the point for us is that in order to get into communion with these beings it was essential for a man to undergo a particular ceremony of initiation into "the Second Sight."

There be odd Solemnities at investing a Man with the Priviledges of the whole Mistery of this Second Sight [writes Kirk]. He must run a Tedder of Hair (which bound a Corps to the Bier) in a Helix (?) about his Midle, from End to End; then bow his Head downwards,

as did Elijah, I Kings 18, 42, and look back thorough
his Legs untill he sie a Funerall advance till the People
cross two Marches; or look thus back thorough a Hole
where there was a Knot of Fir. But if the Wind change
Points while the Hair Tedder is ty'd about him, he is in
Peril of his Lyfe. The usewall Method for a curious
Person to get a transient Sight of this otherwise invisible
Crew of Subterraneans (if impotently and over rashly
sought) is to put his (left Foot under the Wizard's right)
Foot, and the Seer's Hand is put on the Inquirer's Head,
who is to look over the Wizard's right shoulder (which
hes ane ill Appearance, as if by this Ceremony ane implicit
Surrender were made of all betwixt the Wizard's Foot
and his Hand, ere the Person can be admitted a privado
to the Airt); then will he see a Multitude of Wight's,
like furious hardie Men, flocking to him haistily from all
Quarters, as thick as Atoms in the Air; which are no
Nonentities or Phantasms, Creatures proceiding from ane
affrighted Apprehensione, confused or crazed Sense, but
Realities, appearing to a stable Man in his awaking Sense,
and enduring a rationall Tyrall of their Being. Thes
thorow Fear strick him breathless and speechless. The
Wizard, defending the Lawfullness of his Skill, forbids
such Horror, and comforts his Novice by telling of
Zacharias, as being struck speechless at seeing Appari-
tions, Luke I. 20. Then he further maintains his Airt,
by vouching Elisha to have had the same, and disclos'd
it thus unto his Servant in 2 Kings 6, 17, when he
blinded the Syrians; and Peter in Act 5, 9, forseing the
Death of Saphira, by perceaving as it were her Winding-
sheet about her beforehand; and Paul in 2nd Corinth.
12, 4, who got such a Vision and Sight as should not,
nor could not be told. . . . And again, that Men of
the Second Sight (being designed to give warnings against
secret Engyns) surpass the ordinary Vision of other
Men, which is a native Habit in some, descended from
their Ancestors, and acquired as ane artificiall Improve-
ment of their natural Sight in others; resembling in their
own Kynd the usuall artificiall Helps of optic Glasses (as
Prospectives, Telescopes, and Microscopes), without
which asctitious Aids those Men here treated of do
perceive Things that, for their Smalness or Subtility,
and Secrecy, are invisible to others, tho dayly conversant
with them; they having such a Beam continuallie about
them as that of the Sun, which when it shines clear only,
lets common Eyes see the Atomes, in the Air, that without those Rayes they could not discern; for some have
this Second Sight transmitted from Father to Sone thorow

the whole Family, without their own Consent or others
teaching, proceeding only from a Bounty of Providence
it seems, or by Compact, or by a complexionall Quality of
the first Acquirer.

Now this, I suggest, is an account not of something
imaginary, but of the long-preserved ritual of a
hereditary cult whose members actually or professedly
were able to communicate with and enter some other
plane resembling that *Annwn* of which Taliesin's
mystical poem speaks, a long descended Keltic rite
of occult potency, recognized as practicable by men
living only 137 years ago.

I have followed Kirk so long because I desired to
indicate the presence and survival of what I believe
to have been a definite tradition of contact with
another plane, through the medium of a certain cult
in descent from the ancient British mystics. But
before leaving him, there are one or two points which
I should like to allude to more particularly, although
I shall later return to the whole question of the
survival of the ancient cults in Britain. He tells us
that "if invited and earnestly required, these
Companions make themselves known and familiar to
men; otherwise, being in a different State and
Element, they neither can nor will easily converse
with them." This reveals the fact that a certain
ritual of invocation was employed to get *en rapport*
with the "fairy" world. Again, it is stated that men
occasionally employ stratagems "for procuring a
Privacy to any of these Mysteries." This seems to
indicate that mysteries were held, that these were in
line of descent from the ancient British mysteries,
and that they were frequented and continued by
people who actually were, or believed themselves to
be, initiates. Such a condition of broken-down
mysticism, or mysticism employed for evil purposes,

was undeniably in use in connection with the cult of witchcraft, as we shall see later.

Finally, as regards the places in which these rites and mysteries may have been held, certain writers believe them to have been the "Fairy Hills" or "howes" in various parts of Scotland. Indeed the late Mr. David MacRitchie in his *Testimony of Tradition* put forward the theory that the Picts were a dwarfish race dwelling in such hills and earth-houses and were mistaken for fairies or brownies by Kirk and others. Referring to the Fairy Hill at Aberfoyle, where Kirk lived, Mr. MacRitchie writes : "How much of this 'howe' is artificial, or whether any of it is, remains to be discovered."[1] It is much larger than most artificial tumuli, and like most of such mounds, is probably sepulchral. Tales and legends of the entrance of humans into "fairy" mounds where they were instructed in supernatural secrets are so numerous as to defy description.

To return to Arthurian literature. Its more modern phase, the Anglo-Norman, holds a very considerable amount of proof of the survival of a belief in early British mysticism, but that part of it which has an arcane significance is contained in the legends of the Holy Grail, with which I shall deal in the following chapter.

[1] See also his book *The Underground Life,* privately printed, Edinburgh, 1892.

CHAPTER VI

THE MYSTERY OF THE GRAIL

SOME recent writers, among them Miss Jessie L. Weston, who speaks with authority, have given it as their opinion that the legend of the Holy Grail, although of British origin, has certainly been sophisticated by Oriental or alien ideas. That may be so, so far as its later elements are concerned, but in its early form it is demonstrably of British provenance, as I hope to prove in this chapter. I also wish to demonstrate that the legend is in direct association with the secret mystical tradition of our island, of the existence of which I have already afforded considerable proof ; that it has indeed a unity with and was drawn from that venerable body of occult belief which I believe is capable of rescue for the use of British mystics.

As I have shown, the poem of Taliesin on "The Spoils of *Annwn*" described the descent of a body of initiates or mystics into the lowest plane or circle, for the express purpose of recovering therefrom the cauldron of Pwyll, the Lord of *Annwn*. In that poem Pwyll and Pryderi, his son, are associated together by name, and the cauldron is found at a place called Caer Sidi or Caer Pedryvan, "the Four-cornered Castle" in the Isle of the Active Door. Now in Norman Grail romances the Grail is said to be in the keeping of Pelles or Peleur, merely Normanized forms of Pwyll, in the Castle of Carbonek, which is merely Caer Bannauc, the "peaked" or "horned" castle, having reference to the points or corners of Caer Sidi.[1]

The vessel which Arthur and his companions recover from *Annwn* is described in the Taliesin poem as a cauldron, the rim of which is set with pearls. The fire beneath it was kindled by the breath of nine maidens, oracular speech emanated from it, and it would not cook the food of a coward. Compare this with the description of the Grail in the Norman romances, where Pelles and his brother are mentioned. The Grail, when it appears, supplies them at the table with whatever kind of food each desires, but the unworthy were not permitted to remain near it or to approach it without hurt to themselves. Those who worship at the Grail Chapel of Peleur remain young, and to them the passage of time signifies nothing. The Grail, too, heals the sick and wounded. It is thus obvious enough that the Grail was nothing more nor less than the magic cauldron of Pwyll given a later Christian interpretation.

The Grail is said to have been brought to Britain by Joseph of Arimathea, who collected the blood of Christ in the vessel and conveyed it to the West, or gave it to one Bron or Brons to convey thither. Brons, it is clear, is merely Bran the Blessed of Welsh literature. Brons, sailing from Palestine, is said to have floated across on a shirt taken from Joseph's Son. But this is nothing but a later "re-hash" of the voyage of Bran to Ireland, to which he is said to have been wafted. Bran, too, or rather his mystical head, which in his legend takes the place of the Grail, provides in Welsh myth banquet and mirth for eight years to his funeral bearers. Rhŷs,

[1] Some authorities give the derivation as Cor-arbenig, "the sovereign chair".

in speaking of the soundness of the comparison, remarks : " We have in reality to go further : it is not a case of similarity so much as of identity. The voyage of Bron is but a Christian version of the voyage of Bran, and one cannot be surprised to find one of the romances of the Quest of the Holy Grail stating that the vessel was in the keeping of Bron, represented as dwelling 'in these isles of Ireland'."

In the *Mabinogion* story of Kulhwch and Olwen, Kulhwch is commanded by the giant Yspydaden to procure for him the *Mwys,* or dish of Gwyddno Garanhir. This trencher or platter was capable of feeding all the world, nine at a time, and it was thought to have disappeared with Merlin along with the other treasures of Britain "when he entered the Glass House in Bardsey."

But I wish to make it clear that I am here concerned with the Grail romances only in so far as they reveal evidences of the survival of native British mystical tradition. That the Grail tradition was diverted to Christian purposes and therefore penetrated and sophisticated by Christian and Oriental influence is admitted, but with this side of the inquiry I have logically no concern, even with the theory that the Keltic Church in Wales employed the Grail legend to combat the pretensions of the Roman pontiff to British ecclesiastical hegemony. What I look for is evidence of the survival of the original native occult tradition associated with the Grail in its form of a cauldron of inspiration situated on another plane, to reach which initiation into a mystical or Druidic brotherhood was essential.

We have seen that there is actually traditional continuity between the Taliesin poem of "The Spoils of *Annwn*" and the Grail legends, that the one arose out of the other, that the Grail was in the first place the cauldron of inspiration of a Druidic cult before it was thought of as the dish which held the blood of the Redeemer. In one of the later romances it is described as a salver containing a head, in another as a reliquary, again as a "dish" or cup. It matters not in what form it may appear in Christian symbolism, as it still indubitably retains therein the eucharistic character of its new forms notwithstanding the clearest evidences of its "pagan" or Druidic origins as the Keltic cauldron of inspiration and plenty, the cauldron of the Dagda, of Keridwen, of Pwyll. Even its Anglo-Norman name, Graal, a dish made of costly materials used for purposes of festival, is merely a translation of the Keltic word *mowys* or *mias*.

In a striking passage on the folklore antecedents of the Grail, Mr. A. E. Waite writes :[1]

> The antecedents of folklore passed into the literature of the Graal undergoing great transmutations, and so also did certain elements of old Druidism merge into Christianity; Rite and Myth and Doctrine were tinged by Tradition and Doctrine and Rite for things which co-exist tend to dovetail, at least by their outer edges; and there are traces, I think, of a time when the priest who said mass at the altar was not only a Druid at heart, but in his heart saw no reason also for the Druid to be priest any less. Long after the conversion of the Celt, enigmatical fables and mystical Rites lingered in Gaul and Britain, and if one could say that the Cauldron of Ceridwen was a vessel of pagan doctrine, then in an equal symbolical sense it became a vessel of hotch-potch under the strange ægis of the Celtic Church. There were masters of mysteries and secret science, whose knowledge, it is claimed, was perpetuated under the shadow of that Church and even within the pale thereof. The Bardic Sanctuary, by the evidence of some who claimed to speak in its name, opposed no precious concealed mysteries, and perhaps on its own part the Church received into its alembic much that was not of its matter, expecting to convert it therein and turn it out in a new form. In

[1] *The Hidden Church of the Holy Grail*, pp. 176 ff.

the fourth century there were professors at Bordeaux who had once at least been Druids, and for the doctrines of their later reception the heart of their old experience may have been also an alembic. St. Beuno in his last moments is recorded to have exclaimed : " I see the Trinity and Peter and Paul, and the Druids and the Saints !"—a choir invisible, the recognition of which would, if known, have imperilled his canonisation, supposing that its process had been planned in Rome. At a much later period, even in the twelfth century, we have still the indication of perpetuated mysteries, and there is no doubt that the belief in these was promoted generally by the bards. The twelfth century saw also the beginning of a great revival of literature in Wales. There are certain Iolo manuscripts which are late and of doubtful authenticity, but accepting their evidence under all necessary reserves, they refer the revival in question to Rhys ap Twdur, who assumed the sovereignty of South Wales, bringing with him "the system of the Round Table, as it is with regard to min-strels and bards". And when the time came for the last struggle between the Celtic and Latin Rites for the independence of the British Church, I can well believe that all which remained, under all transformations, of that old mixed wisdom of the West was also fighting for its life. When pseudo-Taliesin prophesied the return of Cadwaladr, who had passed into the unmanifest, like Arthur, and, like Arthur, was destined to return, I believe also that this allegory of rebirth or resurrection, if it referred on one side to the aspirations of the Celtic Church did not less embody on another the desired notion of a second spring for the mysteries which once dwelt in Wales, which even after many centuries were interned rather than dead.

But to the tales themselves. The Welsh Perceval or Peredur gives the first form of the Grail legend. We are not here concerned with the story itself, but only with those details in it which illustrate our thesis of the survival of the British tradition.

The mother of Peredur, we are told, had two brothers, Peles and Peleur, as they are called in the Welsh " Seint Greal." These are merely the Pwyll and Pryderi of the old tradition, as has been said. Peredur destroys a monster known as the Addanc or Avanc of the Lake. This was a mighty beaver, which in another Welsh tale was said to have been drawn from the waters of its lake by the god or hero Hu. Now in an ancient Welsh poem, "Cadair Ceridwen", or "The Chair of Keridwen",[1] the goddess mentions this animal as follows :

> I saw a fierce conflict in the vale of Beaver, on the day of the Sun, at the hour of dawn, between the birds of Wrath and Gwydion. On the day of Jove, they (the birds of Wrath) securely went to Mona, to demand a sudden shower of the sorcerers; but the goddess of the silver wheel,[2] of auspicious mien, the dawn of serenity, the greatest restrainer of sadness, in behalf of the Britons, speedily throws round his hall the stream of the Rainbow, a stream which scares away violence from the earth, and causes the bane of its former state, round the circle of the world, to subside. The books of the Ruler of the Mount record no falsehood. The Chair of the Preserver remains here; and till the doom, shall it continue in Europe.

Thus the Avanc and Keridwen, goddess of the cauldron, are associated, and the whole passage unquestionably relates to a part of the ceremony of initiation into the rites of Keridwen, goddess of the cauldron of inspiration, a passage referring to the strife between sun and storm, order and chaos, and one which could be equated from the rituals of more than one secret tradition.

Next the castle visited by Peredur, and which is obviously the Castle of the Grail and the Fisher King (for the Welsh version is later and probably borrowed much of its "machinery" from Norman sources) is merely the Palace of Caer Sidi or Caer Bannauc, the royal seat of *Annwn*, the centre of the mysteries of the Astral Plane, where the cauldron of inspiration (or Grail) was kept. Here he meets the owner of the Castle, his uncle (the "Fisher King" of the Grail versions) who was watching his men fishing in the

---

[1] *Welsh Archæology*, p. 66.   [2] Arianrhod.

lake.   He tells Peredur, in the true accents of one who has arcane knowledge to conceal, that whatever strange things he may see in the castle, he must not speak of.

The late Mr. Alfred Nutt believed that in the original Keltic tradition the surname of the Fisher King had a significance now lost.[1]   Now the brother of this Fisher King is called in the Norman-French Grail romances Goon Desert, Gornumant, and Gonemans, which, as Rhŷs has shown,[2] are merely corruptions of the name of Gwyn, son of Nudd, King of the demons of the Otherworld.   Now Gwyn, in Welsh myth, has a brother or companion Gwydno, whose name seems to have meant "Tall Crane", or "Stalking Person", and he was famous as the owner of a weir in which fish to the value of a hundred pounds were caught on the eve of the First of May each year.   Connected with this story was the legend of the finding of the babe Taliesin in this weir, as recorded beforehand, that Taliesin, indeed, who was the son of Keridwen, born to her after she had swallowed Gwion, the watcher of her cauldron, that very Taliesin who was the "official" bard of the mysteries of Caer Sidi or *Annwn*, and who boasts that he was present with Arthur when he stole the cauldron of inspiration therefrom, whose "rebirth", as Canon MacCulloch acutely observes, "is connected with his acquiring of inspiration".[3]

It is thus clear enough that the whole Grail myth is founded in the central idea of the cauldron of inspiration in *Annwn*, the mystical plane, that this is, indeed, the hub from which all the spokes of the wheel radiate.   *The Red Book of Hergest,* of which the Welsh "Peredur" or "Perceval" is a part, is

[1] *Holy Grail,* p. 123.   [2] *Arthurian Legend,* pp. 315-16.
[3] op. cit. p. 118.

found in a Welsh manuscript of the end of the thirteenth century, so that at that relatively late date we find the initiation story of the *Annwn* Plane, somewhat garbled, perhaps, but still flourishing, if with a Christian interpretation.

The *Conte del Graal* of Robert de Borron and his continuators, commenced about the third quarter of the twelfth century, is "a composition", says Rhŷs,[1] "which cannot help striking a student of Welsh literature and mythology as one of the oldest in point of time and allusion within the whole cycle of Grail romance." It says of the Rich Fisher : "much knew he of black art, more than an hundred times changed he his semblance".

Now the whole turning-point and key of the *Conte del Graal* is connected with the mystic question which Perceval fails to put to the Fisher King, the "suppressed word", as Mr. Waite calls it. "In the *Conte del Graal*," he writes,[2] " the law and order of the Quest is that Perceval shall ask the meaning of these wonders which he sees in the pageant at the Castle of the Quest." The prime question he should have put to the sick Fisher King was : "Unto whom one serveth of the Graal?" and this query would have released the King from his mystical dumbness and have permitted him to pass on the translation of the Secret Words, the keys of the mystery he conserved, and have dispelled the Enchantment of Britain. Because he did not ask the question Perceval was assailed with reproaches.

If we look a little more closely into the story of the Lame Fisher King and his brother we find plenty of evidence that they are the people of the Underworld well defined in myth. In the first place, the ruler of Hades is frequently lame, and Vulcan,

[1] op. cit. p. 117.   [2] op. cit. p. 153.

Weyland Smith and even the mediæval Satan show this deformity. Pwyll, or the Fisher King, is, indeed, the grand black magician of the Underworld, who, still, has the means of fertility, inspiration and regeneration in his mystical cauldron.

The three properties of the cauldron—inexhaustibility, inspiration, and regeneration—may be summed up in one word, fertility; and it is significant that the (Irish) god with whom such a cauldron was associated, Dagda, was a god of fertility. But we have just seen it associated, directly or indirectly, with goddesses—Cerridwen, Branwen, the women from the lake—and perhaps this may point to an earlier cult of goddesses of fertility, later transferred to gods. In this light the cauldron's power of restoring to life is significant, since in early belief life is associated with what is feminine. . . . Again, the slaughter and cooking of animals was usually regarded as a sacred act in primitive life. The animals were cooked in enormous cauldrons, which were found as an invariable part of the furniture of every Celtic house. The quantities of meat which they contained may have suggested inexhaustibility to people to whom the cauldron was already a symbol of fertility. Thus the symbolic cauldron of a fertility cult was merged with the cauldron used in the religious slaughter and cooking of animal food. The cauldron was also used in ritual. The Cimri slaughtered human victims over a cauldron and filled it with their blood. . . .

Like the food of men, which was regarded as the food of the gods, the cauldron of this world became the marvellous cauldron of the Otherworld, and as it then became necessary to explain the origin of such cauldrons on earth, myths arose, telling how they had been stolen from the divine land by adventurous heroes, Cuchulainn, Arthur, etc. In other instances, the cauldron is replaced by a magic vessel or cup stolen from supernatural beings of the Fionn saga or of *marchen*. Here, too, it may be noted that the Graal of Arthurian romance has affinities with the Celtic cauldron. . . . Thus in the Graal there was a fusion of the magic cauldron of Celtic paganism and the Sacred Chalice of Christianity, with the product made mystic and glorious in a most wonderful manner.[1]

[1] MacCulloch, op. cit. pp. 382-3.

In fact the whole myth explains the bringing of the mystical tradition, the Essence of Divine Life, and all that it implied from another plane, just as domestic animals such as the pig, the dog, and the deer were also brought from that plane, or as fire was thought of as having been brought from heaven by Prometheus, or cattle from "Fairyland". Long afterwards, as folk-tale assures us, the notion lingered that all good gifts emanated from the Underworld, and many are the stories told of men and women who penetrated the fairy-hill to gain either hidden lore or magical objects, as we shall see when we come to consider the subject in its folklore aspect. In numerous instances these had first to lose their senses, to become unconscious or fall asleep before admittance to the fairy realm. The Grail legends are merely Christianized versions of this theme, glorified and sanctified to fit them to the more exalted aim. They enshrine the remains of an ancient British code of initiation deflected to the uses of Christianity.

We have seen that in some versions of the Grail legend Peredur or Perceval is told by the Fisher King that he must *not* ask the reason of anything he beholds, whereas in the others he is blamed for refraining from putting the question. The second is manifestly a perversion of the first, obviously designed for later religious reasons. To ask the reason of any mystery in the Land of Enchantment or to put questions to any enchanted person is speedily to meet with disaster. It is a relic of an ancient system of taboos. Peredur must not interrogate the King of *Annwn* on matters relating to the mysteries of the Underworld, simply because the replies to these would instantly have placed that ruler's occult power in the hands of another.

The Grail as a cauldron may for a moment attract our attention. The cauldron is a symbol of the magical brew, and as such has its later counterpart in the witches' cauldron. Now from one point of view the cauldron is obviously, besides being the symbol of inspiration, plenty, and fertility, the symbol of *Annwn* itself, the region or plane in which the lower life which was sooner or later to overflow into *Abred*, the earth-plane, seethed and bubbled. It is the symbol of life, psychical as well as physical, germinating and evolving. Moreover, the myth of Arthur's journey to *Annwn* is an allegory of the ascent from *Annwn*, through initiation, into *Abred*. The "life" which seethes in the cauldron of Pwyll is removed by the initiates to a higher plane. It is obviously a myth of the evolution of life and spirit from a lower to a more exalted sphere. It follows that there was probably a similar story, now lost, of the evolution of soul-life from *Abred* to *Gwynvyd*, the sphere of immortal beings, the whole composing an allegory of the soul's journey.

CHAPTER VII

THE SECRET TRADITION IN RITE AND LEGEND

THE ancient secret tradition of Britain survives in a fragmentary manner in numerous legends, local customs and festivals, in curious rites connected with such localities as holy wells and in other manifestations. It is, of course, questionable how far some of these are associated with the ancient occult tradition of the island, and many of them may be merely survivals of the popular beliefs which constituted its baser side, bearing, indeed, the same relationship to the philosophical part of it, the official cult, so to speak, as do the rites of the Sudra caste of India to Brahminism. For what was preserved by popular favour alone could scarely have been of much mystical value in the higher sense, or have enjoyed much official countenance. At the same time, popular rites and festivals may have conserved certain ideas capable of throwing light on the Secret Tradition, especially in so far as they may be of Iberian origin. With those which have no bearing on the Secret Tradition we are, of course, not concerned.

In the first place, it is notable that the idea of *Annwn*, the mystic plane to which Arthur and his companions were thought to have penetrated, still survives as a part of modern Welsh folklore. The late Sir John Rhŷs, in his *Celtic Folklore*, provides many traditions of *Annwn*, how the "Plant Annwn", or denizens of that realm, were wont to penetrate to this upper world, hunting the souls of doomed men who had died without baptism or penance with their ban-hounds. Indeed, they came into such close contact with the sons of men that the latter were actually able to capture one of their milk-white kine !

Strangely enough we do not find any reminiscences in modern Keltic folklore of the other planes in the mystic circle, but that merely implies that the circle of *Annwn* was believed to lie much nearer that of *Abred*, the dwelling-place of man, than the others, and that therefore communication with it was much more common.

Now there is some evidence that Arthur, in his mythological aspect, superseded, or was a "surrogate" of a certain Hu Gadarn, who, we will remember, was responsible for dragging the Avanc or monster of the lake from his watery abyss by means of large horned oxen. It seems, indeed, that at one time a complete saga must have existed of the Harrying of Hell by this Hu, of which the capture of the Avanc and the raid for the Cauldron were subsidiary parts ; that the manner in which the secrets of the mystical plane of *Annwn* had been recovered by the brotherhood of an occult priesthood had been digested into writing or into these mnemonic poems of which the British Druids were wont to make use. In his *Celtic Folklore* Sir John Rhŷs makes it plain that modern Welsh peasants believe Arthur to have been the hero of the Avanc exploit rather than Hu the mighty. It would seem, therefore, that Arthur has taken over many of Hu's attributes and adventures.

But that the rites of Hu Gadarn or Arthur—for the two are, as we shall see, one and the same— survived until the middle of the sixteenth century at least is plain from several passages in English and Welsh literature. One of the objects of pilgrimage in the Principality prior to the Reformation was the image of Darvell Gadarn in the Diocese of St. Asaph. In a letter from Ellis Price to Cromwell, Secretary to Henry VIII., dated April 6th, 1538, the image is described as follows :

> There ys an Image of Darvellgadarn within the said diocese, in whome the people have so great confidence, hope, and truste, that they cumme dayly a pillgramage unto hym, somme with kyne, other with oxen or horsis, and the reste withe money; in so much that there was fyve or syxe hundrethe pilgrimes to a mans estimacion, that offered to the said image the fifte daie of this presente monethe of Aprill. The innocente people hath ben sore aluryd and entised to worship the saide image, in so much that there is a commyn sayinge as yet amongst them that who so ever will offer anie thinge to the saide Image of Darvellgadern, he hathe power to fatche hym or them that so offers oute of Hell when they be dampned.

Now this idol was taken to Smithfield in the same year and burned. It is obvious, of course, that Darvell Gadarn and Hu Gadarn are one and the same. Besides, it was peculiarly the province of Hu Gadarn to draw souls out of *Annwn*, or "Hell". He was the supreme deity, who by the strength of his emanations (his solar oxen) drew the Avanc or beaver (the sun) out of the lake, an allegory of his ability to rescue life from the darkness of the abyss.

Now all this points to the existence and functioning of the ancient British Tradition in the sixteenth century at least, for the worship of a deity like Darvell Gadarn could not have existed in Wales unless it were associated with a mystic brotherhood or priesthood, without whom it would have had no sanction or status, no binding force. And this is rather borne out by the fact that when the idol was taken to Smithfield there was taken with it a "friar" *who bore the same name as itself*, and who was also committed to the flames. Had he been a friar in Holy

Orders such a fate would certainly not have been meted out to him, nor could he have borne such a name, and it therefore appears as if he must have been not only the living representative of the god, but the conservator of his mysteries and the ancient British Secret Tradition, visited by hundreds of pilgrims, who worshipped the idol as a quite familiar deity.[1]

It is also to be noticed that oxen were offered up to this image. This not only makes it plain that it represented the Hu Gadarn of Welsh myth, but that it was identified with the sacred solar ox or bull symbolic of that deity, and which we have seen was referred to in more than one of the British mystical poems.

In the superstition concerning changelings, we also find a very distinct trace of a belief in the return of the soul to the dreary region of *Annwn*. The superstition ran that the fairies frequently exchanged their offspring for that of human beings, leaving behind a withered and often half-idiot elf in place of the robust human babe which they had spirited away. As we have already seen, the belief in fairies probably originated from the Cult of the Dead. That is, they were supposed to be the (evil?) dead waiting for re-birth, and that they were also associated with *Annwn* is positive. The changeling was thus a soul from *Annwn*, struggling to get a hold on *Abred*, the earth-plane, whereas the belief that it was possible for the fairies to spirit children away seems to have arisen from the idea that the human soul, if its earth-journey were not satisfactory, might once more lapse into the depths of *Annwn*.

In a word, the superstition about changelings is

[1] The worship of Hu Gadarn in Wales at such a late date as 1538 suffices to quash utterly the arguments of the opponents of the theory that Druidism collapsed in Roman times.

undoubtedly a memory of a cult which believed in the progression or retrogression of souls rather than in their transmigration. For after all, there is very little evidence that transmigration in its usually accepted form was believed in by our forefathers, whereas there is abundant proof that a great scheme of psychic evolution underlay their theology. A ceremony which has also obvious relationships to the belief in the plane of *Annwn*, and which, indeed, displays the remains of mystic rites associated with the ancient brotherhood who presided over its ritual, is that of Hallow-e'en.

In his account of the Bards, Owen tells us that in North Wales the first day of November was attended by many ceremonies, such as lighting a large fire and running through it, "running away to escape from the black short-tailed sow", and so forth. He says :

> " Amongst the first aberrations may be traced that of the knowledge of the great Huon or the Supreme Being, which was obscured by the hieroglyphics or emblems of his different attributes, so that the grovelling minds of the multitude often sought not beyond those representations for the objects of worship and adoration. This opened an inlet for numerous errors more minute; and many superstitions became attached to their periodical solemnities and more particularly to their rejoicing fires and the appearance of vegetation in spring and of the completion of harvest in autumn."

Huon is, of course, the same as Hu Gadarn, so that here once more we find him associated with a rite of the Underworld, for the Hallow-e'en fire was nothing more or less than a symbol of that of *Annwn*, as is easily proved by the reference to the "black short-tailed sow". The reader will remember that the pig was one of the "Spoils of *Annwn*", given to the earth by Pwyll. The minister of Kirkmichael in Perthshire, writing in the Statistical

Account, says : " Formerly the Hallow Even Fire,
a relic of Druidism, was kindled in Buchan, various
magic ceremonies were then celebrated to counteract
the influences of witches and demons. . . .
Societies were formed, either by pique or humour,
to scatter certain fires, and the attack and defence
were often conducted with art and fury." It is
surely clear enough that this rite, totally unlike the
more innocent amusements associated with Hallow-
e'en in more modern times, was the memorial of a
very ancient myth interpreted by dramatic action,
descriptive of the attack on the fiery underworld
plane by a society or brotherhood of mystics.
Dramas of the kind were invariably associated with
the Mysteries of the ancient world, in Greece and
Egypt especially. And that these celebrations were
popularly believed to have descended from the Druids
is not only stated by the minister of Kirkmichael, but
by the minister of Callander, who in the same Account
states that : "The people received the consecrated
fire from the Druid priests next morning, the virtues
of which were supposed to continue for a year."

It is by no means a simple task to trace the eroded
outline of the mystical tradition of Britain in folk-
belief and legend, and in many instances the
professional exponents of Folklore have made the
task all the more difficult by their insistence in
regarding all ancient beliefs as having a bearing on
vegetation or other rites, neglecting altogether the
deeper significance which lies beneath these tales. In
order to prove that a recognized caste of celebrants
did actually exist within living memory, I will now
turn to various evidences of their presence, in Wales
at least. In Lewis's *Topographical Dictionary of
Wales* we read that the Well of Fynnon Elian
"Even in the present age is frequently visited by the

superstitious . . . the ceremonies performed by the applicant standing upon a certain spot near the well while the owner of it reads a few passages of the sacred Scriptures, and then taking a small quantity of water gives it to the former to drink, throwing the residue over his head, which is repeated three times.'' Foulkes, in his *Enwogion Cymru*, published in 1870, says that the last person to have charge of the Well was a certain John Evans. Before him a woman had officiated there and many amusing tales of her shrewdness were recounted. Says Rhŷs in his *Celtic Folklore* :

> A series of articles on the Well appeared in 1861 and were afterwards published, I am told, as a shilling book which I have not seen, and they dealt with the superstition, with the history of John Evans, and with his confessions and *conversions*.[1]   I have searched in vain for any accounts in Welsh of the ritual followed at the Well. When Mrs. Silvan Evans visited the place the person in charge of the Well was a woman, and Peter Roberts in his *Cambrian Popular Antiquities*, published in London in 1815, alludes to her or a predecessor of hers in the following terms: " Near the well resided some worthless and infamous wretch who officiated as priestess. . . ." There is, I think, very little doubt that the owner or guardian of the Well was, so to say, the representative of an ancient priesthood of the Well.   That priesthood dated its origin probably many centuries before a Christian church was built near the Well, and coming down to later times, we have unfortunately no sufficient data to show how the right to such priesthood was acquired, whether by inheritance or otherwise; but we know that a woman might have charge of St. Elian's Well.

Sir John also left behind him data regarding a similar site in Pembrokeshire, the Church of St. Teilo. The building, he tells us, is in ruins, but the church-yard is still used and contains two of the most ancient post-Roman inscriptions in the Principality. This well was thought to be good for the whooping-cough,

---

[1] Italics mine.—L.S.

and when Sir John made inquiries as to whether any rite or ceremony must be performed in order to derive benefit from the water, he was told that the water must be lifted out of the well and given to the patient to drink by somebody *born in the adjoining house, preferably by the heir*.   The water, it appears, was drawn from the well in a skull which was said to be the skull of St. Teilo, and, indeed, he was shown the skull.   Sir John learned later that this well is known as the *Oxen's Well*, and that the family owning and occupying the adjoining farmhouse *had been there for centuries*.   Their name was Melchior, by no means a common one in the Principality, and having a sound sufficiently priestly, in all conscience.   There was also current a legend relating to the manner in which the skull came to be used as a drinking vessel.   "In this particular instance," says Sir John Rhŷs, " we have a succession which seems to point unmistakeably to an ancient priesthood of a sacred spring."

Now mark that this well was known as the "Oxen's Well", that is, it was associated in some manner with the cult of Hu Gadarn, the mystic deity of the Brythonic race who with his sacred oxen was supposed to have overcome the powers of evil. Here we have a case, as Rhŷs, a very sound authority, was convinced, *of the survival of a hereditary priesthood in Wales from pre-Christian times until the beginning of the twentieth century!* We seem to have clear evidence not only that such a cult actually existed, but that it was in some way associated with the mystic ox and thus with the occult brotherhood who were led by Arthur into the gloomy abyss of *Annwn*.

Elsewhere on British soil there are evidences of the existence of persons who appear to have been inculcated into a mysterious and magical society whose writings they actually preserved.   A woman attainted by the Presbytery of Perth for sorcery in 1626 stated that she had a book containing magical knowledge which was her "Goodsire's, her Grand-sire's, and was a thousand years old."   Her son, Adam Bell, read it to her.   Again there are many proofs, as we shall see when we come to deal with the cult of witchcraft, of persons being initiated into the ritual of that cult either by their relatives or by friends.

It will be necessary to say a word here regarding Arthur's glass-ship, alluded to in the legend of the descent into *Annwn*.   This vessel has been construed by various authorities as a diving-bell, and so forth, and has been equated with the boat of glass in Irish myth in which Condla the Red was spirited away to the Land of the Everliving by a fairy princess.   But I think it is obvious that the vessel has more a spiritual than a material significance, that, indeed, it more nearly resembles the ship of the Egyptian Osiris, which was supposed to navigate the dark waters of Amenti, the Egyptian Underworld.   The two myths are, indeed, one, and obviously emanate from a common source.   This craft is, indeed, the ship of souls, just as is the barque of Osiris, and in this connection we may recall the myth cited by the late Greek writer Procopius, quoted at the commencement of this volume, in which he describes the passage of the dead souls by ship to the shores of Britain.   This proves that a very ancient myth actually existed relative to the bearing of the souls of the departed into the land of darkness by means of a magical vessel.   This magical vessel was, indeed, the vehicle by which the astral shape was transported into its appropriate plane, and, in the case of Arthur and his comrades, it was obviously able to transport also the astral shapes of the living to an extra-terrestrial sphere. What was the nature of this vessel?

That this ship had a solar significance we may be pretty certain. The similar Egyptian barque which plumbed the depths of Amenti was certainly of solar origin, and its symbolical significance seems to be that of light invading darkness, the ship of the Sun god penetrating the gloom of the world of Death or non-being.

Perhaps the derivation of Caer Sidi, a part of *Annwn*, is, as Rhŷs thought, Caer Shee, "City of the Fairies". It is notable that four organs play around its fire. This instrument has a long association with mysteries, from those of Byzantium to the present day, as in Masonry.

Searching through the detritus of Folklore for evidences of the Secret Tradition, we have now to consider what precisely were its associations, if any, with the cult known as witchcraft. What exactly was witchcraft, and was it intimately associated with the ancient Secret Tradition of Britain? We are now aware that witchcraft was by no means a thing of hallucination, that it did not originate in the imaginations of disgruntled old women. Research has made it abundantly clear that, as known in the sixteenth and seventeenth centuries, it was the last remaining fragment of a very ancient cult, which probably had its origin in prehistoric times. I believe it to have had its beginnings in a caste of women associated with horse-breeding or cattle-raising, or both, as the entire folklore of the cult has reminiscences of association with the horse and with domestic cattle. Some such caste, I think, as that of the Amazons of classical lore may possibly have been the prototype of the witch cult. The tendency of the witch to bespell cattle, her obvious power over flocks and herds, and her traditional aspect as a horse-using sorceress has led me to believe that somewhere in North-West Africa a female religion arose out of the usages of such a body of women as I describe, which later lost its significance with respect to pastoral affairs, and became purely and simply magical and occult. That it was thus of "Iberian" origin is also highly probable, and thus it was bound to have been connected with that general aboriginal body of faith and superstition on which Druidism was founded, that, indeed, it represented the lower *cultus* in Britain and elsewhere, an aboriginal faith.

Although we do not hear a great deal about it in British history, there is no doubt that witchcraft, as a more or less secret cult, persisted in Britain throughout the ages, but I do not believe it to have been part of Druidism or of the Secret Tradition. Rather was it a debased remnant of that still older Iberian magic which to some extent Druidism embraced, but which it also superseded and perhaps tried to weed out. As Sir James Frazer has shown in his *Golden Bough*, the Druids seem to have burned animals whom they believed to be witches in disguise, and *a fortiori*, it seems probable that they also burned sorcerers, male or female, on occasion. The Druidic priestesses of whom we read, those for example of the Island of Sena, or of Anglesey, although perhaps acting as a separate female caste, do not appear to have been of the character of witches. There is, however, one connection between the nine muse-like maidens who kept the Cauldron of Keridwen warm, and who have been identified with the priestesses of Sena, and the cult of more modern witchcraft, and that is the Cauldron itself.

But was the witch's cauldron of tradition the same

as that of Keridwen? The Cauldron of Keridwen was obviously a vessel of inspiration, whereas the cauldron of the witches was a vessel for the brewing of poisonous concoctions. We will remember, however, that the contents of Keridwen's Cauldron were of a poisonous nature with the exception of the first three drops which sprang from it, and this would seem to link it with the magical vessel of the witches. I do not believe, however, that this cauldron was originally part and parcel of the witch's magical apparatus. I rather incline to think, as the evidence tends to show, that it had been adopted by the members of the witch-cult from that which conserved the Secret Tradition.

For these and other reasons I do not think that the witch-cult had any connection, official or otherwise, with that of Druidism or the Secret Tradition. I rather believe, as I have already said, that it arose out of the ancient aboriginal or Iberian body of gross superstition once existing in Britain, Gaul and Spain. But it seems to me extremely probable that it borrowed much from the cult of the Secret Tradition, especially as regards some of its ritual practices, which it would debase and turn to evil uses.

Many of the magical acts of the witches are identical with those which are alluded to as having been practised by the Druids, such as levitation, the raising of storms, the use of herbs, transformation into animal shapes and so forth, and it may be that the lower castes of official Druidism actually employed stratagems of the kind which they had borrowed from the practitioners of the aboriginal religion for the purpose of overawing the people, just as the earliest Christian disciples in Britain and elsewhere seem to have used a certain amount of low-caste black magic for a similar purpose.

We now come to evidence which makes it plain that a strong leaven of the old Druidic cult, the vehicle of the Secret Tradition, survived until what may be called comparatively recent times in Scotland. As late as 1649 to 1678, according to the records of the Presbytery of Dingwall, bulls were sacrificed in the parish of Gairloch in Ross-shire and oblations of milk poured on the hills.

The Rev. James Rust, minister of Slains, in his *Druidism Exhumed,* published in 1871, provides the following valuable evidence of the survival of Druidic belief in eighteenth century Scotland.[1]

As there was in the seventeenth century a number of superstitions prevalent in Scotland, as well as in England, which had come into being in Popish times, as well as a number which had had an existence before Popish times, belonging to the earlier system of religion, the Druidical, and which had been tolerated, connived at, or at least not extirpated, the General Assembly of the Church of Scotland resolved to take action against them. As the most of these superstitions, they said, proceeded from ignorance, they resolved that the most strenuous efforts should be made throughout Scotland for bringing education to the doors of all, even of the poorest, by the erection and extension of Parochial Schools, and by urging that Bibles should be possessed in every family, and the inmates taught to read them. But besides this, they appointed a Commission. The General Assembly of 1649 approving of a recommendation of the Assembly 1647, appointed a large Commission of their own number. Along with the Ministers appointed, there were Sir Archibald Johnston of Warristoun, "Clerk Register"; Mr. Thomas Nicholson, "His Majesty's Advocate"; Mr. Alexander Pierson, one of the ordinary "Lords of Session", Sir Lewis Stewart, Mr. Alexander Colvill, and Mr. James Robertson, "Justice Deputes"; Messrs. Rodger Mowet, John Gilmoir, and John Nisbet, "Lawyers"; with Doctors Sibbald, Cunninghame, and Purves, "Physicians". And they did "ordain the said brethren to make report of the result of their consultations and conferences from time to time, as they make any considerable progress, to the Commission for public affairs. And the said Commission

[1] pp. 38 ff.

shall make report to the next General Assembly". Among other matters, to which they directed their attention, were the Druidical customs observed at the fires of Beltane, Midsummer, Halloweven, and Yuil. All these customs and fires were ordered to be abolished. They succeeded outwardly among the old, although the youth of the country still enjoy in many places some of these same customs and fires, although they have forgotten the object of their institution, and of course the superstition itself. They directed their attention to the Remains of Druidical Superstition and Sorcery practised at the old places of worship, dedicated not only to the greater, but to the lesser gods, the familiar spirits, the household divinities, or demigods of the ancients, who, as was supposed, could be consulted, and could grant charming powers to their votaries, at those pieces of ground which the Druids had consecrated to them, and which had continued for thousands of years untilled. These were ordered to be cultivated under severe church censures and civil penalties, church and state then acting hand in hand in the matter. As one of the results of this Commission, we find some most important minutes in the Kirk Session Register Book of Slains, stating that inquisition was made by the minister and Elders of Slains,—as must have been done by other Ministers and Sessions,—into old Druidical superstitious practices and places within the parish. And from that inquisition, we learn that within Slains there were different pieces of land dedicated to the demi-gods of the Druids, those imps who became the little elfin tricky semidemons of the Christians; and that these places were called after those fancied creatures by words both of Lowland Scots and Highland Gaelic, as the *Guidmanes fauld*, and *Garlet*, or *Garleachd*, connected with Garlaoch, An Elf.

From entries in the Kirk Session Register Book of the Parish of Slains we find that several persons were "delaytit" or summoned before it for practising pagan rites in connection with hallow fires and refusing to till the ancient Druidical fields.

Here then we have the General Assembly of the Church of Scotland only 280 years ago, or but four "lifetimes" since, fully persuaded that Druidism was being practised all over Scotland, and taking steps to put it down. How those steps were received by

L

their congregations is probably well illustrated by Mr. John Buchan's most interesting novel *Witch Wood*.

In writing further of the antiquities of his parish, Mr. Rust deals with the belief that the spirits of the Keltic past were wont to manifest themselves on occasion to the people in old times, who were not infrequently decoyed into the recesses of the earth. There was at least three places within the Parish of Slains dedicated to the "Good People", and these remained uncultivated in the midst of cultivated ground until the beginning of the nineteenth century. " It continued also to be employed for generations for magical superstitious purposes, after the other Elfin places had been destroyed, desecrated, or cultivated by authority. I knew the woman, Mary Findlay, who died a few years ago at a great age, who was the last person laid down in infancy at the Cairn, because she was supposed to be an Elfin Changeling."

But let us examine what he says regarding the Lykar Cairn :

Lykar Cairn lay eight hundred yards N.N.E. of the Parish Church in the south angle formed by the Castle Road, where it diverges from the Turn-the-neuk Road, in a small valley surrounded by natural eminences or knolls, the most striking of which, and to the base of which it was nearest, is *Maidsemaaighe*, which means "The knoll of the very great caldron". It comes from *Maidse*, fem. "A knoll, lump, or hillock": and *ma*, a comparative with a superlative meaning, of *mor*, *great*, and *aighe*, a genitive of *aghann*, fem. a *caldron*. This will turn out, as we shall find, to have the same meaning as Bennachie, and it will contribute to make a most interesting disclosure of the Druidical religious system. We shall therefore reserve the further consideration of this till we come to consider under a distinct branch, and in a subsequent part, the Utensil or Structure called "The Caldron", so much celebrated in Welsh Mythology, but of which no notice has been taken in Scotland, although we might upon the smallest reflection have anticipated that what prevailed, or existed in the one place, did so originally in the other.

So the Cauldron of Keridwen was associated with the survival of Druidic belief in Scotland so lately as the close of the seventeenth century ! Mr. Rust points out that this name "the Cauldron" is connected with numerous localities in Scotland, at Aberdeen (Kettle-hill or Cadhal, a cauldron), where, according to local tradition, the cauldron "was made by the Picts", and was used by large crowds "for religious purposes". Place-names, too, in which enter the word Aden, Eden or Edin, as in Edinburgh, were, thought Rust, connected with the cult of the cauldron, from the Gaelic Aidheann, "a cauldron, kettle, or goblet".

" The drinking of the water of this cauldron," says Mr. Rust, " was one of the rites of the Novitiate's Initiation into the Druidical mysteries and craft, after twenty years of hard study. It was the previous hard study, and not the caldron decoction, which made him so great an adept in the Druidical art and science, and opened up futurity to his view. The Novitiate promised to the admitting Hierophant and his three accompanying Druids, during the dark hours of night, that he would be faithful to the Druidical caste. And the most fearful oaths were undertaken by him, and as dreadful orgies gone through by him."

" In Bennachie, a Druidical locality," says Rust, " is the 'Maiden Casay', or Mha-adhann-casach, 'The Great Cauldron Ascent', and 'The Maiden Stene', or Mha-adhann-lia, 'The Very Great Cauldron Stone', the Cauldron on which has been removed, probably when the modern road was formed." But upon the stone itself is incised a figure which Rust believed to be a representation of the Cauldron itself. "The Structure," he says, "according to the figure, allowed the flames to play below and around the Caldron, which was always seething with its mysterious and wonder-working contents. It is," says Rust, "the holy Caldron, the Caldron of knowledge and initiation, for it has the Z figure passing through it. This Z figure has been erroneously styled sometimes the Broken Spear, and sometimes the Broken Sceptre, and because neither of these was satisfactory it has been sometimes called by others just the Z figure, because it resembles that letter of the alphabet; and they could not think of anything else upon which they could agree. But that Figure is just the zigzag lightning of Heaven, drawn down by the Druids, who pretended to be possessed of this divine power. By this, they alleged, they produced the real celestial fire, which they sold to their votaries for domestic purposes at so dear a rate, but, according to their accounts and belief, so worthy of the price. This belief in the Heaven-produced fire was firm, deep, and universal."

That pagan rites in Scotland were regarded as "common usage" is rendered clear enough from a passage in the *Chronicle of Lanercost* (Bk. II, ch. viii), from which it appears that John, the parish priest of Inverkeithing, in Fife, was cited before his bishop in 1282 for having celebrated Easter Week "according to the rites of Priapus" by collecting the maidens of the town and making them dance round the figure of the phallic deity, singing the while. He pleaded the "common usage of the country" and was allowed to retain his benefice. This is precisely what was done, so far as the date was concerned, by the priest of Darvel Gadarn in Wales, who celebrated his highest rites on April 5th, Easter Day. There is no doubt that the stern battle of the early Keltic Church for a separate Easter arose out of especial veneration for a Keltic seasonal festival of great antiquity.

It cannot but be interesting to us to examine briefly such of the Druidic rites whose details are known in order to discover how much light these may cast upon the Secret Tradition. The rite which perhaps has been described more frequently than any other was that of the ceremonial gathering of the mistletoe. From the accounts of Pliny and Maximus of Tyre we know that the oak tree was sacred to the Kelts, and it therefore follows that the gathering of the mistletoe was definitely associated with the fundamentals of their faith. The Druidical groves were composed of oak trees, and the sacred ceremonies of the Druids were invariably graced by the presence of oak branches. In short, the oak tree was in itself a deity.

The mistletoe is not frequently found on the oak, it is more apt to twine parasitically on the poplar and the willow. Its precise significance, I believe, has been altogether missed by the majority of those writers who have dealt with this aspect of it. It has been thought to be a sign of the especial favour of the god, the symbol of immortality, of lightning, and so forth! But I believe it to be the symbol of the essence of life, regarded by the ancients indeed as the protoplasmic material of existence.

It was culled on the sixth day of the moon. Extraordinary preparations for feast and sacrifice were made beneath the tree which bore it, says Pliny, and two white bulls whose horns had never been bound were conveyed thither. A white-clad Druid climbed the tree and cut the mistletoe with a golden sickle.

As it fell it was caught in a white cloth. The bulls were then sacrificed and prayers offered up to the god. Among the Kelts the mistletoe was known as an "all-heal", and the liquor brewed from it was supposed to make barren animals fruitful, a fact which buttresses my contention that it was regarded as the protoplasm of life. Canon MacCulloch wisely sees in Pliny's account the description of a rite which "was an attenuated survival of something which had once been important, but it is more likely that Pliny gives only a few picturesque details, and passes by the rationale of the ritual. He does not tell us who the 'god' of whom he speaks was, perhaps the sun-god, or the god of vegetation . . . the oxen may have been incarnations of the god of vegetation". I believe the god of the mistletoe and the oak to have been that Hu of whom I have already spoken. Now we will recall that the image of "Darvel Gadarn" which was burned at Smithfield in 1538 had oxen offered up to it. I believe this image to have been the oak tree in an anthropomorphic or man-like shape. It appears to have been of wood, and, of course, we know that Darvel Gadarn was merely another name for Hu Gadarn, the god of Plenty, invariably associated in Keltic folklore with the ox, indeed in his symbolized form the ox itself.

It seems probable that the mistletoe as the symbol of the essence of life was introduced into the ritual of initiation of the Secret Tradition just as wheat was in that of the Eleusinian mysteries. We find it regarded as a cure for many kinds of disorders. It must indeed have been looked upon as the primordial agency of life itself. Were the "pearls" on the rim of the Cauldron of Inspiration mistletoe berries? This may appear very far-fetched, but I believe it to be not improbable. Did Hu or Arthur bring back from *Annwn* not only the Cauldron of Inspiration but the secret of life as emblemed by the mistletoe?

Much has been written regarding the human sacrifice of the Druids. To which god or gods was this sacrifice made? We are informed that huge images of wickerwork were erected, and that these were filled with victims, either criminals or slaves. The only trace of British gods designed in wicker-work which I can discover is that connected with the figures of Gog and Magog, the giants in the Guildhall. In a curious anonymous work entitled *The Giants in Guildhall*, published in 1741, and now exceedingly scarce, it is stated that the figures they replaced in 1708 were made of wickerwork. Let us look for a moment into the genealogy of Gog and Magog.

In wellnigh two thousand years of existence Imperial London has succeeded in retaining a wealth of folklore and legend quite commensurate with her importance and celebrity. It is significant, however, to the student of her tradition that at least eighty per cent. of it is Keltic and pre-Keltic, and of exceedingly venerable origin. Roman, Saxon, and Norman occupations have scarcely coloured London's pristine and native mythology, the associations of which are as Brythonic every whit as those of the folk-tales of Cambria.

Indeed, London's very name seems to be referable to certain British deities, her tutelary patrons. Doctor Henry Bradley, a sound authority, has explained "London" as a possessive formed from some such appellation as Londinos, derived from the old Keltic adjective meaning "fierce", and Mr. Gordon Home, the recent historian of Roman

London, gives it as his opinion that "the only conclusion at which it is possible to arrive is that the
twin hills beside the Thames formed at some remote
period the possession, and doubtless the stronghold, of a person or family bearing the name
Londinos".

This is sound, and clear enough so far as it goes,
but who were the "Fierce Ones" of the twin hills
beside the Thames?   If reference be made to the
names of other British cities more or less coeval with
London, it will at once be seen that a very considerable proportion of them received their names from
tutelary or guardian deities.   Camulodunum, or
Colchester, is merely the dun or hill of Camulus,
the Keltic war-god, the name of Eboracum, or York,
has been traced to the Iberian divinity Ipor or
Hyperion, and Corinium, or Cirencester, was the
city of Corineus, an eponymous deity of the island.
There are literally scores of examples.   Thus it
seems highly probable that London was named not
after any tribe or gens, but from a sub-title of the
gods who presided over the region.

Nor are there lacking the titles and traditions of
gods whose characteristics well merit the formidable
description preserved in the place-name.   From time
immemorial, almost, the names of Gog and Magog
have been associated with the site.   Its legendary
appellation Cockaigne, as indigenous to it as
Lyonesse to Cornwall or Alba to Scotland, has time
and again been explained as "the land or region of
Gog", the pleasant place or paradise of the Keltic
Ogmios.   Indeed, there is no dubiety concerning the
veridically British character of the twin titan-deities
Gog and Magog.   Their figures were formerly
carved into the slope of Plymouth Hoe, the
Gogmagog Hills in Cambridgeshire still embalm the

memory of their names, and the carved and painted statues of them which loom up at the farther end of the Guildhall are the successors of those once carried through the streets of the capital on Michaelmas Day, at the festival of the Lord Mayor's Show.

In his *New View of London* (1708), Hatton assures us that hackney coachmen in the City were wont to swear "by Gog and Magog", and he further makes it clear that a very vivid terror inspired certain Londoners, even at that late date, at the mere mention of them. Some apprentices, he tells us, were as "frighted at the names of Gog and Magog as little children are at the terrible sound of Raw-head and Bloody-bones", and evinced a livelier fear of them than at the prospect of being haled before the Lord Mayor or Chamberlain. Surely a terror so long-established could have survived only on account of an exceptionally powerful folk-memory of ancient sacrifices to the deities in question, and the student of tradition is probably justified in equating the giants of London with Ogmios, the fierce Keltic god of eloquence, who, garbed in lion-skin, and with club in hand, drew all men after him in chains and demanded more than occasional human holocausts. Magog, the "Mother Gog", is evidently his female counterpart, and her replacement by a male figure of Corineus is evidently a late and faltering acquiescence in the bowdlerized British mythology of Geoffrey of Monmouth and John Milton. Probably, too, the name Og, or Ogmios, became confused in later times, and by the same "authorities", with those of Gog and Magog, the Biblical monarchs of the Land of Bashan. On the whole, then, it appears highly probable that the twin hills on either side of the Walbrook were regarded as the duns or mounts of Og and his consort, just as the twin rocks at the extremity of Land's End were once regarded as their citadels.

There can be no doubt that Gog and Magog were deities of fertility, but it is also clear that Gog was one and the same with the Keltic Ogmios, the god of poetry and inspiration. Magog, it may be inferred, was also associated with the inspirational faculty. This would equate her with Keridwen, and indeed I see no reason to think that she is not one and the same with that goddess, who in more than one place is described as "the old giantess". But the important thing for us is that in the capital of England in pre-Roman times the rites of these monstrous deities were actually celebrated, and that the memory of them remained for so long. We are informed by more than one writer that the people of London in the eighteenth century almost worshipped them, and seemed in a sense to regard them as the palladia of the nation. Even now, were these effigies to be removed from their ancient positions in the Guildhall one can envisage something of the anger which would ensue.

Do we not take too much for granted that the passage of time utterly overwhelms ancient belief, and that during the past century we have made such strides in thought and progress as entirely to discount what we label the "superstitions" of other ages? True, there may have been during the past sixty or seventy years a much more wholesale breakaway from old tradition than ever before, but it is certain that only a very few generations ago British people were much more closely in touch with the remnants of the faith ancillary to the Secret Tradition than many moderns imagine. Festivals like Shrovetide and Yule are undoubtedly remnants of Druidic ritual, but it is equally clear that they enshrine many survivals from pre-Keltic practice. At Martinmas Saint Martin is said to have been cut up and eaten in the form of an ox. This is clear evidence that St. Martin merely took the place of the god Hu, who was symbolized by that animal. The Irish Tailteann Games still hold the memory of Tailtiu the fostermother of Lug, who died in the Kalends of August, and Lammas was the ancient Keltic feast of Lug himself. Another ancient British rite, in all probability associated with the Secret Tradition, survives in the annual celebration at Coventry of the Festival of Godiva. Who and what precisely was Godiva?

Godiva's historical existence is by no means at stake. Her personal reality is at once conceded. She was the mother not only of the patriotic Saxon princes Edwin and Morcar, but also of a heroine with associations even more romantic than her own, Edith Swan-neck, wife of that Harold who fell at Senlac or Hastings. But, this notwithstanding, the story of her noble sacrifice is demonstrably of the nature of legend. Roger of Wendover, who first alludes to it, wrote in the beginning of the thirteenth century, or about a hundred and fifty years after the death of the central figure. No previous chronicler makes mention of her unselfish performance, and in the eyes of the folkloreist it embraces so many circumstances obviously connected with ancient British religious rite as makes it evident that it must have arisen therefrom.

It is, indeed, quite unnecessary to prove, as has been done, that Coventry was, at the supposed date of the Countess's famous ride, a village inhabited by some three hundred serfs dwelling in wooden huts, that it had no market-place, nor groaned under the tolls and taxes alluded to in the legend. But it is of importance that Godgifu or Godiva, and her husband Leofric, Earl of Mercia, were the restorers, if not the founders, of its monastery of St. Osburg. For, with the restoration of this religious house, the prosperity of Coventry as a market-town commences. Godiva came to be regarded as a civic benefactress, consequently it is not surprising to find that her fame was confounded at a later date with the myth of the ancient British local goddess Brigantia or Brigit, whose story, during the early Christian centuries, had itself grown dim and confused in the popular imagination. In the Keltic period, this divinity, or her human representative, rode through the village of Coventry at the period of the summer festival at the end of May. But her feast and attributes were in the course of time confounded with and latterly absorbed by the legend of the fair-haired Saxon Countess.

This is a process with which the mythologist is well acquainted. The memory of a god wanes, and his legend is appropriated by a later hero or saint, with modifications of time and place. Just as in Ireland the goddess Brigantia, with whom we have here to deal, became the Christian St. Bridget, there is no reason to doubt that in Coventry a similar process took place, and that Brigantia or Brigiddu became confused with the saintly Godgifu, the "God-given".

For our contention, the salient points of Godiva's legend are that she passed through Coventry innocent of any covering save that of her abundant golden hair, and that in doing so, she was spied upon. There is good proof that the ancient Keltic deity, or a woman representing her, appeared in this condition at her annual festival ; and to spy upon godhead, or its representative, was, of course, the unpardonable sin, punished with the deprivation of sight.

That Coventry was anciently situated in a district in which Druidical rites were practised is generally conceded. At the village of Southam, hard by, the Godiva procession was formerly celebrated with a faithfulness equal to that evinced in the larger township. But curious variations of the ceremony, even more eloquent of its Druidical character than the rite obtaining at Coventry, were celebrated there. The pageant was headed by a personage known as "Old Brazen-Face", who wore a mask representing a bull's head, with horns complete. At certain festivals the hide and head of a sacrificed bull were worn by the Druidic officiants, so that "Old Brazen-Face" may well be regarded as the degenerate descendant of these. His name is, of course, an appellation of the Keltic sun-god, whose burning visage, surrounded by lambent rays, was frequently cast in brazen discs. The expression "Old" is frequently prefixed to the names of discredited deities, as in "Old Scratch", "Old Harry". Then came Godiva in a lace mantle, followed by a second Godiva, whose body was *stained black*. This, Pliny tells us, is precisely how the women of the ancient Britons decorated themselves on occasions of religious festival, smearing their bodies with woad, "so that they resembled the swarthy Ethiopians". At Fenny Compton, not far from Southam, where this Godiva rite is held, is Woad Farm, perhaps the very site where the plants from which the dye was made were formerly obtained. That a preponderatingly British element has survived in Warwickshire has been maintained by generations of archæologists, and what more probable than that it continued the practice of its ancient rites, placating later Christian opinion by their attribution to the saintly identity of a worthy daughter of Mother Church?

Coventry was formerly situated near the southern boundaries of the great British tribe of the Brigantes, the presiding deity of whom was the goddess Brigantia or Brigiddu, the same, as has been indicated, with the Irish Brigit, later Christianized into St. Bridget. She was also known as Danu or Anu, and is undoubtedly identical with that "Black Annis" who was supposed to lurk in the Dane (or Danu) Hills in Leicestershire, and to carry off children and sheep to her cavern—a memorial of human and animal sacrificial offerings. She was a divinity of the earth, a goddess of fertility, worshipped almost exclusively by women. The name "Black Annis" obviously relates to her woad-stained appearance, and accounts for the "Black Godiva". But how to explain "Peeping Tom"? The shrine of Brigiddu at Kildare, in Ireland, was enclosed by a fence which no man might pass *or peep through*, nor was any man permitted to gaze upon the sacred virgins dedicated to the goddess. Thus, when one or more of them rode through the streets of British Coventry at the time of the festival of the goddess, no "Peeping Tom" dared offend, or the outraged deity would summarily have deprived him of sight. To such a custom, then, we may trace the beginnings of the Godiva legend.

There can be little doubt that this rite has a certain bearing on the ritual of the Secret Tradition. Not only does it show its capacity for survival, but I think it reveals part of the representation gone through in the initiatory ceremony, or at least that it is associated with the ritual of the faith ancillary to the Tradition itself. Briginda was a goddess of knowledge, she was worshipped by poets, and had two sisters of the same name connected with leech-craft and smithwork. She was indeed a goddess of culture and poetry, and is the equivalent of the Gaulish goddess Brigindo. The name seems to come from the Welsh root "bri", "honour" or "renown". Her cult until lately was known in the Hebrides, where, on St. Bride's Day, Candlemas Eve, women dressed a sheaf of oats in female clothes, and set it with a club in a basket called "Bride's Bed", to the accompaniment of the cry : "Bride is come ! Bride is welcome !" She was undoubtedly, as Canon MacCulloch says, "an early teacher of civilization, inspirer of the artistic, poetic, and mechanical faculties, as well as a goddess of fire and fertility".

It seems to me that, like Keridwen, she presided over the female department of the ancient mysteries, as Hu presided over the male portion. In all likelihood her worship obtained more in the north and central parts of what is now England and Scotland, and in Ireland. But the fact that she is associated with wells, with inspiration, and with agriculture seems to equate her almost entirely with Keridwen, the goddess of the Sacred Cauldron.

CHAPTER VIII

THE HIGHER PHILOSOPHY OF BRITISH
MYSTICISM

It is now necessary to turn to the higher aspects of the Secret Tradition of Britain as enunciated in its most distinguished document, that *Barddas* already described in a former chapter, only the superficial philosophy of which was touched upon. In the first place it will be necessary to satisfy ourselves regarding the notion of deity as there set forth.

God, we are told, is three things, and cannot be otherwise : coeval with all time ; co-entire with all essence ; and co-local with all mental purpose. He is inconceivable and incomprehensible, the greatest and the most immeasurable of all that are together in place.

But of what god are these statements made? It seems probable that the Welsh bards of later times recognized the God of Christianity as the supreme divinity, but there are not wanting allusions to a certain Hu whose nature has already been touched upon.

Now concerning this Hu there is a considerable diversity of opinion. "The meaning of Hu," explains a note to *Barddas*, "is that which is apt to pervade, or to spread over. It is used as an epithet of the Deity, in reference to His omniscience, and is not unfrequently to be met with as such in the works of the Bards." The bard Cynddelw identifies him with Jesus, and the annotator ventures the opinion that he was identical with the Heus[1] of Lactantius and the Hesus of Lucan, described as a god of the Gauls.

Canon MacCulloch[2] regards him as probably "an old culture-god of some tribes", and adds that the triads referring to him are of later date. Rhŷs[3] speaks of him as a "British Hercules", and thinks that he was superseded by Arthur. In fact, very little notice has been taken of him by the official mythologists. But it is obvious from the constant reference to him in the triads that he was a personage of importance, a culture-god, skilled in the arts of husbandry, a law-giver, probably of solar origin. He is alluded to as the "supreme proprietor of the isle of Britain", and as "a bull dwelling in a sacred stall", a statement which seems to equate him with Osiris. Undoubtedly he is the individual alluded to in the poem of "The Spoils of *Annwn*" as "the brindled ox with the thick head-band, having seven-score knobs in his collar". That such an animal was kept by the Druids as a symbol of this deity in the same manner as the priests of Egypt kept the Apis bull as the representative of Osiris, is proved by a passage in the same poem : " They know not what animal they (the Druids) keep of the silver head." The name of this bull or ox seems to have been Elzen, judging from a poem by Merlin, and its slaughter by the pagan Saxons is deplored by that magus.

This not only equates Hu to some extent with Osiris, but associates his worship with that of Mithraism and the bull-cults of the Mediterranean area. Now the Gaulish god Esus, or Hesus, mentioned previously and alluded to by Lucan, is

[1] Hu, in Welsh, is pronounced Hæ, or He.
[2] op. cit. p. 124, note.   [3] *Celtic Folklore*, p. 142.

depicted on an altar found at Paris as a woodman cutting down a tree, and on the same altar a bull is represented.   There is a similar altar at Trèves. Pre-Roman bronze bulls have been found at Hallstadt in Austria, and at La Tène.   " Many place-names in which the word *taruos* occurs, in Northern Italy, the Pyrenees, Scotland, Ireland, and elsewhere," says Canon MacCulloch, " suggest that the places bearing these names were sites of a bull-cult."   He adds that possibly the animal tended to become the symbol of a god, a tendency perhaps aided by the spread of Mithraism, and states that "a later relic of the bull-cult may be found in the carnival procession of the Bœuf Gras at Paris".[1] We will also recall the sacrifice of bulls at Gairloch and elsewhere in Britain in later times.

That Hu was a culture-god symbolized by the bull (as was Osiris) is therefore clear enough, and that he had a common origin with the Egyptian god in North-West Africa is also extremely probable. Frazer, in a note to the *Golden Bough*, mentions the discovery of a Druidic grave in North Africa, complete with implements, and Westermarck provides many evidences of the survival in Morocco of the rite of Bealtainn, a ceremony for the annual purification of cattle by passing them through the sacred fire or smoke.

Now we are informed in *Barddas* that God alone can endure the eternities of *Ceugant*, and as we know the three circles of the Keltic psychic progression to have been depicted in solar form, as shown on the early British coins, and, according to some, in the stone circles at Avebury and elsewhere, *Ceugant*, the dwelling of the Most High Hu, was probably regarded as the sun itself, *Gwynvyd*, the happy dwelling of immortal beings, as its outer rim, and *Abred*, as the outer darkness. But the drawing of the psychic scheme in *Barddas* shows *Abred* as the central figure, *Gwynvyd* as the outer, and *Ceugant* as corresponding to the rays of the luminary. It may thus be that *Abred* or *Annwn* was regarded as a fiery solar abyss wherein all things germinated, a torrid and burning alembic of life. But as *Abred* is obviously the earth-plane, some confusion may have taken place between it and *Annwn* in the mind of the draughtsman of this plan. In all probability the three psychic planes of man were *Annwn*, the place of germinal existence, *Abred*, the earth-plane, and *Gwynvyd*, the plane of justified spirits. *Ceugant*, the plane of God, was unapproachable and reserved for deity alone. That some confusion certainly did exist is clear from two statements in the *Book of Dwyfyddiaeth*, placed side by side, one of which bears out that the three states of existence of living beings are "the state of *Abred* in *Annwn*; the state of liberty in humanity, and the state of love, that is *Gwynvyd* in Heaven". While the other lays down as the three necessities of all animated existence, "beginning in *Annwn*; progression in *Abred*; and plenitude in *Gwynvyd*".

The three necessary obligations of man are set forth as suffering, change, and choice, and his equiproportions as *Abred* and *Gwynvyd*, necessity and liberty, evil and good, to which he has the power of attaching himself as he pleases. This is no philosophy of fatalism, and as such is differentiated from the Eastern systems and marks the growth and acceptance of the Western doctrine of human free-will, which, indeed, is insisted on. Yet there are obvious associations with the doctrine of escape, as observed in the Oriental systems, for we are told that Man does "escape" from *Abred* and *Cythraul* (evil) to *Gwynvyd* through forgetfulness and death. Thus former states cannot be recalled in the happier sphere, although elsewhere it is explicitly set forth that it is essential for perfectitude that they should be.

There are thus the three planes and no others in our early British mystical philosophy, not seven as in the Eastern. Nor does it seem to have been assumed that man has numerous psychic bodies, as in the Eastern philosophies, although, as has been shown, he is composed of various "materials", or elements.

In the triads of Bardism is an interrogatory which throws considerable light on the early British notions concerning the faculties of the soul. To the question "What is conscience?" the reply is "The eye of God in the heart of man, which sees everything that is perceptible in its right form, place, time, cause, and purpose." Reason is explained as the revolving of the conscience, whilst it contemplates by means of sight, hearing, and experience whatever comes before it, and understanding is described as the working of the conscience whilst it exercises its energies and might for the purpose of acquiring knowledge.

In *The Sentences of Bardism*, written by Ieuan all lives, the spirit of God as the power of all powers, and the providence of God as the order of orders and the system of systems. Truth is the science of Wisdom preserved in memory by conscience, and the soul is the breath of God in a carnal body, while Life is the might of God.

In this questionary God is described as the life of ab Hywel Swrdwal, a poet who flourished about 1450, a good deal of insight is given into the Bardic philosophy of existence. It is indeed strange to find in the Wales of this particular era so much of profound thought as is contained in these sentences, sentiments indeed, which, if they had been known to the doctors of Elizabethan London, might have caused them to revise their opinions of contemporary Keltic civilization! Let us glance briefly at a few of these aphorisms.

That does not but exist, we are told, from which a greater amount of good than evil can be produced, since it cannot be otherwise in virtue of God's power, wisdom, and love. Of that which is neither good nor bad, neither the existence nor non-existence is safe for man, for nothing in reason is known of it. Others say that it is the material of everything. However, there is only God that knows its good and evil, its utility and inutility, whether the good or evil be the greater. Where a great good to all, without harm to anyone, can be comprehended, it cannot be but that it is in existence, since otherwise the three principal attributes of God, namely, knowledge, wisdom, and mercy, would not stand without being opposed by distress and necessity: "therefore Bardism is true".

Truth cannot be had from that in which every truth cannot consist, and which will not consist in every truth, for truth cannot be had from what will contradict or withstand that which is true. The very power of God, we are further informed, is a guarantee that the best of all things are in existence. "The Ten Commandments of the Bards" found in the *Blue Book* have obviously been interpenetrated by Christian thought. For example, we are told to keep Sunday religiously and to beware of worshipping idols, which shows that the tendency to worship idols was actually present. But certain passages betray the Keltic mentality. That, for example, concerning the three deliverances—"there will be no transgression which will not be set right, no displeasure which will not be forgiven, and no anger which will not be pacified, and thence will be obtained the three excellences : first, there will be nothing ill-favoured which shall not be adorned ; secondly, there will be no evil which shall not be removed ; thirdly, there will be no desire which shall not be attained.   And from reaching this mark : in the first place, there can be nothing which shall not be known ; there can be no loss of anything beloved which shall not be regained ; thirdly, there can be no end to the *Gwynvyd* which shall be attained. And it is not necessary that there should be an understanding might and love other than these things, with the careful performance of what is possible."

These latter sentiments particularly display a Keltic bias. Possibly there is nothing Biblical about them, and there is certainly nothing of the hard, dry theology of the Teuton in the yearning beauty they contain.   The core of their philosophy seems to imply that, the struggle of the soul notwithstanding, all will be well in the end.   They reiterate the age-long cry of the poet that beauty cannot die, that somewhere, even though occluded by clouds, it awaits the spirit at the end of its journey, and that despite human agony, there is certainty of gain at the conclusion of the struggle. This is not fatalism, nor has it anything to do with the ugly philosophy of punishment which seems to have a peculiarly Judaic origin and to have arisen through a survival of early barbarous beliefs. It is indeed the philosophy of joy, which shines through all Keltic art, however shadowed it may seem in places.

Wherefore, then, the struggle of man? It seems to me that in our native British mysticism the idea of struggle, of evolution, is stressed more as a

natural and necessitous course than as a series of
phases through which the human soul must pass,
almost, indeed, as an act of psychic growth, rather
than a definite rule which it must observe. The
Oriental philosophies seem to indicate that it is
necessary for man, if he would develop in psychic
stature, to tread a certain path definitely laid out for
him, a path which may take him æons of ages ere it
lead him to the ultimate. At practically every step
of this path choice is afforded him to tread rightly
or wrongly ; but the mysticism of our fathers, or so
it seems to me, lays less of stress on choice. Man
must progress whether he would or not. True, he
may fall back into *Abred* time and again, but
ultimately he must gain *Gwynvyd*. True, there is
a belief associated with the Eastern philosophies that
in the end all life must return to God, but not only
does the process seem to be very much more prolonged, but it does not seem to be so mechanical.
To my way of thinking *Barddas* postulates a species
of evolutionary machine in which, from a low form
of existence, the soul is slowly raised to the heights
of *Gwynvyd*, rather than a specific scheme to which
the conduct of man is chiefly contributory. Not that
in the British system it is not contributory, but rather
that man appears, in virtue of it, to receive more
assistance from supernatural powers. It is, as I have
said, rather that he seems to be slowly born through
the planes of being into the light of *Gwynvyd*, than
that he arrives there entirely through his own
volition and conduct.

It is obvious, too, that enormous stress is laid
upon the value to the soul of man of scientific knowledge in this development, that it is indeed the lever
by which he raises himself from one plane to another.
This alone is proof, in its practical thrust, of a

Western origin.   Good deeds doubtless assist man, but without a knowledge of the secret sciences he may be retarded.   It looks, indeed, as if the process were hastened through such knowledge, and therein probably lay the desire for initiation, that is, it would appear that, given this initiation, man would be assured of entrance into the plane of *Gwynvyd*, and that without it he might possibly fall back into *Abred*. This scheme of things notably resembles the Egyptian idea that without a knowledge of *The Book of the Dead* the human soul could not hope to gain paradise.

So loosely are the tenets of our ancient mysticism set down that it is extremely difficult to systematize them.   They are, for the most part, cast into Triads or groups of three, after the manner of the Welsh bards, and frequently in an arbitrary fashion though never altogether incoherently.   The juxtaposition of some of these aphorisms, too, is often irrelevant.   It is therefore necessary to cull from the mass that which seems important and to the point.

The three laws of man's actions are set forth as necessity, choice, and judgement, according to what is possible, for ever in the circle of *Gwynvyd*.   There are three things, we are told, which are to be found everywhere :   God,   truth,   and   the   Circle   of *Gwynvyd*, and to know this is to be united with them and to have deliverance from *Abred*.   There are again three things the magnitude of which cannot be known, the Circle of *Ceugant*, the plane of the existence of God alone, the length of eternity, and the love of God.

The three principal vigours of man are set forth as *Awen*, affection, and intellect, from which triad all goodness proceeds.   All the efforts of man should be in unison with that which is in the Circle of

Gwynvyd. There are three grades of animation : God in *Ceugant*, spiritualities in *Gwynvyd*, that is "Heaven", and corporalities in *Abred*, that is an water and earth. Here we have the Circle of *Gwynvyd* absolutely identified with the Christian Heaven, and *Abred* with earth rather than *Annwn*. A note to this passage states that : " Some persons profess to discover indications of the doctrine of *Abred* or the metempsychosis in the Holy Scriptures, thus they say that the passage in Job (ch. xxxiii, v. 29-30) : 'Lo, all these things worketh God often-times with Man, to bring back his soul from the Pit, to be enlightened with the light of the living', ought, according to the Hebrew, to be rendered : 'Lo, all these things worketh God with Man, and thrice to bring back his soul from the Pit'." This may be so, yet still, as I have said, I find nothing of the doctrine of transmigration in our ancient mysticism, rather that of evolution, or psychic development.

We come next to the three conditions to which the nature of existence and animation is subject : efficient, as with God and His powers ; effected, as is the case with finite vitalities and mixed beings ; and non-effective, that is what was not made "and will not make", as space, absolute time, mortality, and darkness. These conditions are postulated in another way as follows : " What has not been made, that is God ; what has been made, that is the living and motion ; what has not been made, that is the motionless dead." It is curious to find the theory of relativity introduced into these ancient triads, where the existence of absolute time and space are denied —another instance in which, I take it, the Welsh bards were greatly in advance of thought of con-temporary Europe.

The three stabilities of oneness are given as

universality, for there can be no two kinds of one universality, infinity, for there can be no limits to one whole, nor can anything be whole which is not universal nor omnipresent, for that is not one whole which is not all-comprehensive ; and immutability, for it is impossible that there should be one conjunctive, universal, entire and all-existent, otherwise than they are ; therefore there can be no God but from fundamental and universal oneness.

The manner in which the end of *Abred* or the earth-plane will be accelerated is set forth not so much prophetically as with an air of scientific exactitude.   Three things, we are told, will accelerate its conclusion : diseases, fighting, and becoming *eneidvaddeu*, which has already been explained as a state of being legally punished for offence.   But "eneidvaddeu" in this instance implies a state of punishment which has been justly and reasonably brought about, for example, by war or conflict carried out in a just cause.   We are told that it was for the benefit of and out of mercy to living beings that God ordained the mutual fighting and slaughter which takes place among them, a doctrine which, we will remember, was stressed with no little weight by Wordsworth.   However the modern mind recoils from such a belief, it seems to have commended itself to our British ancestors as a short cut from the miseries of the plane of *Abred,* and this strengthens my theory that the philosophy set forth in *Barddas* by no means found its origin in any of the Oriental systems, which not only prohibit slaughter and regard the taking of life as blasphemy, but rather look upon life as a painful experience to be overcome more by a good train of thought than anything else.   Moreover the doctrine in question shows most distinctly its Druidic origin, for the

Druids, although at times they seem to have intervened in tribal wars, at others certainly inspired their people to combat. But before we blame them for the creation of a doctrine which appears to us barbarous and inhuman, let us remember that even within our own times it has been preached, and not without effect.

The basic foundations of *Abred,* we are told, are the predominance of opposition and *Cythraul* over prosperity and amendment, necessary lawlessness and death ensuing from the mastery of *Cythraul* and from the system of deliverance which is according to the love and mercy of God. Here we find the state of *Abred* set forth as a dreadful necessity, a part of a psychic evolution which must be borne. It is clear that from this philosophy man is expected to realise that life on the earth-plane can never be a happy experience, that he must be resigned to it. This might seem at the first glance similar to the Eastern idea of bearing existence with resignation, but this is rather belied by the preceding statement that such a condition may be shortened by strife and slaughter.

The three necessities of the state of *Gwynvyd,* the spiritual plane, are the predominance of good over evil, memory reaching from *Annwn,* and hence perfect judgement and understanding without the possibility of doubting or differing, and lastly superiority over death. This consists in power derived from knowing the whole of its cause and the means of escaping it, and hence everlasting life. It has often seemed strange to commentators on ancient dogma that the idea of the survival of memory in the last phase of psychic existence should be so greatly stressed. One wonders precisely what the value of such recollection might be, unless it is to render the soul more perfect by providing it with the lessons of experience in full.   I am inclined to think that it signifies that there can be no real happiness without perfect knowledge and experience, that happiness in a higher state is actually relative to the suffering endured in lower phases of existence.   Again, the spell, so to speak, by aid of which man escapes from death, triumphs over it, consists in power derived from knowing the whole of its cause.   That is, the secrets of death must be plumbed and accurately understood before the soul can triumph over it. This throws some light on the allegory of the descent of Hu, or his other form Arthur, into the depths of *Annwn*.   Not only did he penetrate thither for the purpose of seeking the cauldron of inspiration, the source of life, which was naturally located in the gloomy abyss whence life in its early forms was thought to have sprung, but he also sought to gauge the secrets and mysteries of death, the opposite of life, and that this knowledge was part of the initiation of the brotherhood of the Secret Tradition we can scarcely doubt.

We have little data to assure us that the belief in such a secret was held by other ancient brotherhoods.   As regards the Osirian tradition, Osiris was certainly Lord of the Dead, but that the priests of his cult regarded it as essential to probe into the mysteries of death I can discover no evidence. The same holds good of the Eleusinian mysteries and others.   The place of death, the Underworld, was to the hierophants of these cults also the place of the beginning of life, at least of cereal life, to which they likened that of mankind.   At the same time the initiates must pass through the place of death to reach life.   The embalmers of Egypt were wont to imitate the hues and colours of life in the corpse by painting its face red and by giving it artificial eyes. However, the early Osirian alchemy appears to have excogitated a system of thought by which out of dead metals and earths a species of psychic elixir was developed. In some religions, too, we observe the idea that life may emanate from death. The idea of resurrection was known to the Egyptians and is still upheld by the Christian religion, and although this is by no means the same thing as the conquest of death by the discovery of its secrets, it is nevertheless an assertion that death can be conquered.

But we find in both the Egyptian and Christian religions the powers of death definitely overcome by Osiris and Christ, and in at least one Central American religion, that of the Quiches of Guatemala, a similar allegory exists. Death and Hell are overcome by these champions, it is implied, either by material or spiritual weapons. In the allegory of Arthur's descent into *Annwn* we have a similar instance of the Harrying of Hell. The heroes descend into *Annwn* and some even do not return. *Annwn*, in the allegory, was therefore conquered by force of arms, material or spiritual, and this also, we may take it, formed part of the theatric pantomime of initiation through which the neophyte must pass when he became a member of the Brotherhood of the Secret Tradition.

On the whole, then, we cannot deny a veridically British character to the philosophy set forth in *Barddas*. Although certain of its principles appear to have much in common with the mystical philosophies of the East, there is assuredly contained in it a strong leaven of Western thought and idealism, which renders it worthy of the consideration of British mystics as enshrining much that is of extraordinary value to the race from a psychological point of view, and which should not be lightly cast aside.

Why, indeed, should we not strive to study and preserve the mysticism of our early ancestors rather than seek in the records of the East for guidance in things hidden and secret? Are the tenets set forth in the records and chronicles of our own island less lofty or less worthy of consideration, are they not more in consonance with the tendency and genius of British mentality than the mystic systems of the Orient? Are we not carried away in this regard by the hallucination of a specious Oriental glamour heightened by spurious imagination and sham romance? The attitude is on the same plane as that which prefers Continental musical talent to our own, and which has resulted in the decay and almost the death of British music, formerly a flourishing institution. Is there not something weakly, supine, and unimaginative in the fashion which strains for a distant enchantment and can discover none at its own portals? Wherefore has British mysticism been permitted to languish for generations to the behoof of an exotic tradition which is not superior to it and is of no prior authority?

Let the reproach be removed, let us address ourselves to the serious consideration and rehabilitation, the rescue and restoration of the noble Secret Tradition of our fathers. I do not mean to infer that we should entirely neglect other traditions. That would be as foolish as to despise our own. But I emphatically believe that it would be eminently for our psychic advantage to restore and rebuild the ruined edifice of British mysticism, as rendered conformable to Christian belief by the bards, who were the conservators of the ancient Secret Tradition. In its tenets, as purified by them, is little of the barbarous which only too plainly reveals itself in the systems of the East, and which has, therefore, rendered them unacceptable to thousands of British people as suspect of diabolism and the horrors of the lower *cultus* which indubitably cling to them. As set forth in *Barddas* there is nothing in our native mysticism which the most orthodox Christian could not accept. It is, in a word, the native British mystical thought applied to the Christian ideal. The scattered stones are to our hands. Some, indeed, are lost, but search can assuredly restore them. Let them be unearthed, and the Temple of the British Secret Tradition be re-edificated. These are days of restoration, when men in every land, tired of the cosmopolitan with its wearisome affectations, are inquiring into the foundations and origins of those things which have developed their own particular environment. "Far fowls have fair feathers", says the old proverb, illustrating a human infirmity which enlightened men are beginning to realize only too well.

As a patriotic Scotsman and Briton, I would appeal to English, Scottish and Welsh mystics not to let that die easily which must inevitably be to us all of the utmost value. We Britons are a "peculiar people," rapt and divided from our Continental neighbours by tendencies of thought exceptionally remote and individual. In that lies our greatness. And so it was in the beginning. This sacred isle constituted a laboratory of thought and mystery recognized by the races of the Continent as unspeakably hallowed and inscrutable. Can we, if we admit and encourage alien and by no means harmless esoteric systems, do so without damage unspeakable to the psychical integrity of our island? We assuredly cannot. The system to our hands is not only of British origin, but it is more susceptible of response to British mentality than any exotic system, it is capable of such a degree of restoration as may render it of much greater opportunity to British mystics as a gateway to the universalities by reason of a more native, more kindly and more familiar aspect than any alien portal reveals.

It may be that in the higher existence there is neither Greek nor Jew, Syrian nor Ethiopian, bond nor free. But in this of *Abred* we are so much the creatures of our immediate environment, that only by a realization of and agreement with its properties can we hope to accomplish anything, whether material or spiritual. And surely a system which has already sounded and comprehended these properties is of all systems the most fitting and natural for us to adopt as a groundwork of psychic advancement.

" The Secret Tradition of Britain!" Does not the very name stir the heart and appeal to the imagination of the true son of Albion with a thrill more mysterious and romantic than any allusion to the magics of Egypt or Hind? I need no Thebes or Benares, no Vedic Hymns, no *Book of the Dead*, for I am heir to a lore as exalted, as sublime as these, inherited from Druid sires, and in the main restored by pious searching. And in this Tradition restored I believe the future germ of British Mysticism to reside, that from its ash and cinder the phœnix of a marvellous rebirth shall arise on invincible wing :

> Like that self-begotten bird
> In the Arabian woods embost,
> That no second knows, nor third,
> And lay erewhile a holocaust,
> From out her ashy womb now teemed,
> Revives, reflourishes, then vigorous most
> When most unactive deemed,
> And though her body die, her fame survives
> A secular bird, ages of lives!

CHAPTER IX

THE WAY OF INITIATION

FROM the evidence already placed before the reader
it is possible in some measure to reconstruct the rites
of initiation of the Secret Tradition. It is not
claimed that it is here competent to divulge them in
their entirety, as the gaps and lacunæ in the evidence
are only too obvious, but an outline at least can be supplied, and there is no doubt in the mind of the writer
that adequate research would succeed in the recovery
of still further evidence, the lost links of the chain.

Cæsar tells us that the Druids were in the habit
of making their initiates undergo a very long course
of preparation before they reached what may be
described as adeptship. He also states that they
were extremely jealous lest their rites and ceremonies
should be observed or overlooked by the vulgar
herd. Now this can in no sense apply to public
rites. It cannot but signify those more secret
ceremonies associated with magic or initiation.
That an arcane brotherhood, the Pheryllt, actually
existed we have already seen, and doubtless it was
to them that the business of initiation was entrusted.
That this was associated with the Cauldron is
manifest not only from numerous Welsh poems, but
also from the allegory itself, which makes it plain
that the draught of inspiration was the last, or one of
the last, steps in the ceremony of initiation.

Now we have the authority of a poem of Taliesin
entitled "The Chair of Taliesin", for describing
certain of the apparatus and ceremonial associated
with initiation. As it is important, I make no

N

apology for quoting it in full after the translation of Davies :

I am he who animates the fire, to the honour of the god Duvydd, in behalf of the assembly of associates qualified to treat of mysteries—a bard with the knowledge of a *Sywedydd*, when he deliberately recites the inspired song of the Western Cudd on a serene night amongst the stones.

As to loquacious, glittering bards, their encomium attracts me not when moving in the course; admiration is their great object.

And I am a silent proficient who address the bards of the land; it is mine to animate the hero; to persuade the unadvised; to awaken the silent beholder—the bold illuminator of kings!

I am no shallow artist, greeting the Bards of a household like a subtle parasite—the ocean has a due profundity!

The man of complete discipline has obtained the meed of honour in every knightly celebration, when Dien is propitiated with an offering of wheat, and the suavity of bees, and incense and myrrh and aloes from beyond the seas, and the golden pipes of Lleu, and cheerful precious silver and the ruddy gem, and the berries, and the foam of the ocean, and cresses of a purifying quality, laved in the fountain, and a joint contribution of wort, the founder of liquor, supplied by the assembly, with a raised load, secluded from the moon, of placid, cheerful vervain.

With priests of intelligence to officiate on behalf of the moon, and the concourse of associated men under the open breeze of the sky, with the maceration and sprinkling and the portion after the sprinkling, and the boat of glass in the hand of the stranger, and the stout youth with pitch, and the honoured *Segyrffyg*, and medical plants from an exorcised spot.

And Bards with flowers and perfect convolutions, and primroses and leaves of the *Briw*, with the points of the trees of purposes, and solution of doubts, and frequent mutual pledges; and with wine which flows to the brim, from Rome to Rosedd, and deep standing water, a flood which has the gift of Dovydd, on the tree of pure gold, which becomes of a fructifying quality when that Brewer gives it a boiling who presided over the cauldron of the five plants.

Hence the stream of Gwion and the reign of serenity and honey and trefoil, and horns flowing with mead— Meet for a sovereign is the lore of the Druids.

Now it is impossible to credit, whatever the date of this manuscript, that it has not actually come down to us as evidence of the former existence of an ancient system of initiation. For what possible purpose, indeed, could it have been otherwise invented? Its details are too closely associated with what we know of Druidical practice and, indeed, of the rituals of other and similar mysteries not to have had an actual background in reality. Let us examine them a little more closely. The first four paragraphs are obviously prefatory. The name *Sywedydd* is the first hint we receive that we are dealing with something out of the common, something occult and mysterious. It implies mystagogue, or revealer of mysteries, and the word *Cudd* which follows it signifies "the Place of the Dark Repository".

The paragraph which follows these relates to the herbs and other materials which were seethed together in the Cauldron of Inspiration. The "gold pipes of Lleu" obviously allude to some yellow flower, and the "cheerful precious silver" seems to mean the fluxwort, which in Wales is known as *ariant Gwion*, or "Gwion's silver", which in itself proves that it was associated in Cambrian lore with the mystical cauldron. The "ruddy gem" is perhaps the hedge-berry, which was also known as *eirin Gwion*, the Borues of Gwion. The cresses allude to the *Fabaria*, called *berwr Taliessin*, or "Taliessin's Cresses", and on vervain the Druids set particular store, casting lots by its use and employing it in divination. It was usually gathered at the rise of the Dog-star "Without being looked upon either by the sun or moon". In gathering it the earth was propitiated by a libation of honey and it was dug up with the left hand.

The Boat of Glass was a crescent shaped like a half-moon and in all probability was the vessel from which the draught of inspiration was quaffed.

Primroses ranked highly among the mystical apparatus and the *briw* was probably also vervain, which was known by the name of *briw'r March*.

The poem states that the same rite of libation prevailed from Rome to Rosedd. This seems to point to a date for its composition when the Britons were acquainted with the Romans, but while Rome itself was yet pagan. The "deep water" seems to signify the bath for the immersion of the neophyte, and the gift of Duvydd was the Selago or hedge-hyssop, which in modern Welsh is known as *gras Duw*. Pliny says of this plant: "Similar to savin is the plant called Selago. It is gathered without using iron and by passing the right hand through the left sleeve of the tunic, as though in the act of committing a theft. The clothing must be white, the feet washed and bare and an offering of wine and bread made before the gathering. The Druids of Gaul say that the plant should be carried as a charm against every kind of evil and that the smoke of it is good for diseases of the eye."

These, then, were the mystical plants, the ingredients of the Cauldron of Keridwen which produced the stream of Gwion, to which is ascribed the beginning of genius, the power of inspiration and the reign of serenity.

Now we find that these rites, far from falling into desuetude, were actually employed so late as the twelfth century, when Hywel, Prince of North Wales, was initiated into the lesser mysteries of Keridwen in 1171, and that he longed for admittance to the greater mysteries conducted by Gwyddnaw and his son. In a song supposed to be sung by Hywel he addresses Keridwen as the moon, lofty and fair, slow and delicate in her descending course, and requests her to attend his worship in the mystical grove. "I love the place of the illustrious lady near the pleasant shore," sings Hywel, "for the severe discipline which I experienced in the hall of the mysterious god, I have obtained her promise—a treasure of high privilege. . . . I shall long for the proud-wrought place of the Gyvylchi till I have gained admittance. Renowned and enterprising is the man who enters there." "If we may judge from these strains of Hywel," says Davies, " and from many similar passages in the works of his contemporaries, the Cambrian bards were as zealously devoted to the worship of Keridwen . . . in the twelfth century as they had been in the sixth, or in any earlier age of heathen superstition."

Now "the proud-wrought enclosure in the Gwvylchi, in the desert of Arvon in Eryri," or Snowdon, and near the shore, was the Caer or sanctuary of Keridwen and her daughter Llywy. "The topography of this temple is so minutely pointed out," says Davies, "that the spot cannot be mistaken. . . . Dwy-Gyvylchi is still known as the name of a parish in the very spot where the Cambrian prince fixed his Caer Wen Glaer, or sanctuary of the illustrious lady, in the deserts of Arvon in Eryri and towards the sea : and here the remains of the Caer are still to be found." Camden's annotator, Gibson, has described a strong fortress "seated on the top of one of the highest mountains which lies towards the sea", and gives the following account of this ancient temple : " About a mile from this fortification stands the most remarkable monument in all Snowdon, called *Y Meineu Hirion* upon the Plain Mountain within the parish of Dwy-Gyvycheu, above Gwddw Glas. It is a circular entrenchment about twenty-six yards diameter ; on the outside whereof are certain rude stone pillars, of which about twelve are now standing, some two yards and others five foot high : and these are again encompassed with a stone wall.   It stands upon the Plain Mountain as soon as we come to the height, having much even ground about it ; and not far from it there are three other large stones pitched on end in a triangular form.''

Gibson, the annotator of Camden, also informs us that at the distance of about three furlongs from this monument are several huge heaps or cairns and also several cells constructed of huge stones fixed in the ground, each cell being covered with one or two stones of great size.

Bearing in mind the words of Hywel relative to the locality, there can surely be no question that these stones are the remains of the open-air temple of Keridwen, and that the cells alluded to by Gibson were the secret places in which the neophyte was prepared for initiation.   I do not propose to enter into the welter of controversy concerning the question as to whether the Druids actually employed the stone-circles of this island for purposes of worship or not. That they did not raise many of them is obvious, but it is odd that those who have argued so fiercely against their use by the Druids should not have been able to discover the many evidences in literature where they *are* spoken of as using them for that purpose and of which I shall give some account towards the end of this chapter.

The reader will recollect that the Pheryllt, or priests of the Pharaon, had a city or temple on Snowdon known as Dinas Emrys, which has already been described.   Now it seems to me not at all unlikely that this Temple of Keridwen, only about a mile away from the site of Dinas Emrys, must have been under the auspices of the Pheryllt, and this leads to the supposition that they were flourishing in Hywel's time—that is in the twelfth century.

An ancient poem in the *Welsh Archaiology* supplies us with an old formula in obscure language which appears to have been employed on occasions of initiation as an introduction for approaching the gate of the sanctuary. Arthur and Kai are represented as coming to the portal, which is guarded by a hierophant, and the following dialogue takes place :

> Arthur : What man is he that guards the gate?
>
> Hierophant : The severe hoary one with the wide dominion—who is the man that demands it?
>
> Arthur : Arthur and the Blessed Kai.
>
> Hierophant : What good attends thee, thou blessed one, thou best man in the world? Into my house thou canst not enter unless thou wilt preserve.
>
> Kai : I will preserve it and that thou shalt behold; though the birds of wrath should go forth and the three attendant ministers should fall asleep, namely the son of the Creator Mabon, the son of Mydron, attendant upon the wonderful supreme Ruler, and Gwyn, the Lord of those who descend from above.
>
> Hierophant : Severe have my servants been in preserving their institutes. Manawyddan, the son of Llyr, was grave in his counsel, Manawyd truly brought a perforated shield from Trevryd, and Mabon, the son of Lightning, stained the straw with clotted gore: and Anwas the winged and Llwch Llawinawg (the ruler of the lakes) were firm guardians of the encircled mount. Their Lord preserved them and I rendered them complete. Kai! I solemnly announce though all three should be slain, when the privilege of the grove is violated, danger shall be found.

The rest of this obscure dialogue describes the adventures of Arthur and Kai after their initiation, but it is clear that in the part of it I have quoted the neophyte engaged before the heirophant to preserve the laws of the sanctuary, even though assaulted by enemies or deserted by friends. The hierophant in his turn denounces the fate of those who violate the sacred engagement. It is plain, too, from the text that the hierophant was attended by three assistant ministers, each of whom seems to have impersonated a god, and in this the usage seems to have been the same as that prevailing in the Eleusinian mysteries, in which four priests officiated, the hierophant, who represented the Creator, the torch-bearer, who personated the sun, the herald, who took the part of Mercury, and the minister of the altar, who represented the moon.

We must now return for enlightenment to the myth of Keridwen and her Cauldron. This Cauldron cannot but have been one and the same with the Cauldron of Inspiration alluded to in the myths of *Annwn*, to which Arthur or Hu penetrated. It has precisely the same character and is described in the same manner, and when we learn that Keridwen was a goddess of the Underworld, the identity of the vessel seems complete. She is also styled Ogyrven Amhad, "the goddess of various seeds", a statement which equates her with Ceres, and indeed she appears to have been the British Ceres.

We will recollect that when Gwion unwittingly tasted the virtue of her Cauldron of Inspiration she pursued him, that he transformed himself into a hare, when she became a greyhound, turned him, and chased him toward a river. He leapt into the stream and became a fish, but as she pursued him as an otter, he took the form of a bird. Transforming herself into the guise of a sparrowhawk, she was gaining upon him, when he perceived a heap of wheat upon a floor, dropped into the midst of it, and assumed the form of a single grain. Keridwen then changed herself into the shape of a black, high-crested hen, descended into the wheat, scratched him out, and swallowed him, and, as the history relates, he was born of her in due time as the beautiful babe

Taliesin, who was found in the fishing weir of Elphin.

Now the whole myth certainly bears allusions to the rite of initiation. Keridwen first transforms herself into a female dog. Virgil, in the sixth book of his *Æneid*, describing all that it was lawful to reveal of the Eleusinian mysteries, says that one of the first things observed by his hero as the priestess conducted him toward the mystic river were a number of female dogs, and Pletho in his notes upon the *Magical Oracles of Zoroaster*, remarks that it is the custom in the celebration of the mysteries to exhibit to the initiated certain phantoms in the figures of dogs. The dog was, indeed, the guardian of the Underworld, and it seems probable that, as the initiate was supposed to enter this gloomy region when undergoing his ordeal, the presence of dogs may have entered symbolically into the ceremony. Indeed, Diodorus, dealing with the mysteries of Isis, mentions that the whole solemnity was preceded by the presence of dogs, and he even terms the priests of mysteries "dogs", although he believes that the Greeks mistook the Hebrew word *cohen*, a priest, for their own word *kune,* dog. However, the dog of Gwyn ap Nudd, the British Plato, is named Dormarth, "the gate of sorrow", so it would seem that the animals represented in the British mysteries somewhat resembled the classical Cerberus, and that they had a similar significance—that they were, indeed, of the same character as the *Proserpine Limen* which Apuleius approached in the course of his initiation.

Then we find that the aspirant was converted into a hare, a sacred animal among the Britons, as we learn from Cæsar, but perhaps here symbolizing the great timidity of the novice. This hare is turned and driven toward a river. The first ceremony in the

Greek mysteries was that of purification, which was celebrated upon the banks of rivers. The Athenians, for example, performed this ceremony at Agra on the Ilissus, a river of Attica, whose banks were called "the mystical", and whose stream itself was named "the divine".

According to the myth, the aspirant now plunges into the stream, and the otter here seems to symbolize the priest who attended to his lustrations. His form then changes into that of a bird, probably the *dryw*, which means both a wren and a Druid, and, indeed, elsewhere Taliesin informs us that he had once taken that form. His adversary becomes a hawk, reminiscent of Egyptian mythology. At last he takes the shape of a grain of pure wheat, mixing with an assemblage of the same species, and thus assumes a form eminently sacred to Ceres or Keridwen, who receives him into her bosom, whence he is re-born. The meaning of this statement probably resides in the fact that the initiate remained for a season in one of the mysterious cells or caves of the Druidic cult, where he was subjected to a rigid course of discipline, and where he studied the rites and imbibed the secret doctrines of Keridwen, lastly emerging "re-born" into the outer world.

But this description probably applies to the lesser or initial mysteries only. The greater were still to follow. After the initiate had completed his course of discipline in the cell and had been born again of Keridwen, the goddess enclosed him in a coracle covered with skin and cast him into the sea. Now if we compare this procedure with that known to have been followed in the Greek mysteries, we discover a close resemblance between the two. After passing through the lesser mysteries the herald summoned the initiates to the sea-shore. The name of the day on which this took place was entitled "Novitiates to the Sea", after the summons of the herald. The aspirants on this occasion embarked upon the sea in certain vessels, and it was in these mysteries, we are told, that the whole truth was to be revealed. Now we will recall that in the myth of Taliesin he was, while yet a babe, albeit a learned one, launched by Keridwen in a coracle which took him to the weir of Gwyddno, where he was discovered by Gwyddno's son Elphin. He prophesied the future renown of Elphin and his own as well. Elphin bore the babe to the castle, where Gwyddno demanded of Taliesin whether he was a human being or a spirit. The infant Taliesin replied in a mystical song, in which he described himself as a general primary bard who had existed in all ages and was in some measure identified with the sun. "Thrice have I been born," sang Taliesin, the Radiant Fronted one, " I know how to meditate. It is pitiful that men will not come to seek all the sciences of the world which are treasured in my bosom, for I know all that has been and all that will be hereafter."

Now Davies (whom I have closely followed as regards these latter passages, and who was, indeed, very much more competent to speak on these matters than some of the modern mythologists who have rather cruelly sneered at him, owing to his rather tiresome theory that the whole of British myth is to be referred to what he calls "Arkite" theology), believed that Gwyddno and his son were the husband and son of Keridwen. This seems not improbable, when we remember that Gwyddno was the lord and Keridwen lady of *Annwn*. Gwyddno's surname was Garanhir, or the "long, or high crane", or "Stalking Person", to which allusion has already been made in the chapter on the Grail and elsewhere, where it was stated that the bull god of the Continental Kelts was styled Trigaranos, because he carried three cranes. Elsewhere Taliesin alludes to Elphin as "The sovereign of those who carry ears of corn", and later in his life he was to liberate him from a strong-stoned tower in which he had been imprisoned by Maelgwn. Elphin has certainly some solar significance.

One of the poems attributed to Gwyddno appears to have an application to the enclosing of the aspirant in the coracle. The novice is about to be plunged into the waves and he sings : " Though I love the sea-beach I dread the open sea. A billow may come undulating over the stone." To this the hierophant replies : " To the brave, to the magnanimous, to the amiable, to the generous who boldly embarks, the ascending stones of the Bards will prove the harbour of life. It has asserted the praise of Heilyn, the mysterious impeller of the sky. Until the doom shall its symbol be continued." Still the novice is not reassured. " Though I love the strand," he cries, " I dread the wave. Great has been its violence— dismal the overwhelming stroke. Even to him who survives, it will be the subject of lamentation." Once more endeavouring to reassure him, Gwyddno says : " It is a pleasant act, to wash in the bosom of the fair water. Though it fill the receptacle it will not disturb the heart. My associated train regard not its overwhelming. As for him who repented of his enterprise, the lofty wave has hurried the babbler far away to his death ; but the brave, the magnanimous, will find his compensation in arriving safe at the stones. The conduct of the water will declare thy merit."

But to the timid or rejected candidate he addressed himself thus : " Thy coming without external purity is a pledge that I will not receive thee. Take out the gloomy one ! From my territory have I alienated the rueful steed. My revenge upon the shoal of earth-worms is their hopeless longing for the pleasant place. Out of the receptacle which is thy aversion did I obtain the rainbow."

Davies believed this ceremony to have taken place in Cardigan Bay, at the mouth of the Ystwyth. The ceremony was intended to test the constancy and purity of mind of the neophyte. "The old bards," he says, "speak in magnificent terms of the benefits which were derived from these mysterious rites. They were viewed as most important to the happiness of human life. They imparted sacred science in its greatest purity and perfection ; and he who had completed his probation was called *Dedwydd*, 'one who has recovered intelligence', or rather has been brought back into the Presence. It is nearly equivalent to the Greek term *Epoptes*, which describes a person who had been initiated into the greater mysteries." By the course of the tide it was to be discovered whether or no the initiate was worthy to survive, as in the case of Taliesin himself.

Taliesin, in a poem recited immediately after he had gone through the concluding ceremony, describes himself as "thrice-born", that is, once of his natural mother, once of Keridwen, and lastly of the mystic coracle. As a consequence of this regeneration he tells us that he "knew how to think rightly of God", and that all the sacred science of the world was treasured in his bosom.

In a poem immediately following this, Taliesin sings : " I was first modelled into the form of a pure man in the hall of Keridwen, who subjected me to penance. Though small within my chest and modest in my deportment, I was great. A sanctuary carried me above the surface of the earth. Whilst I was enclosed within its ribs the sweet *Awen* rendered me complete, and my law, without audible language, was imparted to me by the old giantess, darkly smiling in her wrath." In the concluding verse he says : " I fled in the form of a fair grain of pure wheat. Upon the edge of a covering cloth she caught me in her fangs. In appearance she was as large as a proud mare, which she also resembled—then was she swelling out like a ship upon the waters. Into a dark receptacle she cast me. She carried me back into the sea of Dylan. It was an auspicious omen to me when she happily suffocated me. God the Lord freely set me at large." This obviously applied to a course of penance, discipline and mystical instruction undergone by the initiate, and must have consisted in scenic or symbolical representation, as language does not seem to have been employed. It appears to have taken place in the Temple of Keridwen, and the goddess seems to have taken various shapes, just as did Diana in the mysteries described by the author of the *Orphic Argonautics*. She transformed herself into the shapes of a dog, a horse, and a lion, according to the particular knowledge she desired to impart.

One of the most remarkable poems connected with Keridwen is that in which her priest deals with certain passages in her history. He tells us that in the dead of night and at the dawn, the lights of the initiates have been shining, and that as to *Avaggdu,* her son, the correcting god has formed him anew for happiness. In the contention of the mysteries, indeed, his wisdom has exceeded her own, and he has become the most accomplished of beings. His bride is a woman composed of flowers, whom, by his exquisite art, Gwydion created.

"When the merit of the presidencies shall be adjudged," says Keridwen through the mouth of her priest, "mine will be found the superior amongst them—my chair, my cauldron and my laws and my pervading eloquence meet for the presidency." "This poem," says Davies, "was evidently intended to be sung or recited by a priest or priestess who personated Keridwen."

Davies concludes his rather rambling criticisms of these ceremonial poems by certain remarks which, whatever one may think of his general method, have a good deal of cogency behind them.   He says it is scarcely to be wondered at that the ancient Britons should have pertinaciously adhered to the rites of the British Ceres as lately as the sixth century, especially during the period between the dominion of the Romans and the coming of the Saxons.   "There seems," he says, "to have been several parts of Wales into which Christianity as yet had scarcely penetrated ; or where, at least, it had not prevailed. Hence Brychan is commended 'for bringing up his children and grand-children in learning, so as to be able to show the faith in Christ to the Cymry where they were without the faith'."   He goes on to say that the Welsh princes, to the latest period of their government, not only tolerated but patronized the old rites, and that the mysteries of Keridwen were celebrated in Wales as late as the middle of the twelfth century.   They influenced the writings of the bards, and the princes were induced by national prejudice to regard these as innocent and to fancy that they might be good Christians enough without wholly relinquishing their heathenish superstitions. The ministers of Christianity thought otherwise, and sometimes refused Christian burial to these Gentile priests, and there are numerous instances of the bards

themselves promising a kind recantation some time
before their death.

We must now turn to the question as to whether
the stone circles commonly attributed to the Druids
were ever employed by them for religious or mystical
purposes.   That they were first raised by the Druids,
as Druids, is, as we have seen, out of the question.
The cult which was responsible for them may have
been proto-Druidic, that is, it may have held the
early germs of Druidism, although there is no
evidence to countenance such a theory.   But that
they were actually employed by the later Druids is
undoubted, whatever recent arguments may have
been brought against this belief.

In the first place, we have early Christian evidence
on the matter.   Pope Gregory in his famous Bull,
and in his instructions to the Abbot Melitus when
he dispatched him to Britain, advised him not to
destroy the British temples or fanes, but only the
idols they contained, as they might be suitable to the
worship of the true God.   William Thorn, the monk
of Canterbury, speaks of a fane towards the east of
that city where King Ethelbert was accustomed to
celebrate heathen worship.[1]   This fane, was are told
by another chronicler, was built ''in the British
manner''.   The twentieth Canon of the Council of
Nantes, promulgated about A.D. 658, provides that
stones in ruinous places and woods raised to the
worship of demons shall be destroyed, and a similar
fulmination against standing stones is given in the
Liber Pœnitentialis of Archbishop Theodore, of
Canterbury (A.D. 602—690).   '' If any may have
vowed or paid a vow at trees, or at fountains, or at
stones, whether at the balusters, or anywhere else,

---

[1] According to accounts received while this volume was in the
Press, this ''fane'' has only recently been unearthed.

excepting in the Church of God". The word "balusters" here means "encompassing rails" or stone balustrade. In Ireland, St. Patrick is said to have incised the name of Christ on three lofty stones on the Plain of Magh Slecht which were associated with heathenish rites.

We know that St. Samson, Bishop of Dol in Brittany, when travelling in Britain actually surprised certain "Bacchanalians" while worshipping an idol on the top of a mound within a stone circle. He endeavoured to dissuade them from the practice, and they were disputing him, when a certain youth passing in a chariot was thrown therefrom and broke his neck. This was taken as a sign that God was displeased with the idolatry, and the pagan congregation broke up.

There is plenty of evidence that in Scotland courts were held at stone circles as late as the fourteenth century. One was convened in 1349 by William, Earl of Ross, Justiciary of Scotland, at the standing stones of Rayne in Garioch, and another by Alexander Stewart, Lord of Badenoch, the King's Lieutenant, in the year 1380 at the standing stones of Easter Kyngucy in Badenoch. This is eloquent of very ancient custom.

Davies provides a lengthy and in some ways a useful disquisition on the question of Druidic circles. He believes that the circle named Caer Sidi was the Temple of Keridwen, and that its prototype was the locality of Caer Sidi in *Annwn*. Of this Chair Taliesin was the president. " Is not my chair protected by the Cauldron of Keridwen?" sings Taliesin, " therefore let my tongue be free in the sanctuary of the praise of the goddess". Davies believed that this sanctuary was modelled on the great circle of the Zodiac. " I have presided in a toilsome Chair over the circle of Sidin whilst that is continually revolving between three elements. Is it not a wonder to the world that men are not enlightened?'' These words of Taliesin, Davies translates as signifying that the sun is the visible president. Taliesin, or ''Radiant Front'', was his earthly representative in that sanctuary, which typified the abode of the god.

Now Davies further believed that these ''Caer Sidis'' were none other than the stone circles. He drags the Ark into his elucidations, but if we discount this, we arrive at some not invaluable conclusions, for, despite his notions regarding ''Arkite philosophy'', Davies was logical enough.

He shows, for example, that when the mystical Bards treat of history and the rites of Keridwen, that they almost invariably allude to the completion of the year and the return of a particular day. He thought that the stones in the circles represented the various constellations, with the sun and the moon in the centre. Now Caer Sidi, as he has said, means the Circle of Revolution, and he notes that at least one Druidic grove, the *Cylch Balch Nevwy*, was known as the ''magnificent celestial circle''. He also proves that Aneurin, Taliesin and Merlin in their mystical poems mention the particular stones which composed certain circles.

Then he reverts to the poem of Prince Hywel in the Desert of Arvon in Snowdon, where stood the sanctuary of Keridwen, visited by the prince as lately as the twelfth century. This was composed of a circle of twelve stones, and like other circles found in Britain, was, he believed, ''constructed upon astronomical principles. In short, it represented either the Zodiac itself, or certain cycles and computations deduced from the study of astronomy.

Hence the frequent repetition of twelve, nineteen, thirty, or sixty stones which has been marked in the circles of these monuments." He indicates that the number twelve is twice repeated in the circle at Avebury, in the circle of Classernish, in the western islands of Scotland, and in certain Cornish monuments.

Lastly, after a long dissertation on Stonehenge, which has been superseded by recent research, he states that the personage or prince known as Seithin Saidi is called "the guardian of the gate of Godo" or "the uncovered sanctuary", which he believes alludes to the typical stone circle.

Now when one recalls the philosophy set forth in *Barddas*, with its cosmography of the universe described in circles, it does not seem at all improbable that the stone circles may have had some bearing upon it. It seems likely that Druidism in these islands mingled with a much older religion, which had as its basis the circular cosmography above alluded to. On the other hand, it may have adapted the stone circles to this cosmography, likening the outer circle to *Abred* and the inner to *Gwynvyd*. I hasten to say that I do not dogmatize on the subject, for where all is so vague it would, indeed, be rash to do so. Moreover, it would be necessary to prove that a similar course was adopted in Gaul and elsewhere. We know that other cults in other countries employed the ancient stone circles built by their predecessors. Thus it was only in the age of Zoroaster, some five hundred years before our era, that the Persians adopted covered temples, having formerly worshipped in open-air circular structures, and even the Greeks themselves, according to Pausanius, are not free from the suspicion of having done so in the early days of the Hellenic religion.

We know that the Druids worshipped in circular groves. What, then, is more likely that, finding stone groves ready erected and to their hand, they employed these for a worship which had probably much in common with the cult which had originally been practised within them? At that I leave the question. A great deal more requires to be known concerning the cult of those who raised these circles before we can speak more definitely upon it. But Mr. Kendrick has given it as his opinion that although the Druids certainly did not build Stonehenge, they employed it as a temple, and on the whole I also conclude that this was actually the case.

One of the most pregnant statements on the use to which certain stone monuments were put is that of Mr. Bernard H. Springett on *Traces of Mithraism and Early Masonic Resemblances in the Stone Remains of South Brittany*, a copy of which he was kind enough to send me in 1924. The remarks in it might with equal reason apply to stone remains in Britain. Many of the stone monuments in Brittany struck Mr. Springett when he visited them as having been erected for something beyond the usual reason assigned, that of sun worship, and so forth. In inspecting the dolmens, by which name the Bretons call those stones covered by a large slab, he noted that they were frequently found in the centre of a tumulus, whereas certain stone chambers or cells were invariably underground. In describing these underground chambers, he says :

> You descend a varying number of steps to the entrance of a passage, the steps being so arranged, with a curve or an angle in them, that it is impossible from the first step to look along the passage. This is roughly lined with upright slabs like the chambers themselves, with appearances of having originally had the interstices filled with chips of stone, or merely earth, perhaps. This

central passage . . . leads direct to the largest chamber of a series of three, two others on the right of the passage having entrances from it, but no intercommunication. On the left of the central passage is a long, somewhat narrower passage running right alongside it, almost to the end chamber, so that anyone could pass direct into this end chamber without traversing, except at each end, the main central passage.

Mr. Springett asked a Masonic friend who accompanied him if the plan of these chambers had suggested anything to him, and he replied that they reminded him of the rooms used by Masons in the Rose Croix Degree. "Then," writes Mr. Springett, "we pictured together the whole ceremony, crude enough, no doubt, most probably terrifically awe-inspiring to the ancient candidates, conducted by a Deacon down the steps, along the central passage, first into one side chamber, to be shown some terrible and fearsome object, perhaps; then into the second chamber; finally into the larger chamber at the end, no doubt for an Obligation, and then admission. Meanwhile, officiating priests, on the other side of the left hand wall of the central passage, were probably producing 'stage effects'."

Mr. Springett believes that the cult which made use of these underground initiation chambers was that of Mithraism. There are, he says, two legendary periods for the erection of these stones in Brittany. One tradition asserts that they were erected by Druids, who came from Britain for this express purpose and imitated the structures used by them for religious ceremonies in their own country. The other is that they were erected by a people who came from the East.

It seems to me, however, that these cells of initiation were Druidic. Mr. Springett gives as an evidence of the existence of Mithraism in Brittany the legend of St. Cornely, the patron saint of Carnac, who is always represented as accompanied by two bulls—the symbolic beast of Mithraism ; but this animal, as we have seen, was also symbolic of Druidism.   He thinks that the smaller underground chambers were used for outer degrees, while the interiors of the tumuli were employed for the more arcane rites of higher degrees.   Many of these latter were not employed for sepulchral purposes, and the bones of burnt cattle were discovered within them. Moreover, on the walls of these chambers are rude carvings of serpents and ears of corn, both accompaniments of Druidism as well as of Mithraism.   On an ancient covering stone of a tomb reclining against the south wall of Plouharnel Church Mr. Springett observed a carving which seemed to him to represent an initiate before an altar which supports a volume and a square.   Behind the altar stands the Master's Light, which, like the chalice behind the candidate, springs from a base supporting cones of increasing size, symbolizing the three stages to be passed through before reaching the vault below, from which the cope-stone is removed.   Beneath are the skull and cross-bones, the level and twenty-four inch gauge.   Mr. Springett takes care to mention that certain stones in Britain gave him much the same impression as these Breton monuments, the cells associated with which seem to me to be similar to, if not identical in form with, those alluded to by Camden's annotator as occurring at the Circle of Keridwen in Arvon.   In all probability they were the cells in which the lesser mysteries were revealed to the initiates, a conclusion which it will be seen Mr. Springett shares with Davies and other writers on the subject.

CHAPTER X

THE WRITINGS OF "MORIEN"

TOWARDS the end of last century Druidism was actually revived in Wales by an organization known as "The Druids of Pontypridd", which claimed a fair number of adherents in Wales, but a much greater following in America. Myfyr Morganwg, the Arch-Druid, publicly proclaimed the creed of his forefathers after thirty years' preaching of Christianity, and James Bonwick in his *Irish Druids* states that he was an absolute believer in the tenets he taught. He recognized his Druidic principles in the Jewish, Hindu, and Buddhist religions as well as in classical mythology. He was followed by Owen Morgan, better known as "Morien", whose version of Welsh Druidism can be studied in *The Light of Britannia*, published in 1894. He believed Druidism to be prior in antiquity to any of the world's religions. His work and that which followed it, *The Royal Winged Son of Stonehenge and Avebury*, are certainly extraordinary storehouses of Druidic lore, but the facts they contain are so inextricably mingled with classical and Eastern mysticism that it is frequently difficult to disentangle them. Moreover, the sources from which Morgan drew his Druidic material are only occasionally indicated throughout the volumes, and although the origins of some of them are obvious, we are left absolutely in the dark as to the source of others. This notwithstanding, these works are of primary importance in such a quest as ours, because of the great and varied acquaintance they reveal with the faith and mythology underlying the British Secret Tradition, and an endeavour will be made in these pages to summarize the system of which they treat.

To the Creator the Druids gave the name Celi (Concealing), and to his consort the name of Ced (Aid) or Keridwen. They believed that the firmament was one vast wheel, in which wheel, seated in a chair, the sun made his daily round. Celi and Keridwen are incomprehensible spirits, but are the originators of crude matter, which came in an embryonic condition from across the ocean, from the source of all elements. This essence is feminine and passive in its nature, and was brought every spring over the seas in a sacred boat shaped like the crescent moon and propelled by Keridwen, who applied intense heat beneath it, so that it also became a cauldron. Its work done, it returned once more to its source for a fresh cargo.

The active warmth of the male principle, Celi, the Druids personified under the name Gwion Bach, the Keltic Bacchus, and the wine of which he is god is simply the liquid employed in their mysteries to symbolize the fertilized sap of fruit. This principle was introduced into the cauldron as the three drops mentioned in the allegory concerning it. The Druids believed that the sun and the earth had emanated from two separate eggs in the Boat of Keridwen, but the sun was believed to be a later product than the earth. He was known as Taliesin, but great confusion has been caused by the fact that various names were given to the sun at different stages of his annual progress, such as Hu Gadarn, Arthur, and Taliesin. Formerly the Druids probably symbolized the sun as a bull and the earth as a cow, but in his later type he seems mystically to have been known as Taliesin or the High Hesus. As Arthur, he was the cultivator of the garden-earth.

All titles of the sun, except Hu Gadarn, are comprehended in a Triad known as Plennydd, Alawn, and Gwron. The earth, for its part, was known as the three queens of Arthur, spring, summer, and winter. The negative or evil principles were three males Avagddu, Cythraul, and Atrais, which signified Darkness, Pulverizer, and Soddener, and three female principles, Annhras, Malen, and Mallt, or Graceless, Grinder, and Soddener.

In the system of Nature the Druids regarded the space traversed by the sun from the first day of the solar new year (December 22nd) to the equinoxial line, or the vernal equinox (March 21st) as the kingdom of God's system of lives, occupied also, the Druidic philosophers thought, by evil influences until chased away by the marching up of the sun's Divinity. Man, they believed, occupies during the present life the middle line of that system (the equinoxial line of the moral world). He is entrusted with free-will, and is a free agent; . . . the space from the equinoxial line of the moral system *downwards* to where the old sun *disappears* on December 20th (25th) is, in the moral world, occupied by the "lives" of the animal kingdom in their tribes or divers species, in the moral system of Nature. They cannot innovate, or change, or improve their condition, but are bound by the rules of an unerring fate or law, which is called instinct, and *Greddy* by the Druids. But the nearer certain species of animals are to the "line of liberty" occupied in that system by Man, the more evidence of intelligence they manifest. This animal space is called in Druidism, *Cylchau yr Abred*, or, in classic writings, the Circles of Transmigration.

It was thought that when the sun was "re-born" as a babe from Keridwen on December 22nd myriads of lives apart from physical existence emanated at the same time from Keridwen. They were led by the sun from a district of *Annwn* and evolved through the animal creation up to the human. Intellectually, they were inert without *Awen*, inspiration, or the reasoning faculty, imparted to them direct from God through the sun. The bottom rung of the circle was in *Annwn*, the South, from which all development arose. An evil man was relegated to that depth in the circles of progress for which he himself had qualified during his state of free-will in life which was regarded as a condition of probation. On the northern side of the equinoctial line on which human existence is stationed was *Gwynvyd*, the Heaven of the Druids. It was situated, apparently, at the point attained by the sun at the summer solstice, or in the Tropic of Cancer.

The Druids believed in the eternity of matter in an atomic condition, and also in the eternity of water, and further that the passive or feminine principle of the divine nature pervaded both. They thought that at some inconceivably distant period the active principle of Celi concentrated its energy in the passive principle of Ced or Keridwen, and as the result of contact the sun was produced. Under its influence the atomic elements took solid shape and became a plastic chaos known as Calen.

The Druids had a zodiac of their own, and the names of their zodiacal signs are those of the deity's various emanations which come to the earth through the sun. Thus they named the vernal equinox Eilir (second generation), the summer solstice Havhin (sunny temperature), the autumnal equinox Elved (harvest), and the winter solstice Arthan (Arthur's season) when Arthur was engaged in fighting the powers of darkness. He is the Sun as Archer, armed with a bow and arrow, combatting the darkness of winter.

The whole earth was known as Buarth Beirdd, or the Bovine Bardic Enclosure. That is, the earth's fertility was symbolized by a white cow and the generating sun by a white bull. The Avanc or Beaver is said to have been drawn ashore by Hu Gadarn, and typified the sun disappearing every evening in the western seas. There were three cows and three bulls employed as symbols by the Druids in their sacred cattle-pen or circle. The three bulls are the aforesaid Plennydd, Alawn, and Gwron, and the three cows Morwyn, Blodwen, and Tynghedwen-Dyrraith, who are also found later as the three sister-spouses of Arthur, personifications of the earth at the three stages of the year.

The Druidic trinity, whose operations were illustrated by the three rays, were the emanations of the great Creator and not of the sun itself. The sun was the first begotten of Keridwen, the feminine or passive principle, and became the agent of the Almighty in the work of creation, who died allegorically on every 20th of December, falling into the sea at St. David's Head. His three fertilizing attributes were symbolized by three apples whose juice contained the divine essence. When the Druids regarded him as a beaver drawn out of the lake by the oxen of Hu Gadarn, it was implied that the Creator drew him forth by his emanations and that the change was not effected by the sun's own energy, for when the sun grew weak the Creator had to come to its aid.

The divinity of the sun was symbolized among the Druids by the wren. A mode of levying contributions at Christmas in Wales was to carry a wren through the village in a small box or paper house, the bearer singing a song about its poverty. In the Isle of Man it was customary to hunt the wren at the winter solstice, the bird being fixed to a long pole with its wings extended, and afterwards buried. The symbol really refers to the death of the old sun.

Taliesin, in one of his poems, alludes to himself as a wren, and that the Bard represented the sun seems clear enough.

Coming to the legend of Taliesin himself, it would seem that the seventh century bard who calls himself by this name was really named after the solar deity who bore the same title. The myth of his being placed in a coracle alludes to the vessel of the sun, which was believed by the Druids to be launched in St. George's Channel at Arklow on the Irish coast and to arrive at Borth in Cardigan Bay. On the east side of Borth is a vast morass, on the edge of which is a spot called the Grave of Taliesin, and a village close by is named Taliesin. This morass was covered by high tides before the present railway bank was constructed. This inlet, or cove, of Cardigan Bay was evidently in ancient Druidic times sacred to the mysteries of Taliesin, or the sun, exactly as Byblus in Phœnicia was to the death and restoration as a babe of Adonis, who reached that place in an ark of bulrushes. In the same manner, Taliesin in his coracle reached the Weir of Gwyddno. The coracle is one of the symbols of Keridwen.

Dealing with the myth of Keridwen, "Morien" goes on to say that the personages in it represent a solar and cosmic allegory, the dramatis personæ of the ancient solar drama of the Druids. Avagddu is night, Keridwen's first-born, the Sun, Taliesin, was still uncreated and the Cauldron which was to assist his appearance boiled for a year and a day— that is, from December 22nd until the following December 20th, and forty hours over. The circular half of the globe above the rational horizon, the receptacle of the feminine Divine Essence, is the Cauldron, the two halves of which are the northern and southern hemispheres above the rational horizon, with the equinoctial line dividing the earth into two halves. The northern half, when the sun is between the east and the northern point of the heavens, is under the dominion of Taliesin, the sun. The southern half, when the sun is between the east point and the shortest day, is claimed by Avagddu. It is a contest between summer and winter.

The three drops which inspired Gwion are the Triune Word or Logos of the Creator, the three golden apples and the three bulls. Gwion is the water lord, the Druidic title of the Creator in the work of making order out of chaos. The localities between Pontypridd and Tonyrefail are associated with the allegory, and no doubt rites associated with it were performed on Pontypridd Common, with the Rocking Stone as the symbolical coracle of the mysteries.

"Morien" also likens Arthur to Osiris, and draws several parallels between Arthurian and Osirian myth. He then proceeds to deal with the egg as the symbol of the earth and the emblem of the coracle of Keridwen. The earth's inertness in winter and that of the sun at the same season was supposed to be due to the principle of Evil, but Keridwen by brooding over the world-egg was supposed to reintroduce its vital force.

In Druidism [says Morien] it is supposed that all souls have had their generation and birth from Keridwen and Awen in Gwenydva or Elysium and that to come from thence to this world they must cross Gwyllionwy or the Keltic Styx, traverse Annwn and ascend in the train of the sun on his return on the morning of the solar New Year. Inside the sun is the Ancient of Days, Hu Gadarn, and the luminary's body is his and Keridwen's offspring. Hu Gadarn is the son of the creator Celi, who is both his father and mother. The descent is where the sun descends on the shortest day of winter, and the left and right of his descent are Annwn and Gwenydfa, with the

River Gwyllionwy flowing between. In Druidism souls do not return at the dissolution of their bodies either to Annwn or Gwenyddfa, but go either to heaven, or return to the animal circles of transmigration.

Such, in effect, is the general trend of "Morien's" writings, which are, in a measure, valuable so far as his great knowledge of Druidism is concerned, but which are somewhat diffuse and far too greatly mingled with Biblical and classical parallels of doubtful value. He has also much to say regarding the divine name and the resemblance of Hebrew to Welsh mythology, as well as the symbolism of the stone circles, but only here and there do we encounter anything of value in respect of the actual theology of the Druids, although their mythology is copiously enough explained.

CHAPTER XI

DRUIDISM AND THE SECRET TRADITION
IN IRELAND

IT has frequently been stated that Druidism in Ireland had not the same official sanction as in Britain. However that may be, there can be no question that it flourished there exceedingly. There are numerous allusions to Druids and Druidism in Irish literature, and at these we may perhaps briefly glance in the first place.

Three Druids are said to have accompanied Partholan, the first colonizer of Ireland, and the Nemedians and Fomorians are also said to have brought Druids with them to Ireland, who pitted their spells against those of the original inhabitants. In this case "Druid" may simply mean priest or medicine-man. The Nemedians are said to have visited the northern parts of Europe, where they made themselves perfect in the arts of divination, Druidism, and philosophy, returning after some generations to Ireland under the name of the Tuatha De Danann.

The chief deity of the Tuatha De Danann was Dagda, who is believed to be the same as the Cromm Cruach, the great idol overthrown by St. Patrick, and that his worship was Druidic is unquestioned. He possessed a cauldron, which differed somewhat from that of Keridwen in that it was the source of a plentiful food-supply. The Danann people had three chief Druids, Brian, Iuchar, and Iucharba, and two chief Druidesses, Becuill and Danann, besides a number of subsidiary priests and priestesses. Endless tales are told of the magical contests of the Danann Druids with those of the Firbolgs. On one occasion the Danann Druids prepared a magical bath at the battle of Magh Tuiraidh, which seems strongly reminiscent of that of the initiates.

We also read of Druids accompanying the Milesian colony, who are said to have come from Greece and to have passed through Scythia and Egypt in their travels, and thence into Spain, from which they travelled into Ireland, the Druid Caicher leading them from the Iberian peninsula to Erin. On their arrival the Danann Druids raised such a tempest as drove them out to sea again, but a Druid of the Milesians chanted a song so powerful that the tempest abated.

The earliest reference to a Druidic ceremony in the ancient Irish writings is that which tells of the fire lighted by Midhe on the Hill of Uisnech in West Meath, which continued to burn for seven years. The Druids of Ireland, however, said that it was an insult to them to have this fire ignited in the country, whereupon Midhe had all their tongues cut out and buried in the earth of Uisnech. The legend of Etain, the Queen of Eochidh, who was spirited away by a mysterious stranger to the Land of Faery, throws some light on Irish Druidical practice. She was sought by the King's chief Druid, Dallan, who wandered throughout Erin for a year without finding her. At last he came to Slieve Dallan, where he cut four wands of yew and carved an ogham on them, when it was revealed to him that Etain was concealed in the palace of the Fairy King Midir, in the Hill of Bri Leith, in the County of Longford. Her husband had the hill dug open, but the Fairy King sent forth fifty women so closely resembling her that Eochidh could not recognize his wife until she made herself known to him personally. The tale makes it plain that Irish Druidism employed written or carved magical characters.

We also read of the Druids giving draughts of oblivion to certain heroes, and divining dreams by holding a bull-feast and eating of the animals' flesh and broth, after which heavy repast divinatory visions were vouchsafed in sleep. A great many references are made to a certain Cathbad, an Irish Druid of celebrity, who kept a school or college for instruction in Bardism and Druidism. Equally numerous tales are told of the arguments and magical conflicts of the Druids with Saint Patrick, who converted several of them, and it is strange to read in the Leabher Breac that a Druid was the first tutor of Saint Columba.

The rites of the Irish Druids are the constant topic of the ancient Hibernian writings. A method of producing "illumination" practised by them was known as the *Imbas Forosnai*, or "illumination by the palms of the hands", as described in the *Glossary of Cormac mac Cullinan, King and Bishop of Cashel*, compiled about A.D. 890. He who wishes to discover a truth must chew raw red flesh and then retire with it to his bed, where he shall pronounce an oration upon it and offer it to his idol gods. If he does not receive illumination before the following day he pronounces incantations upon his two palms and takes his idols into his bed so that he may not be interrupted in his sleep. He then places his two hands upon his cheeks and falls asleep. The object of this ceremony seems to have been to have turned the palms of the hands into illuminating agencies which would permit the seer to have anything revealed to him which he sought.

It is told of the Druid Ciothruadh that when he made a Druidic fire against the men of Munster his enemies retaliated with a similar conflagration, which produced a shower of blood. Their priest, Moghruith, called for his "dark grey, hornless bull-hide and white-speckled bird head-piece" and other Druidic instruments, and flew up into the air to quell the flames. Ciothruadh also ascended, but the Druid of Munster prevailed and he fell to earth. Moghruith on this occasion was drawn in a chariot by wild oxen, and turned the Druids of Cormac into stones, "which are the Flags of Raighne to this day". This particular Druid, Moghruith, is mentioned in documents known to be historically veracious, and is said to be the ancestor of several of the ancient families in Cork, the O'Dugans, O'Cronins, and others.

The Irish Druids practised augury from the notes of birds, the croakings of ravens, and the chirping of wrens. They observed the stars and clouds for omens, and also practised poetical divination. They employed the yew trees, the rowan, and the black-thorn as sacred wood for personal ordeals. They appear to have been frequently employed as tutors to princes, and frequently as law-givers. But their organization seems never to have been so thorough or so orderly as that of the Druids of Gaul or Britain. At the same time it must be borne in mind that practically everything we know of them comes from sources subsequent to the introduction of Christianity.

Several ancient nunneries are conjectured to have been the retreats of Druidesses, especially that of St. Bridgit at Kildare, which was once almost certainly a community of this kind. At this place the *Ingheaw Andagha*, or "Daughters of Fire",

ministered to the sacred conflagration of the ancient
goddess Briginda or Brigantia, which was never
permitted to go out, and which was surrounded by a
fence or stockade over which no man might climb,
or through the bars of which he might not even peep.
A similar institution may have existed at Tuam, and
O'Connor mentions the Cluan-feart or sacred retreat
for Druidical nuns.   The Synod of Drumceat in
A.D. 590 laid certain restrictions on the Druids, who
were officially abolished after the Battle of Moyrath
in 637. So many Druidic ornaments and instruments
have been discovered in Ireland that it is clear the
number of priests maintained in the island must have
been considerable.   Nothing, however, is clearer
than that St. Patrick engrafted Christianity upon the
pagan superstition then prevalent in Ireland.
O'Brien, in his book on the Round Towers of
Ireland, observes :

> The church festivals themselves in our Christian
> Calendar are but the direct transfers from the Tuatha
> De Danann ritual.   Their very names in Irish are identi-
> cally the same as those by which they were distinguished
> by that earlier race.

Massey tells us that "an Irish name for Druidism
is *Maithis*, and that includes the Egyptian dual
Thoth, called Mati, which, applied to time, is the
Terin or Two Times at the base of all reckoning".
But the etymologies advanced in his interesting *Book
of the Beginnings* are suspect, to say the least of it.

That, as in Wales, Druidism, or at least the
tradition of it, was preserved in Ireland for ages is
obvious enough. Walker in his *Irish Bards* affirms
that the "Order of the Bards continued for
many succeeding ages invariably the same", and
Buchanan, the Scots historian (ca. 1580), found
"many of their ancient customs yet remain ; yea,

there is almost nothing changed of them in Ireland, but only ceremonies and rites of religion".

But in Ireland, as in Britain, we find the bull, ox, or cow the symbol of worship. The ancient camps or sites of the Grey Cow of the Dananns are still remembered by the peasantry, and King Diarmuid Mac Cearbhail, who is described as "half a Druid and half a Christian", killed his son for destroying a sacred cow. Owen Connelan, who translated "the proceedings of the great Bardic Institution", tells of a cow which supplied the daily wants of nine score nuns or Druidesses, concerning which story Hackett remarks : " The probability is that they were pagan Druidesses, and that the cows were living idols, like Apis, or in some sense considered sacred animals." This evidence collates Irish Druidism with British, and seems to point to the existence of some such ox-worship in Ireland as that of Hu.

That Irish Druidic superstition long survived and is by no means yet defunct is well known. There are numerous instances of folk-beliefs in the efficacy of certain stones, for example the Stones of Speculation, from which it was thought fire could be drawn. The Brash or Bullan Stones in the County of Cork and at Glendalough were indented with hollows in which the devotee placed his knees, dropping an offering into a basin in the front of the stone, for the cure of rheumatism. Milligan saw women at Innismurray kneeling before standing stones in worship. Spenser, writing in the time of Queen Elizabeth, states that he saw the Irish drink blood in connection with certain arcane ceremonies.

These are all the remains of Druidic belief, or at least of that lower *cultus* with which it mingled. In many parts of Ireland it is only recently that the peasantry ceased to believe in transformation into animal form. All Saints' Day was merely a perpetuation of the pagan *Samhain*, which was sacred to the spirits of the dead. On the evening of this festival it was considered dangerous to be out of doors, and funeral games, the remains of the Cult of the Dead, were held in the houses. The Irish practice of keening has frequently been considered a survival from pagan times. Mrs. Harrington, writing in 1818, was assured that the keeners were descendants of pagan performers. As in other countries, well-worship could not be put down in Ireland, and even to this day pilgrimages to wells are not infrequent, especially to such fountains as are presided over by Saint Brigit. Within these wells there were thought to reside mystical fishes, probably the familiars or spirits who guarded it. Offerings were made to the spirit in charge of the well and to the priestess thereof. Now this custom is entirely associated with districts where megalithic monuments prevail, and this justifies the belief that it was certainly Druidic.

As in Britain, so in Ireland, the cult of the Culdees followed that of Druidism. The early Christian priests appear to have been distinctly "bad" Christians. In the manuscript of McFirbis we read that : " The clergy of Erin held many synods, and they used to come to these synods with weapons, so that pitched battles used to be fought between them, and many used to be slain." This is reminiscent of the custom of the Druids, who were, as Cæsar tells us, occasionally wont to settle their disputes by the sword. In Ireland the Culdees wore the white robes associated with Druidism, and certainly occupied localities which had a Druidical reputation. As Dr. J. Moore writes : " The Culdees seem to have adopted nearly all the pagan symbols of the neighbourhood." They are, indeed, mentioned as the Ceile Dé in the *Annals of the Four Masters*, in connection with events in the year A.D. 806. The Rev. W. G. Todd, in his volume on *The Church of St. Patrick*, says that : " The earliest Christian missionaries found the native religion extinct, and themselves took the name of Culdees from inhabiting the Druids' empty cells." So lately as 1595 certain friars in Sligo were alluded to as Ceile-n-Dé, and there is frequent mention of certain Keledei in the thirteenth century. They upheld the institution of marriage amongst the clergy and their abbacies were frequently hereditary. That they were suspect of paganism is clear from the language of Bede, who says of them that they would "as soon communicate with pagans as with Saxons". Archbishop Ussher asserted that the Northern Irish "continued in their old tradition in spite of various Papal bulls".

Archbishop Lanfranc of Canterbury was horrified on hearing that they did not pray to saints, dedicate churches to the Virgin, nor use the Roman service, and even St. Bernard in his distant retreat was greatly distressed at what he heard of the Irish Culdees. In his righteous wrath he stigmatized them as "Beasts, absolute barbarians, a stubborn, stiff-necked, and ungovernable generation and abominable ; Christian in name, *but in reality pagan*". One of the Papal entreaties by which Henry II was induced to conquer Ireland related to the possibility of bringing the Irish into the Christian Church.

Wild stories were told of the performance of secret rites by the Culdees, and it was whispered that, like their Druidical fathers, they buried persons alive beneath the fanes where they worshipped in order to propitiate the powers of darkness. St. Bernard, in his *Life of Malachy, Archbishop of Armagh,* states that up to the year 1130 there was none worthy of being called a Christian monk in the whole of Ireland. Two islands are situated in the bog of Monincha. One of these was a monastery for men, their wives occupying the neighbouring women's island. Giraldus Cambrensis, writing of this community in the twelfth century, called it "The church of *the old religion*", and described its inhabitants as "demons".

The round towers of Ireland are associated by tradition with the Culdees. That they are not "Christian" in the modern sense is sufficiently proven by the fact that only in three out of sixty-three have Christian emblems been found, and even these have been regarded as modern additions. Nor are they mentioned in Irish hagiography. They appear to be in the same architectural line of descent as the *nuraghi* of Sardinia and the brochs of Scotland, although probably of later date than these. That is, they were almost certainly referable to a more or less distant Mediterranean origin. That they may have been of late Druidic—that is, of Culdee origin —seems not at all improbable.

For centuries afterwards the medical knowledge of the Druids survived in Ireland. Druidic medicine is chiefly known from its Irish examples. It is scarcely surprising to find that the ancient Kelts of Ireland regarded all medicinal substances as the gifts of the gods. In early Irish literature we find the god Diancecht credited with all the potentialities of a Keltic Æsculapius, a reputation he continued to enjoy well into Christian times. His name signifies "Swift in Power", and many are the legends recounted of his healing skill. Incantations penned in the eighth century reveal him as a god who had long been regarded as a fount of medicinal and herbal lore, and his son and daughter, Midoch and Airmida, even appear to have excelled him in the leech's art.

But the jealousy of Diancecht pursued them, and he slew Midoch, the innovator. From the younger leech's grave, however, there sprang 365 herbs from the 365 joints and sinews of his body, each possessing a mighty virtue to heal the diseases of the part whence it grew. His sister Airmida gathered the herbs, classified them and concealed them in her mantle. But Diancecht discovered them and mixed them up so hopelessly that no leech might henceforth understand their peculiar properties.

The surgeon figures conspicuously in the romantic tales of the Irish Red Branch Knights. In time of war an entire medical corps under one chief physician accompanied each Irish army, every leech bearing a *les*, or bag, of salves and herbs at his girdle.

Although the craft seems to have been recognized in Ireland from the earliest recorded ages, we encounter no mention of any individual physician until the death of Maelodar O'Tinnri, "the best leech in Ireland", in A.D. 860. After that period, however, records of Irish mediciners and surgeons are frequent, and not a few of them could boast of Continental as well as national reputations.

Van Helmont, a physician of Brussels, writing on the state of European medicine at the beginning of the seventeenth century, remarked that the Irish nobility had each their domestic physician who was appointed not because of his learning, but because of his ability to cure disorders. These doctors, he says, received their instruction chiefly from *hereditary writings bequeathed to them by their ancestors,* and employed as cures the productions of their own country. "The Irish," he concludes, "are better managed in sickness than the Italians, who have a physician in every village."

A large number of Irish medical manuscripts are still preserved, and the whole body of ancient medical writing in Irish is probably the largest in existence in any language. *The Book of the O'Lees*, preserved in the Royal Irish Academy, was written in 1443, partly in Latin, and partly in Irish. *The Book of the O'Hickeys* is even more venerable, having been translated into Irish in 1303 from the Latin work by Bernard Gordon.

In these and other books practically all the principal diseases and epidemics we are now acquainted with are described and specifics for their cure recommended. Bubonic plague, phthisis, alluded to as *serg*, or "withering", and described in Cormac's glossary as the disease of "those without fat", erysipelas, or the *teine-buirr*, the "fire of swelling", and *tuthle*, or cancer, are all enumerated, and mention is also made of palsy and ague.

Indeed, the training of a surgeon in ancient Ireland seems to have been a matter of prolonged and arduous application. He had perforce to go through a long apprenticeship with a skilled practitioner before he was licensed to "kill or cure".

That the medical system of ancient Ireland was of Druidic origin is undoubted, as was that of Wales, and its continued practice must have served to keep the Secret Tradition alive, as we may be sure the one could not very well have existed without a modicum of the other.

CHAPTER XII

SUMMARY AND CONCLUSIONS

WE have now reached a stage when the material at our disposal seems to lend itself to the process of being summarized in such a manner that we can draw conclusions therefrom. Some such general condensation of the facts already gathered may then be attempted, and such deductions made therefrom as will justify the hypothesis not only that a peculiarly British form of the Secret Tradition actually existed, but that it is capable of reclamation and reconstruction.

In the beginning we observed that the island of Britain possessed an almost unique sanctity for the peoples of the ancient world as a land of mystic and occult tradition, and this in itself tends to buttress the main theory set forth in this volume. Surely such reverence could not have been forthcoming had not the general reputation of our island been one of peculiar sacredness. That the tradition thus celebrated was of almost exclusively native origin, in respect that its tenets came to their fullest fruition on our soil, was also insisted upon.

That the Iberian race from North-West Africa were the original disseminators of this tradition, carrying it to Britain on the one hand and Egypt to the other in the guise of the Cult of the Dead has, I think, been demonstrated, especially in its historic aspect as associated with "Iberian" Neolithic culture and its introduction to the British Isles. The voyages of early New Stone Age and Bronze Age men to our shores, and the erection by them of stone monuments, leads to the assumption that they must also have imported their religious and occult beliefs.

The long barrow men were traders, voyaging from Spain to Britain, at a period generally placed at about 2000 B.C., and that they had embraced the Cult of the Dead is proved by their burial customs. Other races followed them, but although their religious beliefs have left certain traces, the aboriginal Cult of the Dead remained the official faith, and absorbed all others of later introduction, the Keltic peoples embracing its principles and grafting their mythology upon it to a great extent. This it was which rendered the faith of Britain unique in Europe, and caused the peoples of the Continent to regard it as the exemplar and prototype of the ancient faith of the West.

The argument that it is "absurd to argue that the Western barbarians taught the Egyptians and Cretans the Cult of the Dead" was countered by the theory that it emanated from a common centre in Iberian North-West Africa, and proofs were brought to bear to justify this contention, especially the colonization of Egypt by people of Iberian stock and the existence of certain survivals, like that of the supposed Keltic rite of Bealtainn in Morocco at the present day.

The theories of Mr. T. D. Kendrick relative to the cult of Druidism were then reviewed, and a justification of the theory that Druid traditions did survive was attempted. Moreover, his argument that no official caste of Druids existed in Britain was contested. At the same time it was agreed that the circles of Britain were not built by the Druids, although the development of Druidism was associated with them, and the Druids made use of them.

Druidism, it was concluded, arose out of a Cult of the Dead which had gradually been taking form during the Old Stone Age, and which in the New Stone Age had been disseminated from North-West Africa to Britain on the one hand and Egypt on the other. At the commencement of the Iron Age it became segregated in this island and took on the colours of its environment. Classical passages were adduced to buttress the theory that Druidism was the Cult of the Dead in another form, and instances of Keltic beliefs connected with the Cult were also brought forward, stress being laid on the fact that it did not so much embody the Pythagorean doctrine of metempsychosis or the transmigration of souls, as that of direct rebirth as observed in the ancient belief that fairies were the souls of the dead awaiting re-introduction into a new mortal existence.

The Druidic Cult of the Dead arose from an admixture of Keltic religion and the faith of the older *cultus*, the Iberian religion which had preceded it in Britain. It was, in a word, the North African Cult of the Dead localized and, later, Kelticized. It passed through the same early phases as in Egypt, but later began to take on the hue of its environment.

The Druids were a well-defined priestly class with sub-divisions having different functions, magical, administrative, and bardic, but that the cult practised by these ministers was fairly high in the scale of religions is indubitable. They possessed a system of writing which they appear to have developed of themselves, and which was known as the Ogham. Under Roman persecution they only seemed to disappear, and there is good evidence both from Wales, Ireland, and Scotland that they confronted the Christian missionaries, and it seems not at all improbable that they flourished for centuries after that under the name of Culdees.

Reviewing the material, documentary and otherwise, which helps us to a proper understanding of the mystical literature of the British Kelts, we find this, so far as the Brythonic Kelts of Wales are concerned, derived from the *Mabinogion*, the Welsh triads, dating probably from the twelfth century, but containing lore greatly more ancient, the so-called *Book of Taliesin*, and so forth.   I think I have shown that the criticism directed against the *bona fides* of these works was decidedly strained, and that there was nothing inherently impossible in the idea that they enshrined fragments of the ancient British mysticism. Negative criticism has to explain the presence of hundreds of surviving superstitions in Britain at the present time which are known to be of Druidic origin.

In *The Book of Taliesin* we encounter the mythological group Keridwen, her son Avagddu, and her servant Gwion, whose allegory has been mentioned so often as to need no recapitulation here. The Druidic bards who lived and sang under the Welsh princes unanimously represent Keridwen as presiding over the mysteries of their ancient cult, which also seems to be associated with the caste of the Pheryllt, who dwelt in the city of Emrys, in the Snowdon country. The rites of Keridwen were certainly those of initiation, and her myth is an allegory of the initiatory ceremony, of which there are many notices in Welsh literature and in classical writings on the subject of the Kelts.

We next come to the consideration of the volume known as *Barddas*, collected by Iolo Morganwg and published by the Welsh MSS. Society in 1862, which purports to be a collection of original documents illustrating the theology of the Druids. Its editor, the Rev. J. Williams ab Ithel, gives it as his opinion that the bards from the fourteenth to the seventeenth century viewed the traditions of the Gorsedd as the genuine remains of ancient Druidism, and that there is every reason to believe that in their main features they were so. The material of *Barddas*, its editor believed, had been collected chiefly from the works of these bards, who seem to have regarded Christianity as the fulfilment of Druidism.

The first book of *Barddas* deals with the origin of letters and the secret writing of the Bards and with the name of God. The second book bears on their theological ideas and mystical teaching, wherein it is set forth that God or goodness is opposed to *Cythraul* or darkness.   God united Himself with helplessness with the intention of subduing it to Life or Goodness, which began in the depths of *Annwn*, made its way into *Abred*, from which it was possible for it to reach the circle *Gwynvyd,* the cycle of immortal beings, the still higher circle of *Ceugant* being reserved for God alone.

Included in the section on the theology of the Druids is the "Book of Bardism" by the Bard Llywelyn Sion which he states has been extracted from more ancient writings which he specifies.   It is couched in the form of question and answer between the Bard and his disciple, and contains the allegory of the progress of Life from *Annwn* upward. Here also is described the nature of *awen* or inspirational vision from God.

In the third book, the "Book of Wisdom", we find the doctrines of the elements, the parts of man, the cycles of the years and months, which are followed by the "Book of Privilege and Usage", dealing with the laws and regulations of Bardism. The superficial resemblance of the ideas found in *Barddas* to certain systems of Eastern philosophy and theology must not, however, lead us to suppose that it had in reality an Oriental origin.

Turning now for the evidences of the survival of native arcane beliefs to the mediæval literature of Britain, we find in the work of Geoffrey of

Monmouth a certain residuum of these. He mentions
not a word about Druidical training or practice, but
there are references to pagan priests or flamens in
his volume which appear to me to refer to the
Culdees. It is also of interest that it is in his pages
that we first meet with the legend that the building
materials of Stonehenge were brought from Africa
by the giants of old, and I think his account is a
distorted memory of the manner in which they were
conveyed from West to East.

Arthurian literature may be divided into two
sections, that which was the work of Welsh bards
and arose out of Welsh tradition, and that composed
in English and Norman-French. The occult
traditions which it enshrined were clearly defined in
the literature of the Grail. Its dramatis personæ is
Keltic, and derives both from Brythonic and Goidelic
sources. That Arthur was a god of the culture-hero
type is obvious enough. Attempting to discover
remnants of the mystical tradition relating to him in
the ancient Welsh poems, we find him mentioned in
five of them by name, and especially in that known
as "The Spoils of *Annwn*", which is a poem of the
type of the "Harrying of Hell", and probably
constituted a description of part of the ritual of the
candidate for adeptship into the mysteries. The
cauldron seized by the expedition to *Annwn* is
obviously the same as that of the goddess Keridwen
and the Grail vessel. It is plain from this that
Arthur, like Osiris, was the god of a mystical cult
who must periodically take a journey through the
Underworld for the purpose of subduing its evil
inhabitants and of learning their secrets and magics.
Arthur, indeed, has probably a common origin with
Osiris. In British myth and literature there are
evidences of the survival of a belief associated with

rites which necessitated a real or allegorical passage through a lower plane from which mystical secrets and treasures might be reft. Such instances may be found in the legend of Thomas the Rymour, Merlin himself, and in the book of the Rev. Robert Kirk, Minister of Aberfoyle in 1691.

The literature of the Grail also contains certain evidences of the survival and continuance of this tradition in Britain for centuries. Its dramatis personæ are merely those of Keltic myth in another shape, the Cauldron of *Annwn* is, indeed, the Grail itself. The whole legend of the Grail, though diverted to Christian uses, is indeed entirely derived from sources which may well be described as Druidical, and there is actual traditional continuity between the poem of "The Spoils of *Annwn*" and the Grail Legend, which also contain a large number of references to the personages of Welsh myth. The Grail Castle is merely the Palace of Caer Sidi in *Annwn*.

Examining later British legend, custom, and festival for evidences of the survival of ancient cult, we find that a good deal of material concerning it has survived through these media. The idea of *Annwn*, for example, still survives as a part of modern Welsh folklore, although strangely enough that contains no reminiscences of the other planes in the mystic circle. There is considerable evidence that Arthur in his mythological aspect superseded a certain Hu Gadarn, the hero responsible for dragging the Avanc from the lake by means of his oxen. By some means Arthur became confounded with this Hu and took over his attributes and adventures ; both were, indeed, phases and "names" of the solar deity, and it is clear that the rites associated with them survived until the middle of the sixteenth century, the image of Darvel Gadarn being adored in the Diocese of St. Asaph so lately as 1538, when his idol and priest were taken to Smithfield in London and burned. In the superstition concerning fairy changelings, too, we seem to find a distinct trace of a belief in the return of the soul to *Annwn,* the changeling being a soul struggling to get a hold on *Abred*, the earth-plane.

In the popular superstitions, too, associated with sacred wells we find good evidence that a recognized caste of celebrants or priests actually existed within living memory, as statements by Lewis, Fulke, and Rhŷs clearly demonstrate, and it seems, too, that the cult of witchcraft retained certain associations of the aboriginal beliefs with which the Secret Tradition had to a certain extent become interpenetrated. There is also a good deal of evidence that a strong leaven of the ancient cult of Hu survived in certain parts of Scotland until a relatively late period, and the Cauldron of Keridwen seems to have been known in the same localities in which these ideas flourished.

Many of the Druidic rites, the details of which are known to us, cast light upon the nature of the Secret Tradition. It seems probable that Hu was the god of the oak and mistletoe cult, the oak-tree in an anthropomorphic or man-like shape, as the idol of Darvel Gadarn, burned at Smithfield, appears to have been. Bulls were sacrificed to the mistletoe-bearing oak in Druidic times, and these, we know, were symbolic of Hu. It seems probable, too, that the mistletoe, as the symbol of the essence of life, its protoplasm, so to speak, was introduced into the ritual of initiation of the Secret Tradition, just as wheat was into that of the Eleusinian mysteries, and it is possible that the "pearls" on the rim of the Cauldron of Inspiration may have been the mistletoe berries. Thus Hu probably brought back from *Annwn* the Secret of Life as symbolized by the mistletoe.

We find in the rites associated with the festival of Gog and Magog some reminiscences of the Secret Tradition and also in those of Godiva a certain bearing upon them, for Ogmios and Briginda were deities of knowledge, and the latter may have presided over the female department of the mysteries.

If we turn now to the higher philosophy of British mysticism as expressed in *Barddas*, we find the Supreme Power described as inconceivable and incomprehensible. The allusion seems to be to Hu, who is further identified with the Heus and Hesus of the Gauls, alluded to as the supreme proprietor of the Isle of Britain in Welsh myth, and who appears to have been symbolized by the ox, much as the Apis bull represented Osiris. That Heus was also represented in ox form is practically certain, and a number of Keltic place-names suggest that they were sites of a bull cult. His abode was in *Ceugant,* which was probably regarded as the sun itself.

The necessary obligations of man are set forth as suffering, change and choice, and his equiportions as *Abred* and *Gwynvyd*, necessity and liberty, evil and good, to which he has the power of attaching himself as he pleases. This assumes a Western doctrine of human free-will, although there seem to be certain associations with the "doctrine of escape", as observed in Oriental systems. In the "Sentences of Bardism" and the "Ten Commandments of the Bards" in the *Blue Book* the penetrations of Christian thought are obvious, but at the same time there is certainly a residuum of more pristine theology. In the native British mysticism the idea of struggle, of evolution, is stressed more as a natural and necessitous course, an act of psychic growth, rather than a definite philosophical path, such as is set forth in the Eastern philosophies. There is indeed less stress of choice placed on Man in the British system, the entire cosmic machinery appearing to be more imperative or arbitrary, although great stress is laid upon the value to the soul in this development of scientific knowledge, which seems to hasten the process of psychic growth, and it was probably for this reason that the desire for initiation was so strong.

At the same time we find that a certain amount of contributory action is essential on the part of man, and that his efforts must be in unison with that which is in the circle of *Gwynvyd*.

The basic foundations of *Abred*, or the Earth-plane, are the predominance of opposition in *Cythraul* over prosperity and amendment, necessary lawless-ness and death ensuing from the mastery of *Cythraul*, showing that the state of *Abred* was regarded as a dreadful necessity, that life on the Earth-plane could never be a happy experience. In *Gwynvyd*, the happier plane of spirits, good predominates over evil and memory reaches from the beginning of the soul's evolution of *Annwn*, so that perfect judgement and understanding may prevail. That is, the secrets of Death must be plumbed and accurately understood before the soul can triumph over them. This casts light on the allegory of the descent of Hu or Arthur into the depths of *Annwn*, showing that not only did he seek the Cauldron of Inspiration, but sought to gauge the secrets and mysteries of death, which knowledge was part of the initiation of the brother-hood of the Secret Tradition. In both the Egyptian and Christian religions the powers of death are definitely overcome by Osiris and Christ, and in all probability the allegory of the descent of Hu, or Arthur, into *Annwn* was enacted by the neophyte in the course of his initiation.

An attempt was then made to reconstruct the rites

of initiation of the Secret Tradition. Cæsar assures us that Druidic initiates underwent a very long course of preparation before they reached adeptship, which can only signify that the rites in connection with this were secret. An arcane brotherhood, the Pheryllt, actually existed, and that this was associated with the rites of the Cauldron is clear. The poem "The Chair of Taliesin" describes the apparatus and ceremonial associated with initiation, and we find that these rites were actually in use so late as the twelfth century, when Hywel, Prince of North Wales, underwent initiation, the actual site of the ceremony being indicated in the poem which speaks of the event.

The question whether the Druids actually made use of the stone circles in Britain was touched upon, after which an ancient poem was described which appears to have been used on occasions of initiation as a formula of introduction for approaching the gate of the sanctuary, and which has a resemblance to the usages prevailing in the Eleusinian mysteries. The myth of the Cauldron of Keridwen was then dissected, in view of certain passages in it which seem to have reference to the transformations of the goddess in the allegorical portion of the mysteries, lesser and higher, and that part of them in which the neophyte was plunged into the waves in a coracle was further described as revealing the last ordeal of the initiate.

With regard to the question as to whether the stone circles commonly attributed to the Druids were ever employed by them for religious or mystical purposes, we found that though they were certainly not built in what we now call Druidical times, that they may have been proto-Druidic, and that a good deal of evidence exists that they were made use of at a later period in connection with the Secret Tradition. Davies believed that the stone circles were modelled on that

of the Zodiac and that Taliesin or the sun was represented by the stone in the midst of them, whilst the
surrounding monoliths symbolized the constellations.
Caer Sidi, he says, means the Circle of Revolutions,
an astrological reference, and one Druidic grove at
least was known as the "magnificent celestial circle".
It is also clear from the poem of Prince Hywel that he
made use of the stone circle at Arvon which, Davies
believed, was constructed upon astronomical principles.

But the stone circles appear to have some bearing
upon the philosophy set forth in *Barddas*, with its
cosmography of the Universe described in circles,
and it seems likely that Druidism mingled with an
older religion which had as its basis this circular
cosmography, or, alternatively, it may have adapted
the stone circles to this cosmography, likening the
outer circle to *Abred,* and the inner to *Gwynvyd*.
In any case we know that the Druids worshipped in
circular groves, and finding stone groves ready
erected and to their hands, they may have adapted
them to their worship.

So far as the writings of Owen Morgan or
"Morien" are concerned they exhibit an extraordinary knowledge of Druidic lore, but are almost
inextricably mingled with classical and Eastern
mysticism. He tells us that the Druids believed the
firmament to be one vast wheel, in a chair in which
Hu Gadarn was seated, but that the principal spirits
of the Universe were Celi and Keridwen. Embryonic
matter was wafted across the ocean in a sacred boat
shaped like the crescent moon, the coracle of
Keridwen. The sun was known as Taliesin, but
confusion has been caused by the fact that various
names were given him at different stages of his annual
progress. Taliesin implies "High Hesus". The
topography of Earth and Heaven is then given and

the evolution of animal species commented on. The Druids had a Zodiac of their own and the names of its signs are those of the deity's various emanations. The whole earth was known as the "Bovine Bardic Enclosure", and was symbolized by a white cow, and the generating sun by a white bull. The Druidic trinity, whose operations were illustrated by the three rays, were the emanations of the Creator and not of the sun itself, who was supposed to die allegorically on every twentieth (25th) of December. His three fertilizing attributes were symbolized by three apples, whose juice contained the divine essence. The divinity of the sun was symbolized among the Druids by the wren.

The myth of Keridwen, says "Morien", represents a solar and cosmic allegory, and the three drops which inspired Gwion are the triune word of the Creator, the three golden apples and the three bulls. In Druidism all souls are supposed to have had their birth from Keridwen and Awen, and to come from thence to this world they must cross the Keltic Styx, traverse *Annwn* and descend in the train of the sun on his return on the morning of the solar new year. On the dissolution of their bodies souls do not return to *Annwn* or Elysium, but go either to heaven, that is *Gwynvyd*, or return to the animal circles of transmigration.

If now we attempt to draw conclusions from the mass of facts brought together in this book, we will hardly be able to refrain from the admission that the British islands have been the home of a Secret Tradition originating in prehistoric times and probably in North-East Africa. Probably between A.D. 200 and about A.D. 600 there flourished in Britain an Iberian religion associated with a solar *cultus*, the priests of which raised the great stone circles which stand in the more deserted portions of the island. On the invasion of the Kelts about 600 B.C., this religion was to a great extent adapted to their peculiar psychological needs.

If we examine the pantheon which seems to have been more peculiarly sacred to the initiated Druids, we do not find it to be quite the same as that more generally to be encountered in Brythonic myth. We have, indeed, considerable difficulty in tracing its origin. In this peculiar *cultus* we hear little or nothing of the Children of Don, of Llyr, Manannan, and the other more conspicuous deities of the Brythons, many of whom are said to have been more or less of local origin only. Hu Gadarn is undoubtedly one and the same with the Continental god Esus, but Keridwen, Gwion or Taliesin, Arthur, Avagddu and the rest appear to have no Continental affiliations. Indeed they, too, seem to be localized in Wales, though we certainly find strong resemblances to Keridwen in the goddess Brigantia of the English Midlands and North, and in the Irish Danu. But the pantheon of the cult appears to be in some respects equated with that of the Irish Dagda, who also owned a magic cauldron, and whose myth, as well as that of Bran, helped to the making of the Grail story. Now there is nothing more positive than that the Grail literature, or at least a considerable portion of it, represents the allegorical compositions of a body of poets who were members of an arcane society. These must have had sources to draw upon which are now lost, as well as those of which we know, and that the cult to which they belonged was none other than that of the Druids, altered by Christian ideas, seems to me far from improbable in view of all the evidence.

I think we may safely conclude that the matter contained in *Barddas* has undoubtedly been handed down from very ancient sources. We have evidence of the descent of manuscript and traditional material being bequeathed from century to century in a very much ruder state of civilization than that which obtained in Wales from the time of the sixth century to 1860, therefore there is no good reason for regarding the material of *Barddas* with dubiety. It represents, indeed, precisely what might be expected from a collection of manuscripts dealing with a national cult and handed down from century to century, that is, it constitutes a strange blend of "period" ideas. The marks of many centuries are on it, and the acute student will see for himself the evidences it bears not only of frequent transcription, but of epochal fashion.

The general resemblance of the philosophy set forth in *Barddas* to certain systems of the Orient is scarcely to be accounted for by any far-fetched theories of early Eastern influence in Britain. We certainly do hear of Mithraism and of the worship of Serapis and the introduction of other Oriental cults into Roman Britain, and it is not at all improbable that Druidism may have been coloured by their ideas. Moreover, the Druids of Marseilles were certainly closely in touch with Hellenic thought, which they must have passed on to their Gallic and British brethren. But all this is far from saying that these cults had a powerful or lasting effect on the general *corpus* of Druidic belief. The Druids were by no means barbarians, and were probably equally well versed in religious lore with the priests of Mithraism or any of the other contemporary cults, and, judging from this, it seems to me highly improbable that they would embrace the tenets of a foreign faith in preference to their own. There were, of course, points of resemblance, but I for one certainly do not subscribe to the notion that Druidic religion was a thing of flux, unfixed as regards its ceremonial, and shadowy in its mythology. The whole evidence, indeed, points in the other direction. The entire efficacy of a rite resided in the traditional manner in which it was carried out, and that the Druids deliberately adopted Mithraic, Serapic or other exotic rituals is, to me, unthinkable. The "foreign" introduction had taken place centuries prior to the coming of the Romans, and the resemblance between Druidism and some other systems is obviously due to a much more early common origin.

Perhaps a reconstruction of the broader aspects of the ancient British mystical cult might follow some such lines as these : The sun was regarded as the seat and centre of the divinity, Hu, Hesus or Taliesin, who, it was believed, occupied a chair or throne in the hub of its golden wheel. His demiurges, Celi and Keridwen, were responsible for the drudgery of material creation. The earth was the Cauldron of Keridwen, the matrix, as it were, of the divine mother, into which the fecundating essence of Celi was introduced. In its other aspects this cauldron was a sacred coracle, the moon, which brought embryonic matter to the earth across the ocean. Symbolically, too, the sun was regarded as a white bull and the earth as a white cow. Now these several ideas make it plain to the student of mythology that the cult which embraced them all must have done so at rather widely different periods, that they are, indeed, myths edited so as to fit in with one another by an able and fully conscious priesthood. The same phenomena are severally to be found in nearly all mythologies. The myth of the bull and cow is most assuredly North African or Aurignacian, and of very primitive character indeed. That of the moon as a boat has affinities both in Egyptian and

Anglo-Saxon mythology, but that is not to say that it arose from these sources, although it may well have had a common origin with them. The beginnings of the Cauldron story have more than once been attributed by Keltic scholars to Norse influence on the coasts of the Principality. But there is more than one serious objection to the acceptance of such a theory, the chief being that it does not at all account for the existence of a similar myth on the Irish side of St. George's Channel, which is authenticated as having had an existence long before the Norse invasions of Ireland and Wales.

So far as the "topography" of the various circles, spheres or planes alluded to in the Brythonic mystical writings is concerned, we must imagine this to have been modelled in the first instance upon the line of the sun's passage through the heavens. Man was thought of as occupying the equinoctial part of that line and the sun appeared to rise from *Annwn*, which bears a strong resemblance to the Egyptian abyss Nu, through which Ra-Osiris, the sun-god, passed nightly. He traversed *Abred*, or the physical world, and sank at night into *Gwynvyd*. This was possibly the earliest and most materialistic type of the myth, but later these regions or planes must have been regarded as having a less positive aspect. Moreover in subsequent centuries, *Annwn* appears to have been located in the south and *Gwynvyd* in the north. This is, for example, the exact reverse of the Norse idea of the places of reward and punishment. At a still later period, however, it is almost certain that *Annwn* and *Gwynvyd* were not localized any more than the heaven or hell of Victorian theology, although at a decadent period later folklore placed the latter in various Welsh localities.

For these are only the rude beginnings of our

British mystical system, as is the conception that the earth was a "Bovine Bardic Enclosure". The learned priests of the Secret Tradition of Druidism had undoubtedly by the twelfth century soared far above such primitive notions, and had come to regard the entire mystical topography of their predecessors as useful only from the point of view of allegory. They had become states of the soul, psychological planes, rather than precise and definite regions. Briefly, life was regarded as evolving in its lower forms from the plane of *Annwn*, the great cauldron or abyss of unspecialized soul-force, and as materializing on the world-plane of *Abred*, the sphere of trial, test, and experiment. On this plane the whole drama of *material* evolution was worked out, from animal to human form. If found worthy, it passed on to *Gwynvyd*, the sphere of the conscious and wholly developed spirit.

The scheme underlying the whole conception is thus fully apparent. *Annwn* is the sphere in which crude psychic material or soul-force is stored and created, *Abred* that in which it takes physical form, the stage in which it is rudely hammered into shape, and *Gwynvyd*, the plane in which it reaches perfection. It will thus be seen that the first two are not ends in themselves, but are merely contributory to the last, that Druidic philosophy did not believe that man was an end in himself, but that he was only a phase in the work of psychic production and perfection. The intention of the Creator was to shape and refine the spirit of man in various crucibles. It was a process of psychic refinement at the hands of a conscious Artist-Creator, to which Man was only partly contributory, but which he could assist by the acquisition of arcane knowledge.

From the above, it is plain that the entire significance of the initiatory ceremonies of our British forefathers must have been associated with the endeavour to assist the soul out of its travail on the earth-plane of *Abred* into that of *Gwynvyd*. It is also clear that the intention was to fit the human spirit for passage into *Gwynvyd while still alive,* and it would seem, from what we know of the Druidic course of tuition, which we are told often occupied twenty years, that this initiation may have frequently taken place rather late in life; indeed that, just as a bard was not admitted to the higher circles of his office until he had "grown a long beard", in all likelihood religious initiation would not occur until he was of fairly mature age. The initiatory ceremony was, indeed, the end of a long spiritual course of instruction and meditation which prepared the neophyte for the higher soul-life.

As we have seen, the allegory of the descent into *Annwn* was certainly enacted during the celebration of the lesser mysteries, and it is only reasonable to suppose, although we have no proof of this, that the higher mysteries opened to the adept the spiritual gates of *Gwynvyd*. We must bear in mind that the Cauldron of Inspiration, although situated in *Annwn,* contained the three drops of inspiration which had fallen from the creative deity, and which were later, through skilful priestly mythical interpretation, defined as the three golden apples and the three sacred bulls. These drops contained the logos or Word of God, afterwards translated by Christian symbolism into the rich sacramental pabulum of the Grail. It was, indeed, the mystical influence of that divine essence partaken of during the rite of initiation which made the initiate free of the higher plane.

These drops, which, I believe, were symbolized by the mistletoe berry, were regarded not so much as the essence of material but of spiritual life. Once only had they fallen from the sphere of *Ceugant*, and then into *Annwn*, the Cauldron of soul-force, where alone they could be obtained. Rescued from thence, they became the obvious mystical means of union with the Creator, for to partake of His essence was to be of His train. It is the act of Sacrament in another form, the idea that if the flesh of the god is partaken of psychic unity with him is attained.

Of course, it is obvious that there has been a great deal of confusion as regards the several planes of Kymric mysticism. For example we find *Annwn* in some places regarded as a horrible abyss, a kind of Sheol, at other times as a mere germinating place for life, yet again as a dim territory not unlike this world and even as a species of Avallon. These different phases apply, of course, to different periods of belief, and in the end *Annwn* has become the abode of folklore fairies. But its real character is as a species of psychic crucible, a matrix of souls, and all the legends which have clustered round it are merely accretions on the original belief. *Annwn* is the Cauldron of Keridwen itself. In short, it *is* Keridwen herself, the great teeming Mother of Nature.

Into this cauldron, or matrix, the three fertilizing drops fall from Celi, the male counterpart of Keridwen. Now, to anyone with only a 'prentice knowledge of mythology the basic nature of the myth we have here becomes perfectly plain. It is the myth of Sky-Father and the Earth-Mother over again, the self-same myth as is found in ancient Egypt, and indeed in many other mythologies. It is, indeed, the most primitive type of creation myth known to us. In many cosmologies the earth is formed out of the remains of a giant or monster, and in others is merely an "extension" of a god's soul-force. In still others, the earth is merely raised from the primeval abyss. The cosmology which the creation story of the Druids most resembles is that of the Hindus as given in the Rig-Veda, in which Karma, the primal germ of mind, the bond between entity and non-entity, shot its kindling ray across the drear abyss, energy or desire impinging upon chaotic matter. Just as the learned Hindu pundits very speedily embroidered this primitive story by superimposing upon it all kinds of erudite speculations, so did the Druids in the case of their own particular myth. But perhaps the best reason for stating that they owed nothing to either Egyptian or Hindu sources is that we find practically the same story in the Japanese Nihongi, where the egg of chaos in its clearer part became Heaven, while the yoke became Earth, an object like a reed shoot appeared between Heaven and Earth, and life began. We find the self-same ideas among certain American tribes, in Peru, among the Zuñi Indians and elsewhere, proving conclusively that it is a type of creation-myth exceedingly venerable. There is, indeed, nothing so dangerous as to posit relationships and borrowings between early mythical systems. The probability is that they sprang from a distant and common origin. As I have shown elsewhere, we find the idea of a primeval abyss common to Egypt, Babylonia, India, Scandinavia, the Kelts and some North American Indians, and the creation of life or matter either by spoken word or the dropping of the fertilizing agency among Egyptians, Hebrews, Kelts and Central Americans. But there is *always a distinction*, and the Keltic myth bears in its terms an individuality, and in its subsequent elaborations an original treatment which we do not find reproduced elsewhere.

A study of the material preserved in *Barddas* will show that the philosophy set forth therein must have

developed through many generations and centuries
on peculiarly Keltic lines. It is altogether beside
the point to say that here and there, as for example
in the doctrines of the, Elements, and the Materials
of Man there are reminiscences of Egyptian or
Oriental thought. One might as well say that Keltic
thought obtrudes itself into Egyptian theology.
These resemblances merely *arise from the circumstance of a common origin* and nothing else can
explain them. The notion that Egyptian thought
leavened the whole earth is not only exceedingly
crude, it is entirely gratuitous. No doubt, fragments
of Egyptian belief found their way to Britain as
elsewhere, but that they arrived here at such a period
as seriously to affect British religious thought while
in its creative phase is a little bizarre. That a similiar
theory of Egyptian influence has been applied to
American religion is sufficient to prove its absurdity,
even though the association is alleged to have been
at a relatively late period. Not only would Egyptian
philosophy have found itself faced with prejudices of
the most powerful kind, but as it could only have
penetrated to Britain at second or third hand, its
influences must have fallen harmlessly against the
defences of the entrenched native faith. Those
Druids who battled so strenuously against Roman
invasion and the proto-Druids, their predecessors,
were certainly not easily amenable to novel ideas.
Indeed, everything points to the conclusion that they
met the Romans as intellectual equals, as the writings
of Cæsar, Cicero and others amply bear witness.

Abaris, Priest of the Hyperboreans, mentioned by
Diodorus and Hecateus, who travelled to Greece and
became the friend of Pythagoras, was almost certainly
a Druid, and it is very much more probable, as Suidas
suggests in the *Pythagorean Colloquies*, that the

Greek learned more from the Briton than the reverse, and that the so-called Pythagorean Doctrine was neither more nor less than an adaptation of the ancient British philosophy instead of the contrary.

We Britons are much too prone to look for excellence outside of the boundaries of our own island, and to impute to alien sources the origins of our own *palladia*. In the preceding pages I have striven to put the case for the native evolution of a very original and individual type of mysticism as well as the extraordinary difficulties of the subject permit, and I believe that even the most biassed protagonist of the superiority of Oriental and other mystical systems will admit that there is much to be said for the thesis I have advanced. I cannot pretend that that thesis is complete in all its parts, but I am convinced that a sure foundation has been laid and that subsequent research will not only justify the methods I have pursued but, if properly directed, will succeed in the restoration of the entire fabric of British native mysticism. The missing stones of that fabric lie directly beneath our feet in the soil of our own island, and it depends entirely upon our patriotism and our vigilance whether they shall be recovered and once more fill the gaps and seams in the ancient edifice of British arcane wisdom. That we should so weakly rely on alien systems of thought while it is possible for us to re-establish our own is surely miserable. In no individual born in these islands does there not flow the blood of the Druid priests and seers, and I confidently rely on British mystics, whatever their particular predilections, to unite in this greatest of all possible quests, the restoration of our native Secret Tradition, so that :

In the white secret island the Druid shall dwell once more,
And the Bard, the slave of the harp, utter the speech of the Gods.